Who's Guarding the Gates?

Regaining Possession of Your Gates and the Gates of Your Enemy

by

Nancy L Robinson

This book will have you convinced that not everything that was lost, or stolen by the Enemy, is gone forever. By a divine strategy of radical obedience – you can recover all that God intends for you to recover.

PRESS

Who's Guarding the Gates?
Regaining Possession of Your Gates and the Gates of Your Enemy
by Nancy L Robinson

Printed in the United States of America

ISBN 9781624191848

www.xulonpress.com

*F*oreword

*I*t was E.M. Bounds who said, **"The greatest benefactor this age could have is the man who will bring the teachers and the church back to prayer."** Bounds said "the man," but in the case of "THE WORD" Church, it was a *woman* that brought us back to prayer. For over a decade, Nancy Robinson has had my ear concerning the things of God.

As pastor of a megachurch, I receive a number of people who sincerely believe they have a word from God. Over the years, I've learned to filter through the many words that supposedly "came from on high" and settled on those voices that I specifically sense God has placed in my life. Without question, Nancy is one of the few voices I trust. I trust her because of her prayer life. Many Christians pray to live, not many live to pray! I have never met anyone with the kind of monastic persona that she exudes on a daily basis. Nancy is more comfortable in His presence than she is in the presence of people. I've watched her commit to a life of celibacy because she felt she was missing valuable prayer time and in a sense, cheating on God whenever she attempted to date. Though I have taught her a lot, I've learned much from her - especially as it pertains to the criticality of not striving toward public success while being a private failure in prayer.

From time to time, in a very respectful but honest manner, she will drop me a note on something she's sensing from God regarding our ministry or me. Recently, I received a powerful email from Nancy challenging me on the necessity of having a consecrated place for our members to pray 24 hours a day. She reminded me that we created a place for our kids to skate and play sports, restaurants and bookstores for our people to enjoy, but yet for nearly a decade she had been asking for a place to pray with no avail. It was because of that bold request, and my personal conviction, that we constructed a 50,000-dollar prayer room debt-free for our church, and things will never be the same! Our prayer room is overflowing with people before and after every service. The power of God and his presence is evident throughout all of our campuses. I had no idea how badly our people wanted a place to pray! Not only that, the Spirit of God led me to hire her full-time as our church's first C.P.O (Chief Prayer Officer). That's right, she now gets paid to pray all day!

With many reflections on the disciplines of prayer, **Who's Guarding The Gates** captures an insightful and profound study of the five senses, or ***"gates,"*** that we must all guard with diligence. This masterpiece on the *gates* will quickly become a must-read among serious intercessors in our nation and across the world. This book will challenge anyone who is serious about recovering all that God intends for them to have; motivating them to be more intentional in guarding the strategic portals of Kingdom power and authority – the eyes, ears, mouth, heart, and mind. I can bear witness that this book on the *gates* was birthed out of prayer. Elder Nancy challenged me to a new level of seeking God and the urgency of *guarding the gates*. I'm blessed to be her pastor.

In His Name,
R. A. Vernon, D.Min.

Preface

*T*his book is written for those Christians who have ever lost anything precious to them, or had anything of great value seized or stolen from them. On the top of the list of precious things that many of us have lost is a dynamic, powerful, intimate relationship with Jesus, the Lover of our souls. If you are anything like me, I am certain that you have grieved the loss of those precious things that once enriched your life and have wondered if there is any way to regain possession of them.

We lose many things along the way on our pilgrimage from earth to glory. Our journeys take us from rocky mountaintops to lonely valleys. We must find creative ways to hang onto our precious things. We wade through waters so deep that we fear we will never resurface. What do we do with our valuables during these times? We pass through fires of affliction so hot that we believe we will be burned alive. At times, we discover that we are lost in the wilderness, stuck in the back side of dry, desert places, desperate for water. Wherever we find ourselves on this pilgrimage, we always have something of value in our backpacks, whether we are aware of it or not. Some things we drop from clumsiness, or simply by accident. We are completely unaware that they are gone until the day comes when we need them, only to discover that they are nowhere to be found. Some things we give away foolishly, failing to realize their value until much further down the road, when we have grown older and wiser.

Other things of value have been violently ripped out of our hands and we had absolutely no say in whether we would be allowed to keep them or not. Times such as these leave us feeling shattered, fragmented, violated and utterly confounded. The devastation and disorientation that result from this type of loss can leave us feeling as though we are doomed to wander around aimlessly in some sort of mental and emotional intensive care unit for the rest of our lives.

Then, of course, there are the precious things that we lose through our own neglect, the result of a misguided focus or a twisted vision. It begins with an insignificant minute spent here and there on the worthless things we think are worthwhile and before we know it, that minute becomes an hour; that hour turns into four hours and four hours turn into a day. That day quickly becomes fourteen years and the rest is history. After spinning our wheels, we reevaluate our vision and regain our focus too late one day. When we finally look up, the precious things that were once right there in front of us are gone! There we sit, stuck with the worthless.

If you fit into any one of these scenarios, this book is for you. From the cradle to the pulpit, precious things have been turning up missing in the camp of God's people. Somewhere, someone left a gate open. Somewhere, someone failed to guard a gate and the Enemy seized the opportunity, crept in and ran off with the good stuff. Now the people of God everywhere are waking up to the realization that we are a dispossessed people. We have been robbed of our valuables, plundered and looted because of our failure to guard our gates.

There is a holy roar in the kingdom of God amongst His people. We're awake and we want our stuff back! We are willing to fight for it, but we need a divine strategy against the Enemy of our souls. Everything that was stolen Satan took by way of an unguarded gate. Everything that was lost to our Adversary, was lost by way of an unguarded gate. Everything valuable that was neglected or dropped, you had better believe the Devil has possession of it by way of an unguarded gate and he will not give it up without a fight to the death. We can take heart in knowing that God always equips the willing warrior to stand rough and ready against the Adversary. "From the days of John the Baptist, until now, the kingdom of God suffers violence, and the violent take it by force!" (Matt. 11:12)

God has given us a divine strategy to regain possession of our gates. That strategy is found in our radical obedience. He told Abraham, "...and your descendants shall possess the gate of their enemies. In your seed all the nations of the earth shall be blessed, because you have obeyed My voice" (Gen. 22:17-18, NKJV).

We have been given the strategy to dispossess the gates of our enemies and take back everything that belongs to us. The battle begins with the reconstruction of our own gates. As you undertake the fight to regain possession of your precious things, some of you may have already come to the conclusion that some things that you have considered lost are lost forever. I challenge you to read this book. You may come to a different conclusion. It is my fervent prayer that you do.

Acknowledgments

*T*o the One who came after me, time after time, leaping over the mountains, bounding over the hills like a gazelle. Peering through the curtains of my life, You said to me, "Arise, my darling, my beautiful one, and come away with me." I have never regretted one moment spent with You. Every encounter with You has left me longing for more. You are my one true Love, Jesus Christ. This is my Lover. This is my Friend.

To Ariel, my son, and to Akira, my daughter; the two most beautiful reasons God ever gave me to pray. A mother's love and prayers never cease. Make it in! I love you.

To my granddaughters, Aiyana, and Tiasha, I hope to pass on to you the legacy of intercession. Remember my prayers...Make it in! Nana loves you.

To my brothers and my sister, God has given each of us something to do. We can do it. Finish what He placed in your hands to do, and let us all glorify the Father. "Hold fast. Let no man take thy crown" (Rev. 3:11). Thank you for your encouragement.

To my Mother and Father, I'm here doing what God has called me to do because of you. I love you.

To my pastor, Dr. R. A. Vernon, and First Lady, Victory Vernon, thank you for all you do for the kingdom. Your tireless efforts to do all that God has commissioned you to do have kept me encouraged that "I *can* do all things through Christ who strengthens me" (Phil 4:13), and it's not over until God says it's over. I love and appreciate you.

To Dr. William Myers, and Dr. Otis Moss, Jr., I cannot tell you how much God has used your influence in my life and your words of encouragement to help bring the completion of this project to pass. Thank you ever so much.

To all those who ever gave me a reason to pray, good or bad. You challenged me to discover a glorious life behind the veil. Thank you.

To every precious intercessor out there standing guard in the gap, by your prayers you are saving lives, homes, churches, pastors and first ladies, unborn children, communities, cities, states, and nations. Your prayers are freeing the captives, bringing deliverance to the oppressed, and ridding the land of injustices. You are bringing the kingdom of God to bear upon the issues of our time. Your prayers help to maintain the standard of righteousness and holiness in the land. The cry of your prayers is heard around the world. God is looking for those who will faithfully guard the gates to the kingdom in the place of prayer, and continually cry out to Him. Your labor in the Lord is not in vain.

The things that we long for and yet always seem out of reach,
pale in comparison to the awesome things that God places
right at our fingertips.

– Nancy Lynn Robinson

In loving memory of:

Tyrone Robinson, my beautiful big brother, who went home to be with Jesus in February of 2002. Your last indelible words to me, composed on a single sheet of paper, written from the place of your confinement, were:

"Pray, pray, pray – John 15:7."

Your passing and commission to me marked the beginning of a new season in my life and bound me to the altar forever. Yours, second only to God's, was the most profound commission that I received to never cease to pray. I thank you, and will never forget you. We will never forget you. Love, with all my heart... your baby sister.

Contents

Endorsement

*N*ancy, you have written a book with the amazing strength of a profound believer in Jesus Christ. You have the sensitivity of an artist, the gift of a poet, faith of a pilgrim, the commitment of a servant-leader in the hand of God. "It does not yet appear what you shall be" to the glory of God. *Who's Guarding The Gates?* is a relevant question anchored in the Holy Scripture (the Bible) and the book will be a blessing to many. I pray for God to continue to guide you and speak through you.

- Dr. Otis Moss Jr.

Part One

Defining the Gates

"Though we are willing to offer ourselves completely to God, we are just starting on the spiritual road. It is like entering the gate. After consecration, there must be the discipline of the Holy Spirit – this is the pathway. It takes consecration plus the discipline of the Holy Spirit to make us vessels fit for the Master's use."

- Watchman Nee, *The Release of the Spirit*

Chapter 1

The Significance of the Gates

"...and your descendants shall possess the gate of their enemies..."

*I*n Genesis 22:15-18, the promise from God to Abraham is
this: "...and your descendants shall possess the gate of their
enemies, and through your offspring all nations of the earth will
be blessed, because you have obeyed My voice." The implications
behind this promise are weighty and highly strategic; therefore, it
became important to me to gain a clear understanding of exactly
what it was that God promised to Abraham and to his descendants.

When I first looked at this scripture, I had several questions
for the Lord: "Who are the descendants of Abraham? What are
these gates? What is the significance of the gates to me and to my
Adversary? What does it mean to *take possession* of the gate of my
enemies?" Finally, "What divine strategy would be used to win this
war?"

To answer the first question, my studies revealed that I am a descendant of Abraham. If you are reading this book and you are a Christian, a believer in the Lord, Jesus Christ, you can also consider yourself to be a descendant of Abraham. This promise is for us. As for what the gates are, as revealed to me for the purpose of this book, they are the strategic openings through which valuable possessions are either gained or lost. These gates are the eyes, the ears, the mouth, the heart and the mind. Those valuables can include a number of things, such as your relationship with God and others, your divinely appointed destiny in God, your integrity, your family, your personal property, your health and your emotional stability, to name a few. Since one of his goals is to take God's place (Isa. 14:13-14) and since he is a thief and a liar (John 8:44; John 10:10), it is not difficult to see why the Devil would want full possession of all our gates and why we must do everything within our power to maintain and regain possession of them. It is not the will of God that His children lose anything that He said we could have, nor anything that He has given to us. David said, "O LORD, You are the portion of my inheritance and my cup; You maintain my lot. The lines have fallen for me in pleasant places. I have a good inheritance" Psalm 16:5-6 (NKJV).

As a single mother of two children, I can only imagine how I would feel if I saw another child in unlawful possession of something valuable that I had purchased for my child with my own blood, sweat and tears. Somehow, some way, as long as it was in my power,

I would find a way to help my child regain possession of that stolen property. In the same way, the Lord's zeal is stirred for us to help us get back what has been stolen and against Satan to overcome and ruin him when He sees him running off with our inheritance.

The Hebrew word for "possess" is *yaresh* (yaw-raysh'). It means "to occupy (by driving out previous tenants and possessing in their place); to seize, to rob, inherit, expel, impoverish, to ruin, cast out, disinherit, dispossess, to make poor, and to succeed."[1] In many ways, this is what has happened to the people of God. We have been robbed, disinherited by Satan and his demonic hosts. We have allowed him to drive us out of our own land. He has been allowed to come in and sit as an encroacher, ruling over property, lands, territories, and regions that belong to the children of God. We have allowed him to succeed in bringing many of us to utter ruin through our failure to guard our gates. We have to turn the tables on the Enemy of our souls and take back everything that God intends for us to have, from finances to businesses, to properties, to our communities, nations, families and ministries and our mental, physical, and spiritual wholeness. How do we get from ruin to royalty again? What is the strategy for the people of God? As it was with Abraham, so it will be with us – we must exercise a *radical obedience* to the voice of God. As with all of the promises from God, certain conditions must be met before the promise can be fulfilled. One of the first and most important building materials that we will need to rebuild our gates is radical obedience.

You see, the Israelites were God's chosen people, set apart to be an example in obedience and holiness to the rest of the world. Abraham displayed this unusual obedience when he took his only son to the region of Moriah to offer him up to the LORD as a burnt sacrifice at the commandment of God (Gen.22:1-14). Abraham never once argued with God concerning His unusual request. Instead, he chose to give God radical obedience. It was through his obedience that the promise of Genesis 22:15-18 has been secured for us, but we must meet the conditions of obedience before our gates can be rebuilt.

In every area of our lives where we deliberately chose to disobey God, we must be willing to repent, turn and radically obey God's instructions to us. God told the Israelites in Deuteronomy 30:11-14 that His commandments were not too difficult, not out of their reach, but, He said, "The Word is very near you; it is in your mouth, and in your heart, so you can obey it." We know that we can give God radical obedience because God says we can and He will empower us to do so as we surrender our wills to the control of His Spirit. However, the choice to walk in this kind of obedience is entirely up to us! Our failure to guard our own gates has put us in the predicament of now having to go to war to regain possession of those gates. The battle will be intense, but as we trust and obey our God in the process, He will grant us the victory. Let us now begin the journey to this reconstruction by gaining a better understanding of what the gates are, as well as their significance to us and to our sworn Enemy – Satan.

We can begin this journey by defining what a gate is. A simple dictionary definition tells us that as a noun, a *gate* is a "beginning, an entrance, or a mouth." As a verb, a *gate* is "a stronghold, a fortress, a prison, or a hedge." When we consider the definition of the word *gate* from a spiritual perspective, it doesn't take very much to see that the gates of our Adversary, the Devil are designed to set up inescapable strongholds, fortresses and prisons in our lives. Again, God's Word exposes Satan as a thief and a liar whose purpose is to rob, kill, and destroy (John 10:10). Jesus said in John 10:7-9, "I tell you the truth, I am the gate for the sheep...whoever enters through me will be saved. He will come in and go out and find pasture." Jesus is the gate to a victorious life for the believer. He desires to be our stronghold, our fortress and the hedge of protection about us. However, because the people of God have failed to guard the gates to the kingdom of God, we have become, as Isaiah 42:22 says, "...a people plundered and looted, all of them trapped in pits or hidden away in prisons. They have become plunder with no one to rescue them."

From the little that we know about the gates, simply from our dictionary definition, we can already begin to see why this promise from God to Abraham and his descendants was so significant. In order to get a full appreciation of just how strategic this promise was and still is today, we need to delve much deeper into the spiritual aspect of these gates.

A journey through the Old Testament reveals to us that the gates were positioned at the entrances to the cities. They were considered places for city officials to discuss current events and to transact business (1 Kings 22:10).

- **Legal business** was handled at the gates. (Ruth 4:1-11)
- **Criminal cases** were solved at the gates. (Deut. 25:7-9)
- **Proclamations** were made at the gates. (Jer. 17:19-20)
- **Festivities** took place at the gates. (Ps. 24:7)
- **Political strategies** were carried out at the gates to the cities. (2 Sam. 15:1-6)

The gates to the cities were representative of:

- **Places of authority** where one could both see and be seen. (Gen. 19:1-2; Judg. 18:14-17)
- These gates are also figurative for **satanic power**. (Matt. 16:18)
- They are figurative for **death**. (Isa. 38:10)
- They are figurative for **righteousness**. (Ps. 118:19)
- They are figurative for **salvation**. (Matt. 7:14)
- They are figurative for **heaven**. (Rev. 21:25)

There were also various kinds of gates. There were gates of wood, the kind that we find in Nehemiah 1:3. These gates were easily burned down with fire. This brings to mind the kind of gates that we build: flimsy gates, gates erected with absolutely no constitution behind them. These are the gates that would "come down if a fox climbed upon them" (Neh. 4:3). You know the kind, because we all have them. Sally tells Tommy that she's not the kind of girl that kisses on dates, until Tommy plants one on her and she immediately melts in his arms. Then for the next five minutes, Sally and Tommy are engaged in a French kiss.

Then there's good old Bill, a man of the highest integrity when it comes to money. Bill always pays his boss for using the stamp machine at the office. Even if it's just for one first class stamp, Bill's going to put that $0.45 in the petty cash box before he leaves the office at the end of the day. If he uses the copy machine at the office for personal copies, Bill pays $.05 per copy to petty cash. However, when it comes time to pay his taxes, you will find Bill claiming dependants that he does not have. How about Julia, the most pleasant greeter in your church? Always with her arms open to hug those who enter the church doors, Julia greets everyone with a pleasant smile and cheerful words, "Good morning, and welcome to our church. I hope you enjoy the service." At the conclusion of the worship service, Julia goes to the parking lot. So committed to her Christian service, she is one of the last to leave church that afternoon. To her dismay, Julia finds that someone has scratched the door to her car. With all kinds of foul expletives, Julia expresses her feelings about the person who defaced her automobile. Julia's gates are made of wood. At the slightest hint of temptation, we are all prone to fling these gates wide open. A hint of the fires of adversity would burn these gates down to the ground.

Then there are gates made of bronze (Ps. 107:10-19), designed to keep the people of God imprisoned. The gates of iron found in Acts 12:10 and in Isaiah 45:2 are designed to keep God's people from receiving His divine provision. Our LORD says in Isaiah 45:1-3, "I will open doors before him so that gates will not be shut: I will go before you and will level mountains: I will break down gates of bronze and cut through bars of iron. I will give you treasures of darkness, and hidden riches stored in secret places." Finally, there are the gates of precious stones. These are spoken of in Revelation 21:12. These are the gates to the Holy City, Jerusalem; they are God's gates. God's gates are durable and they cannot be destroyed! It is vitally important that every believer in Jesus Christ understands the significance of these gates. Knowing when to allow access to the gates and when to disallow or prohibit entrance to the gates is paramount to our effectiveness as gatekeepers to the kingdom of God that exists both within and without.

We have to ask the question, "Who gets to come in these gates and who has to stay outside?" If it is determined that he, she, or it has to stay outside the gate, then they or it must stay outside the gate. This is not the time to exercise mercy. God told the Israelites in Deuteronomy 7:1-2, "When the LORD brings you into the land that you are entering to possess and drives out before you many nations... and when the LORD your God has delivered them over to you and you have defeated them, then you must destroy them totally. Make no treaty with them and show them no mercy." Now, more than at any other time in the history of the Church, we must be on guard and we must be willing to do whatever the Holy Spirit instructs us to do. No price can be too high to pay when the strategy for victory is our radical obedience to our God.

Consider Moses. He was used mightily of God and was called of God to intercede for Israel and to stand in the gap time and time again on their behalf. Though he himself was raised by royalty and had position and power, he humbled himself in obedience to the voice of God, enabling the Israelites to position themselves to dispossess hostile nations and to reclaim the gates to their cities. We mustn't fool ourselves into thinking that Moses did not at least consider what he was walking away from and into, but his heart was humble and like Abraham, he exercised that same radical obedience to the instruction of his God. So it is with us if we are serious about regaining possession of what we have lost; no price can be too high. When the Lord allows us to step back into territory that we have lost, by whatever means, we must be discerning enough to recognize it as a divine opportunity to take back what is rightfully ours.

Kevin, a young man in his late thirties, was introduced to Sheri, a lovely, intelligent and God-fearing woman. Upon their first meeting, both Kevin and Sheri were attracted to each other and continued to date with the prospect of marriage. A year into the relationship they hit a rocky point. There were a few issues that they just could not seem to agree upon. Although Sheri tried to get Kevin to open up to outside intervention in the form of a Christian counselor for pre-marital counseling, Kevin was not receptive to the idea. Inevitably, the issues became insurmountable and one day, Kevin blew up in a fit of rage, becoming rude and verbally abusive towards Sheri. Heartbroken, Sheri feeling that it was in her best interest to move on, tearfully walked away from what she believed would eventually become a physically abusive and toxic relationship. Over the next thirty days, Kevin brooded over the loss of his relationship with the woman whom he believed God had sent into his life to be his wife, but his pride was too strong and would not allow him to apologize to Sheri. Later, Kevin would admit that not only was it his pride that cost him a beautiful, potential godly wife, but he also confessed that he believed he would have had to work too hard to win back Sheri's trust and confidence in him. It was easier for him to just let the flame die and move on to another relationship.

It may be easy for us to judge Kevin's behavior as immature, selfish and short-sighted; however, are we not just like Kevin when we resist the Holy Spirit's nudge to mend a broken relationship with a family member, coworker, or a brother or sister in Christ? Are we not like Kevin when we harden our hearts to the Holy Spirit's voice directing us to seek reconciliation to the husband or wife that we are in the process of divorcing? Are we not like Kevin when we fail to reach out to that child that we abandoned some years ago for fear that we will be rejected by them? What price is too high to pay when it can mean the difference between life and death, blessing and cursing? For Kevin, it was pride and the unwillingness to address his own issues from the past. We may also find the price of sanctification and holiness to be too high. It is easier to move in compromise with the masses and remain unchallenged in these areas, than to make a sudden break and run for the altar. Jesus said, "Blessed are the hungry. Blessed are the thirsty" (Matt. 5:6). Those who are desperate for righteousness will have their fill, feasting at the table of holiness.

There is a high price to pay to walk in deliverance from bondage to people, places and things, from crippling habits and addictions. Remember how in Numbers 11:1-20, the anger of the LORD burned against the Israelites when they complained against both God and Moses in saying, "We were better off in Egypt! Why did we ever leave Egypt?" Here they were, on a journey from ruin to royalty, walking out from under the cruel bondage of Egyptian slavery to a promised land flowing with milk and honey and all they could think about was the good food they enjoyed in the land of their captivity. They were being fed fresh heavenly bread every day, straight from the hot and holy ovens of heaven, but to them, having to eat the same thing day in and day out was too high a price to pay for freedom. They preferred the bondage of slavery in Egypt. Apparently, the Devil has discovered that a little meat makes slavery a lot more palatable.

This is how the Devil treats us, too. He feeds us occasional delicacies in the land of our captivity to numb us to the fact that we are indeed in prison. As we unwittingly chow down, we get comfortable being in bondage. Our royal priestly garments slowly become nothing more than dirty, dusty, tattered rags. Our scepters, given to us to rule in the midst of our enemies (Ps. 110:2), become nothing more than splintered, old walking sticks as we hobble along in the dark, musty caves and strongholds of our cunning Adversary, ingloriously blind. A lengthy stay in prison can rob a person of vision. We perish for lack of vision (Prov. 29:18). We forget that we are "a chosen people, a royal priesthood, a holy nation, a people belonging to God, that you may declare the praises of him who called you out of darkness into his wonderful light" (1 Pet. 2:9).

Once again, lest we become too judgmental of the Israelites, we should think back to a time when we, too, preferred to remain in bondage rather than walk in liberty. I personally knew several godly women who chose to stay in abusive relationships with angry men rather than face the prospect of life without a man. They decided that the price for freedom was simply too high to pay. When every voice of reason warned them to trust God with the unknown and break away from their abusers, they continued to listen to and heed the voices that instilled fear within them. This was a satanic trap that kept them tied to these dangerous men and sadly, ultimately resulted in tragedy for them.

This same thing can be said of the one who was once a crack addict, or an alcoholic, or the one who at one time was addicted to pornography. These roads lead only to death. Paul said, "Such *were* some of you. But you were washed, you were sanctified, you were justified in the name of the Lord Jesus Christ and by the Spirit of our God" 1 Cor. 6:11. Surely, before we were enlightened, before we were washed, some of us who engaged in such practices can remember how we preferred the bondage over liberty. Back then, to desire freedom from the bondage of our sinful addictions was not even on the radar. Captivity felt too good to walk away from it. The things our eyes beheld while we were in bondage just looked too good to abandon. The price to obey God's commandment to forsake evil was too high, so we wasted precious years sitting in prison behind the Enemy's gates. Let me tell you, the Devil is no fool. He knows how to design a gate so well that he will not have to seize you against your will, blindfold, or handcuff you to get you behind his gates. No! He designs his gates so that you will walk in freely, shut and lock the gate behind you, toss the key over your shoulder and pull up a comfortable seat to stay a while.

If you have ever caught a small rodent, you will know that the best way to trap them is to set a trap baited with something that it will like. Just before feeding time, you put a small amount of the irresistible bait just on the outside of the trap door and put the bulk of the food just inside the trap door. Bait that is good and sticky, like honey or peanut butter, will keep them eating for a long time, long enough for the trap to do its job. The rodent will smell the food, walk right up to the trap and begin eating the lure, or the small amount of food on the outside of the trap door. Once the lure has done its job of drawing the animal to the trap and whetting its appetite, then the smell of the larger portion of food will call it all the way inside the trap and the mission has been accomplished. Satan lures us in the exact same way. When our flesh begins to crave the delicacies of sin, the Devil understands that it's feeding time. He will design a lure of something tailor-made for us, something really sticky that we will not be able to break free from easily once we have had a taste. His lure will draw us and hold us in bondage behind his gates for years and years, because he will see to it that we always have easy access to the larger portions of sin. Through our own lustful desires, we are held captive behind the Enemy's gates.

In many, many instances, we can probably all testify to times when we were not able to regain possession of our gates simply because we considered the price to be too high to pay. We shut our heart gate to God by hardening our hearts. We shut off our ear gates to God by either pretending that we do not hear His instruction, or when we do hear Him, we make the decided choice to ignore Him. We shut off our mind gate by insisting on having our own way and resisting the mind of Christ. All of these responses are indicators of a spirit of radical *disobedience* and a clear failure on our part to understand just how strategic our gates are. In 1 Peter 2:8, we read that those who stumble do so because they choose to disobey the message from God, and so this becomes their destiny. We must be very careful that we do not continue to respond to God in this manner, or we can expect only to remain a disinherited people. The more we understand of the significance of the gates, the various types of gates and the strategies that Satan uses as he and his demonic hosts operate at the gates, the more empowered we will be to thwart satanic attacks against the kingdom of God within us and around us. The Lord will be our strength and will equip us with counter strategies that will enable us to seize possession of our Adversary's gates and take back everything that is rightfully ours. With so much at stake, we must step up the pace. Like Joshua, we, too must be concerned about how long it is taking us to possess what God said we could possess.

In Joshua 18:3, Joshua asked the Israelites, "How long will you wait before you begin to take possession of the land that the LORD, the God of your fathers, has given you?" The time factor is vitally important to us because, unlike God, we exist within the constraints of time, the chronos – the tick-tock of the twenty-four hour clock, the seven-day week, the thirty or thirty-one days of the calendar, the fifty-two weeks of the year, the seventy, or eighty years of life we are allotted here on earth. There is coming a day for each of us when time will be no more on this side of heaven. In addition, our evil Adversary will be strategizing to frustrate the plan of God for our lives by attempting to change or delay the set times and laws established by God, divinely ordained for our breakthrough (Dan.

7:25). We must be wise about redeeming the time. Moses reminds us in Psalm 90:10-12 that the years of our lives "quickly pass and we fly away... So teach us to number our days aright, that we may gain a heart of wisdom." We must remove every barrier that stands between us and our inheritance. There is a host of contributing factors, which we will discuss in later chapters, which have resulted in the delay of the promise of Genesis 22 for the people of God. Among them are our own fears, our rebellion and disobedience, our unbelief, wrong motives and hidden agendas. Our grumbling and complaining against God and our mistaken attitudes concerning the character of God have also caused us painful delays.

We have yet to take hold of the promise because we, the chosen of God, are yet burdened down with many sins. Our sins stand as the "giants" in the land that we must eliminate before we can claim the land as ours. We are behind schedule and time is running out. May God give us a sense of urgency to get in the thick of this battle and to thoroughly ruin our Enemy. We are engaged in an unimaginable spiritual warfare. The sooner we wake up to that fact, the quicker we will get into position to engage our Adversary, overcome him and come into our inheritance.

Part Two

The Ear Gates

"A dog that wants to go astray will not wait to listen to the voice of the master."

-African Proverb

Chapter 2

Unclogging the Gates

"Faith comes by hearing, and hearing by the Word of God."

Rom. 10:17 (NKJV)

"The tragedy is that our eternal welfare depends upon our hearing
and we have trained our ears not to hear."

-A.W. Tozer, *The Pursuit of God*

*E*very saint of God must be cognizant of the fact that spiritual warfare is incessant until Jesus returns, fights and wins the last battle! The flesh constantly wars against the spirit and the spirit against the flesh. They are sworn enemies; so says Paul in Galatians 5:16-17. It is Satan's job to ensure that your flesh is so well fed that it will always maintain the upper hand in spiritual warfare. He tirelessly strategizes to gain possession of all our gates. If ever you feel that you are struggling to walk in the spirit, you might want to check your spiritual diet. There is nothing like a tall, cool, slimy glass of gossip every now and then to make you slip from the spiritual heavyweight category down to the lightweight category. Or perhaps you have just not spent any time waiting in the presence of the Lord, meditating on His Word and listening for His voice. This, too, will weaken your spiritual defenses and set you up for invasion by the Adversary. Our own spiritual apathy has allowed Satan to clutter and clog the strategic entrances to the kingdom of God within, to the point where we cannot see, hear, or discern God in any way. Admittedly, with all that we have been listening to of late, some of our ear gates could use a good flushing.

Our flesh is already antagonistic to the Spirit. Take gossip for example. Gossip is enticing. Once you have had a taste of it, you want more. All it takes is a little juicy morsel to enter our ear gates and we can quickly become hooked. "Not me. I would never indulge in gossip," you say. In 1 Corinthians 10:12 we are warned, "If you think you are standing firm, be careful that you don't fall!"

Paul said in 1 Corinthians 5:6, "Your glorying is not good. Do you not know that a little leaven, leavens the whole lump?" (NKJV) You are not even a habitual gossip, or one who lends herself to gossip, but see what happens to an unfortified ear gate once a tasty little morsel of gossip has entered into it. Something is stirred up within that causes a pull, a tug, or a desire to hear more. "He began to say to His disciples first of all... 'Therefore, whatever you have spoken in the dark will be heard in the light, and what ye have spoken in the ear in the inner rooms will be proclaimed on the housetops'"

Luke 12:1b-3 (NKJV). Not many people can keep a secret. Don't be fooled, most people will tell what they hear, especially if they consider the gossip to be juicy. With an unfortified ear gate, we will find ourselves becoming party to a vice that we never even considered to be ours. Paul warns us that we should be careful, lest we become partakers in the sins of other men (1 Tim. 5:22). You are not obligated to let anyone plant their garbage in your ears. You have every right to resist invasion and block your ear gates to gossip. Anything sensual arouses our fleshly nature and gossip most assuredly allures our sin-filled flesh. We cannot afford to consider listening to gossip a mere minor infraction of God's commands. James says, "For whoever shall keep the whole law and yet stumble in one point, he is guilty of all" James 2:10 (NKJV). If we stand faithful in the little things, God will make us ruler over much. Conversely, if we are unrighteous in little, we will be unrighteous in much (Luke 16:10).

Now if a gate is, by definition, an origin as we have discovered that it is and "faith comes by hearing, and hearing by the Word of God" (Rom. 10:17, NASB), then that makes our ears the origin of our faith. By guarding this gate we are literally guarding our faith. This is a very important gate to guard, for the Word of God says that, "Without faith it is impossible to please God" (Heb. 11:6). "Everything that does not come from faith is sin" (Rom. 14:23) and "The just shall live by faith" (Heb. 10:38, NKJV). It is absolutely essential that as God's dearly beloved children, we learn how to guard our ear gates with all diligence so that we will be able to hear from the heart of God concerning the many issues surrounding our lives. Unfortunately, we are easily distracted by all the things on our calendars and all the things in our hands. With one, single electronic toy, a smart phone, an iPod or iPad, we have all that we need to keep us occupied, self-indulged and out of the presence of God, *all day long*!

I can recall when I first started seeing people wearing Bluetooth headsets in their ears with the blue light flashing. I had no idea what they were. It just seemed as though, all of sudden, everyone had this blue light flashing in their ears. It was a little scary, at first. I saw people walking across parking lots, going to their cars, with the blue light flashing. I saw mothers with these blue lights flashing in their ears, pushing their grocery store carts, babies in tow. I saw people in the church parking lot, exiting church, walking towards their cars with the same blue light flashing in their ears. It was kind of surreal. Since I was one of the last people that I knew to get rid of my rotary phone, this blue flashing light thing began to fill me with anxiety. One of the first things that I thought was, "What message is being transmitted into their ears that I am missing out on?" To me, everyone looked as if they were all in some sort of hypnotic state. They all appeared to be moving along like robots, all receiving the same very important, esoteric message from some being from another galaxy and here I was the only one not getting the message! Then, the very next thought that came to mind as I regained sobriety of spirit was, Wow! If only we were all that anxious to receive a word from our Lord. If only we were that poised to hear from God! How much more God-centered our lives would be if we were in that constant state of readiness to receive His instructions spoken directly into our ear gates. How much easier it would be for us to locate and stay on the road that marks our divine destiny in God if we were to grant Him at least the same access that we grant others to our ear gates.

Christians have a built-in GPS that they very seldom even use. The fact that we seldom use it accounts for why we are often found pulled over on the side of the road of life with our hazard lights flashing. The sign we hold up reads, "Lost, Broken-Down, Confused Traveler. Need Direction." Think about it: Are we not much quicker to lend our ears to the many other voices that tug on them before we will lend them to the Lord? God will not compete with any other voice to get our attention. Jesus tells us in John 10:1-5 "...his sheep follow him because they *know* his voice, But they will never follow a stranger; in fact, they will run away from him because they do not recognize a stranger's voice." "'Why,' the LORD asks, 'when I came, was there no man? Why, when I called, was there none to answer?'" (Isa. 50:2) It is because we have given our ear gates over to be accessed, occupied and clogged up by many strange voices. Those voices are speaking perversions, profanities, lies and vain things into our ear gates. Those voices are leading us down pathways to sin. Sadly, we have grown to love these other voices, even to prefer them. It is nearly impossible for us to hear the voice of our Lord, which is the voice of truth, the voice of conviction, the voice of holiness, the voice of rebuke, of direction and of love and compassion; what we do hear we shut out because it offends our listening preference.

Our personal lives require that we hear clearly from God. The Father talks to us about our personal struggles. We need to be able to hear what He is saying. The Father talks to us about our children. We need to be able to hear what He is saying. He talks to us about our communities. Can you hear what He is saying? He talks to us about our schools and our churches, our government, our nation, but are we able to hear what He is saying to us? The Holy Spirit talks to us about the depressed person who appears to have taken a random seat next to us in church. He talks to us about the grumpy coworker in the cubicle behind us. Can we hear what He is saying? Someone is on the verge of suicide. Someone else is contemplating taking another person's life. There's a desperate single father thinking about robbing a bank to put food on the table tonight. There is a single mother who is considering prostituting her body so that she can pay for college and make a better life for her family. The Holy Spirit is speaking to someone somewhere about all of these individuals. Is anybody listening? Is anyone in the position to hear? In all of these areas, our Father is tugging at our ear gates. He is giving us instructions and strategies that will empower us to regain possession of our gates and take possession of Satan's gates. He is looking to commission us, equip us and empower us with divine strategies as we walk, as we sit, as we interact with others, as we work, as we minister and as we pray. Sadly, many of us would be hard pressed to hear anything that the Spirit of the Lord God is proclaiming at our ear gates because we have been lending our ears to Satan with the music that we listen to, the dialogues from unwholesome movies that we watch and with negative or unwholesome words that we allow others to plant into our ears.

Then too, we have been listening to Satan's lies for so long that we have come to believe them. Isn't it true that most times we recognize his voice much better than we do the voice of the Good Shepherd? We have all been guilty of believing his lies at one time or another, lies such as, "You will never have integrity." "God is never going to use you. You've done too much dirt in the past." "Even though you say you're a Christian now, you will always be a fornicator." "You will always be broke." "You will always be a liar." "You're never going to drop those extra ninety pounds." "You will always be bitter, angry, depressed and lonely." Do any of these proclamations sound familiar to you? Satan is good at what he does. The Bible calls him a formidable foe. His influence over our gates is not to be underestimated.

Isn't it odd that although we do not like to hear negative things spoken about us, sin has so crippled and conditioned us that we quickly fall prey to a lie, embracing it, believing it and claiming the lie as ours? Jesus wants us to have enough presence of mind to immediately go to war against such demonic assaults, just as He did in His encounter with Satan in Matthew 4. He will train our hands to war so that we will learn how to take up arms against the Devil's lies with God's truth. However, Satan has managed to fortify his position at the gates to our ears and for many of us he now has the supreme authority at this very strategic passageway. He can decree whatever lies he so desires by right of his illegal entry. We *will* have faith to live by his decrees until we latch onto a strategic truth from the Word of God that will both destroy Satan's lies and empower us to regain possession of our gates. Remember – our faith comes by our hearing. We will have faith for whatever we incline our ears to hear. God wants us to have faith to walk in what He has decreed for us. "He who has an ear, let him hear what the Spirit says to the churches" (Rev. 2:17).

Any audiologist will tell you that most hearing loss is gradual, thus causing many people who suffer from hearing loss to be in denial of the loss. So too, relinquishing the full authority of our gates to Satan is a gradual process. It does not happen overnight and we, too, experience that same denial that we are losing the battle at our ear gates. Many Christians think that they can listen to sensual lyrics in secular music and not fall prey to the types of temptations that those lyrics are designed to foster. Each time you lend your ear to such lyrics, Satan takes strategic ground from you.

Secular music involves fantasy and in the world of fantasy any and everything can happen. It is a world that the Devil has created for our sensual pleasure. In it we can have the ideal, perfect man or woman. Fantasy allows a woman to be in a relationship with a married man and suffer no consequences. It fools us into believing that we can have such torrid, forbidden romantic relationships and that no one will ever discover our dirty little secrets. Fantasy will have us believing that if one man doesn't work out, we can have another one better than him in a minute. The world of fantasy is also dangerous because it will take us down a dark path, foolishly chanting the woeful dirge that if the man we love walks out on us, we will never breathe again.

The world of fantasy that revolves around secular music will keep us tied to a daydream, to a castle in the sky that will ultimately crash down upon us. In reality, we know that the perfect man and the perfect woman do not exist. The only perfect man is Jesus. The only perfect woman will be the spotless and wrinkle-free bride of Christ. The truth about forbidden, unholy, adulterous relationships is that eventually everyone who is involved in them will be hurt, especially the unsuspecting spouse. The lie that men are disposable and quickly replaced is one of the most absurd. First of all, men are not disposable items like paper cups or plastic spoons and if we follow God's order as godly women, we would never go out and just quickly grab another man. Second, every woman knows that even if she were to go outside of God's order of bringing a man and a woman together, that it sometimes takes years before a man comes along who is to our liking. The last fantasy, that if the man walks out on us, we will never breathe again, is especially dangerous to a young woman and can be dangerous as well to a young man. The truth is that if they walk out on you, not only will you keep breathing, but you also "will not die but live and will proclaim what the LORD has done" (Ps. 118:17). The LORD will give you "beauty for ashes, the oil of joy for mourning, and the garment of praise for the spirit of heaviness" (Isa. 61:2-3, NKJV). The truth is that "the joy of the Lord is your strength!" (Neh. 8:10) God will lead you beside still waters and He will restore your [wounded] soul (Ps. 23:2-3).

When we lend our ears to the lyrics of sensual music, we set ourselves up to be led around captive by the spirits of fantasy and delusion. These two spirits will drag us around by the neck to deep despair and disappointment, straight to our own doom. If the Devil can keep us chasing a daydream, he knows that we will never wake up and get a real vision for our lives. Daydreaming is a huge time-waster and time is running out. In Job 14, Job reminds us of the brevity of life with these words: "Man who is born of woman is of few days, and full of trouble. He comes forth like a flower and fades away; he flees like a shadow and does not continue" (vv.1-2, NKJV). We also must be mindful of the short span of our years and get busy rebuilding our gates. Every time we listen to gossip, we allow the Adversary to fortify his position at the gates to our ears. Every time we listen to someone tell us something about ourselves that is contrary to what God says about us, we increase Satan's reign of authority at our ear gates. Every time we indulge ourselves with unwholesome secular music, we set ourselves up to be held captive to a hallucination. We give up territory to the Devil to which he is not entitled!

It is critical that we remember that relinquishing the control of our ear gates to the Devil is a process. Satan knows how to whet our appetites. When we have found ourselves in the position of listening to the Enemy, we need to know that we are dealing with more than the fact that we have decided to simply tune in to his station for a minute. It goes much deeper; in fact, it goes right to the heart. Listening to the Enemy is a sure sign that our hearts are in the process of turning away from God. Whenever we wander into the Devil's territory, the stakes are high, much higher than we ever considered. We will never have enough wages to post our own bond. Jesus, our Savior, Redeemer and Deliverer will always be the one to rescue us from the Devil's strongholds. As we move in defense of our gates, our Lord will give us the weapons of war that we need to win the battles and ultimately to win the war.

"Behold, I give you the keys..."

"The most common way people give up power is by thinking they don't have any."

-Alice Walker

Every gate has a key that has been custom designed for the exclusive purpose of either locking or unlocking that gate. Jesus said in

Matthew 16:19, "I give you the keys of the kingdom of heaven; whatever you bind on earth will be bound in heaven; whatever you loose on earth will be loosed in heaven." Jesus tells us that we have heavenly license, or authority, to lock out, or lock in, to allow and to disallow. The keys represent authority. Therefore, whoever has possession of the keys is the one who possesses the authority! Whoever has the authority has the final word on the matter. The authority comes as a by-product of our obedience, which we will see with more clarity in later chapters. Before we move on however, I want to ask again, *"Who is really guarding the gates?"*

Let us first get a better understanding of what it means to "guard." Webster's Dictionary gives us the definition of the word *guard*. It means "to move in self-defense, to resist, to screen, to shield, to beat off, to resist invasion, to show fight, to stand one's ground, and to stand in the gap." These definitions give a picture of a wide-eyed, calculated, aggressive and purposeful resistance! All too often we give up ground too quickly. Perhaps that is because we do not understand the value of what it is we are fighting for. We read in Matthew 13:44-46:

The kingdom of heaven is like treasure hidden in a field. When a man found it, he hid it again, and then in his joy went and sold all he had and bought that field. Again, the kingdom of heaven is like a merchant looking for fine pearls.

When he found one of great value, he went away and sold everything he had and bought it.

The value of what we are fighting for is priceless, but no one can convince us of that fact. We ourselves must be fully persuaded of its value for us to act in ways that show the world that it is worth giving up all that we claim as ours to inherit it. The same can be said of the power and authority that Jesus gave to us when He handed us the keys to bind and to loose. We treat those keys like we do our house keys, at times. We set them down carelessly on store counters, park benches, or on a friend's sofa and there they lay. We tend to forget all about them until we arrive back home and realize that we have misplaced them and cannot access our stuff; then we get desperate to locate them.

When Jesus handed us that set of keys, they came with His verbal guarantee prefaced by one powerful, all-inclusive word – *"whatever."* The emphasis in Matthew 16:19 is on the "whatever." That means anything that is in line with the will of God, we have the power to allow or to disallow. We have all this power contained in this set of keys and most of the time we don't even use them! We allow anything to enter our gates and to sit there and defile us when we have the power to disallow it! We do not fully understand or appreciate the value of holiness. We do not understand how important holiness is to God and what a heavenly and earthly benefit it is for us. We do not understand how rich it is to be a consecrated vessel, set apart for God's use in His kingdom. We cannot grasp how significant the work of sanctification is in the life of the believer and so we fail to resist demonic invasion of our gates. We fail to stand our ground in the face of compromise and we fail to show fight and take the kingdom of God by force when Satan comes to invade our land.

How radical are we willing to be to resist the invasion of our ear gates by the Adversary? Are we willing to change the radio station, no matter how good the beat sounds, to protect the rest of the members of our temple from becoming polluted by the sensual lyrics? To what extent will we stand our ground when Ephesians 6:13 tells us that we are to "continue to stand" after we have done all that the crisis demands? Sadly, that's just when many of us give up. Would we stand in the gap for our own bodies that we might be vessels, sanctified for God to use for the benefit of someone else? As a musician, formerly a nightclub singer═turned worship leader, I have a testimony of how my own failure to guard my ear gates had put me in a place of tremendous grief and sorrow.

I grew up in an era when, arguably, some of the best R&B music was being created. This was the music of the late 70s and 80s, which, when compared to today's music, would have been considered quite clean by the world's standards. I had a love relationship with the music of great artists such as Smokey Robinson and the Miracles, Gladys Knight and the Pips, Aretha Franklin, Diana Ross and the Supremes and Anita Baker, to name a few. If I had any vice back then it was R&B music. My Dad had just about every Nat King Cole album and I fell in love with his velvety smooth vocals as well. I remember many nights playing Nat's records on the stereo, lying down on the floor with my ear as close to the speaker as I could get it and just listening to him sing for hours on end. I wanted the music to run through every fiber of my being. Something about the music made me feel alive and happy. As a young girl who was surrounded by a traumatizing environment, I remember the overwhelming feelings of fear that characterized my world and gripped my soul. Most of the time I was very sad. I would lock myself in my room or in the bathroom; there I would weep and talk to a Jesus who never seemed to be listening to me. In spite of His silence, I somehow believed He was always there with me. The music gave purpose to my life. It erased the fear and gave me peace. I needed to hear the music every day of my life.

After I graduated from high school, I moved away to New York City in pursuit of a career in the secular music industry. To strengthen my vocals, I began studying opera at the Harlem School of the Arts. My vocal coach was so impressed that she began making preparations to send me overseas to study with an elite group of promising opera singers. It was then that God stepped in and redirected my path. My gifts, He told me, were to be used to bless and benefit the kingdom of God. Although I continued to sing in the nightclubs of New York for a period after that, I eventually changed direction and became a worship leader in the church. I walked away from the nightclub scene and never looked back.

Over the years of being a secular vocal artist, I had accumulated a large collection of secular albums, tapes and CDs. At the direction of the Holy Spirit, I gave all of my music away. I began to purchase, listen to and sing only Christian worship music. For the next 18 years, I made it my goal, primarily, to listen only to the purest worship music. Occasionally, I must confess, I would listen to jazz on the radio. It took me a little longer to completely break away from listening to jazz, but eventually I did.

As a worship leader, I noticed that the secular music had left a deposit of sensuality on me that influenced what I conveyed as I ministered in song, a sort of strange fire. Countless hours spent on my knees before the presence of the Holy One, living a fasted life, soaking up his Word and filling my spirit with the purity of worship music had succeeded in cleansing my system of the sensuality of secular music. I was sold out to Jesus, to purity, to sanctification and to holiness.

During my years as a nightclub singer, although I was a Christian, I had married a man who was an agnostic. Eight years into the marriage, we found ourselves filing for divorce. I remained single, choosing to focus on raising my children and serving Jesus. Some time after my children were grown and had moved out on their own, I was introduced to a Christian man. I will call him Robert to protect his identity. We were mutually attracted to each other and began dating. The very first time I went to Robert's house, he played an old secular love song for me and asked me to dance with him. He had the lights turned down real low in his house. Almost immediately, I felt like I had walked into a trap, but the old familiar spirits that were associated with that music from an earlier time in my life had wooed me into a place of strange comfort. I should have felt uncomfortable with the low lights, the sensual music and his body pressed uncomfortably close to mine. However, the music that had made a once-frightened little girl feel alive and safe now made a grown woman who was perfectly within her rights to be uncomfortable feel safe instead, in a scenario created to stir up ungodly passions between two people who were only dating, not married.

Robert quickly picked up on the fact that music relaxed me, so every time we got together he would play another old love song from the 70s or 80s. I was always caught off guard. We would end up slow dancing in the dark and singing to each other. I would dedicate songs to him and he would dedicate songs to me. To my shock, I found myself going out looking for those old songs of the 70s and 80s, remade and now on CDs. I was playing the music that I had sworn off in my car and in my house. I was singing it at the top of my lungs when I was at home alone. The Devil was slowly, but surely regaining possession of my ear gates. He was moving back in. I knew it. I felt it. I was well aware of it, but the trap was tailor-made for me. Music had been my comfort when I was afraid.

It now served as a blindfold to a snare that the Devil had designed especially for me.

While the music was lulling me into a false sense of security, I failed to see that Robert was nothing of the man of God that I thought he was. In truth, Robert was an angry man still carrying around deep hurts from his childhood and from a failed marriage. The brunt of his unresolved anger would often fall upon me. He was extremely needy, requiring excessive amounts of my time. He seemed put off by my spirituality and was constantly trying to violate any boundaries that I had put in place to maintain my integrity. I saw all of this about Robert, but I had allowed the sensual music to strip me of the power that was mine to use my keys to disallow him any more access into my life.

Robert was not a bad man, just a deeply wounded man who had yet to really experience the healing hand of God upon his life for his damaged soul. Yet, he was one of those that I should have sent right back out the gate as soon as I detected that he was not the godly man I assumed he was. I failed to stand my ground and resist invasion of my ear gates; for that reason I took full responsibility for any hurt that I suffered as a result of having allowed him access to my ear gates. I continued to date Robert for several months and over the course of our dating I began to compromise my integrity. Although we never had any kind of sexual encounter, I allowed myself to diminish from the woman of God that I had become before I met Robert. My relationship with Jesus Christ, which was vitally important to me, had all but faded away to nothing. I was so distracted with trying to give Robert all the time that he needed, that I had all but ceased to spend time with the True Lover of my life and my soul, Jesus.

I was praying and reading my Bible only sporadically. A woman who once enjoyed a powerful and dynamic relationship with her God, I now felt like Samson after Delilah cut off his hair (Judg. 16:17-19), just like any other man (or woman, in my case). I felt regular, powerless and un-anointed. I felt robbed, but in actuality, I had handed my anointing over to the Enemy and it all began with a sensual lyric being allowed to enter into my ear gates without a fight. I want to note here that while men are largely seduced by what enters their eye gates, women are seduced by what we allow to enter into our ear gates.

The Devil creates hallucinations at our ear gates. I am sure we can all recall many times when we heard a sound and thought it was one thing, but it turned out to be something else. A great example of this can be seen on one of my favorite television shows, America's Funniest Videos. They feature a segment in which they will play a very weird sound and an audience member will have to guess what or who is making the sound. I am always surprised to see that what I may have thought sounded like one thing was actually something quite different. Once, they played what sounded to me like a creaking door, but in actuality, it was the cry of an agitated cat. On a deeper level, if we are not tuned in to the Holy Spirit's voice, we may think that we are discerning the voice of God, when all the while it is the Devil in disguise. How many women have married men thinking that they had heard from God, only to discover once they'd said "I do," that they wished they had said, "I don't!"? How many men have taken on big salary jobs, thinking they had heard from God, only to discover that that job was designed by the Devil to take him away from his family and ultimately ruin his marriage?

We have to be very, very discriminative of the things that we listen to. We must ask God to give us spiritual discernment into the heart of that man or woman we are dating. In addition, we must obey the voice and the promptings of the Holy Spirit as He reveals the red flags to us that warn us to abandon ship immediately. Admittedly, it took longer than it should have for me to wake up to the fact that I was being robbed, but I did finally wake up. Isaiah 54:16-17 gives us God's promise that though the Enemy tailors a weapon with his heart set on using it to thoroughly ruin us, He will not allow that weapon to have its intended effect upon our lives. Hallelujah! We may feel the blow, but with our God's help, we will survive and go on to glorify the Father.

The Holy Spirit had to shake me out of my stupor. The day that I walked out from behind the Enemy's gates, I felt like I was walking in slow motion. My feet felt like they were encased in cement, but the Holy Spirit gave me strength in my weakness. He walked with me and with every step that I took I kept repeating to myself, "You are a better woman than this. You are royalty. You are a daughter of the Most High God. You deserve better treatment than this. You don't have to settle for the crumbs under the table. You don't have to take this!" I said these words over and over in my mind as I walked away from that relationship, out of the land of my captivity, out from under the stronghold of secular music and fantasy, back into freedom and truth. Once I stepped back over onto holy ground, I repented to God of my disobedience. He washed over me with His Word. It felt so good to be free and on the road to recovery. I got busy repairing my ear gates. I saturated myself with worship music every moment I could. I had learned my lesson the hard way, but I had learned it. With God's help, I will never allow my ear gates to be violated in that manner ever again. I learned the importance of godly discernment and how to trust my God-given instincts when it comes to guarding my ear gates.

When we strongly consider what it means to guard our gates, we have to ask ourselves: Are we really doing all that is required of us to maintain possession of our gates? Are we giving up our power and authority because somehow the Devil has weakened us, picked at our wooden gates, lied to us and convinced us that we have no power or authority, or that his power is greater? Scripture reminds us that the One who is in us is far greater than the one who is in the world (1 John 4:4). This is a truth that we must cling to with all that we have within us. We have to keep reminding ourselves that the battle is raging and that Satan has murder on his mind, with many felonies under his belt. Even when we feel weak, it is still important that we continue to fight. The weakest punch that we throw at our

Adversary does *some* damage *somewhere*. If nothing else, it reminds us and him that we still maintain our position on the Lord's side of the battlefield. Every blow counts. Paul said that we do not fight as one who simply "beats the air" (1 Cor. 9:26). Every blow that we throw means that our gates are still intact and the thief cannot come in and steal, kill, or destroy.

All praise to God and to Jesus Christ, our Savior and our Redeemer, who stormed the gates of hell and snatched back a stolen set of keys. He has given those keys to you and me so that we can exercise our God-given authority at every strategic entrance to every strategic gate. We have got to understand and be confident that we have been given this power in Christ Jesus, not simply for head knowledge, but for us to use wherever and whenever necessary. When we begin to operate in that power, that authority, then we will be able to experience victories in reclaiming our valuables. We will see Satan and his demonic hosts expelled from our territory, just as when God booted Satan out of heaven, so that he fell, as the scripture says, "as fast as lightning" (Luke 10:18). We must ask the Lord to reveal to us the full realm of authority of what we hold in our hands so that we will begin to use our keys with confidence. There is an ancient African proverb that says, "A weapon which you do not have in your hand will not kill a snake." The keys of authority that Jesus gave to us must be kept in our hands at all times. We cannot afford to lay them down somewhere carelessly and give the Devil an opportunity to enter our territory unchecked. When we are careless with our authority, we grant our Adversary the license to trample our gates and to wreak havoc on our land, stealing, killing and destroying whatever he sees uncovered, unlocked and unguarded.

I want you to use your imagination for a minute. Let's say you are going on a lengthy vacation and you leave your beautiful home in the care of a trusted friend. You turn your house keys over to that friend with careful instructions on how to care for your home: i.e. no strangers in my house, no parties while I'm gone, no loud music disturbing the neighbors, lock the doors whenever you leave the house and before you retire at night, etc. You would expect to see your house in the same condition upon your return as it was the day you turned your keys over to your friend. If, upon your return, you find the front door broken down and all your goods strewn about on the floor, some valuable items missing, the windows broken and glass all over the floor, your friend would most definitely have "some explaining to do!" It is the same way with our Lord. He gave us His keys with explicit instructions on how to use them. When Christ returns in all of His glory, we will have to give an account to Him for how we guarded or failed to guard His goods. If we have been good stewards, we will be greatly rewarded. If we have been careless and slothful, there will be rebuke, weeping and gnashing of teeth (Mark 13:32-37; Matt. 25:14-28).

God requires us to be faithful stewards. He requires us to be watchful over what He has entrusted to us. He has not placed a responsibility on us that is more than what we can handle. He has made us watchmen on the walls. By giving us the keys, He has also made us keepers of those keys and guardians of the city's gates. He told His disciples in Matthew 13:12, "Whoever has will be given more, and he will have an abundance. Whoever does not have, even what he has will be taken from him." If we are not being wise stewards of our keys, we can expect to be robbed.

An old Latin proverb says, "We perish by permitted things." We cannot afford to self-destruct by carelessly permitting what we have been given the authority to prohibit.

Chapter 3

When Reason is Asleep

"Then, after desire has conceived, it gives birth to sin; and sin, when it is full-grown, gives birth to death." James 1:15

"Man is born free, but is everywhere in chains!"

- Social Contract (Jean-Jacques Rousseau, 1762)

Scholars who have studied Art History have recorded the phenomenal rise of a movement known as Romanticism, which began in 1750 and ended around 1850. The following gives a synopsis of the genesis and belief system of the Romantic era:

> Romanticism emerged from a desire for freedom – not only political freedom, but also freedom of thought, of feeling, of action, of worship, of speech, and of taste, as well as all the other freedoms. Romantics asserted that freedom is the right and property of one and all, though for each individual the kind and degree of freedom might vary. Those who affiliated them-

selves with Romanticism believed that the path to to freedom was through imagination rather than reason, and functioned through feeling rather than through thinking. For people living in the 18th century, the Middle Ages were the "dark ages," a time of barbarism, superstition, dark mystery, and miracle. The Romantic imagination stretched its perception of the Middle Ages into all the worlds of fantasy open to it, including the ghoulish, the infernal, the terrible, the nightmarish, the grotesque, the sadistic, and all the imagery that comes from the chamber of horrors when reason is asleep. [2]

"When reason is asleep..." "Reason" is otherwise defined as "discernment, foresight, or good judgment." Genesis 1 tells us that God separated the light from the darkness. The all-wise Creator never intended for the light and the darkness to co-exist. In establishing the order of Creation in this manner, God tucked away an important spiritual truth for us. What He joins together, no one should separate and what He separates, no one should attempt to rejoin. However, when reason is asleep, the creature begins to think that it knows better than its Creator. Thus, the lust for more knowledge, this unholy desire to feel something, anything, deeper and greater; the imaginations that lead us to think that we can be more than what God created us to be, even like God, are antagonistic towards God. This evil craving to know more than God knew we were able to handle in our finite state causes us to seek to establish another kind of order; that order would otherwise be known as *disorder*.

In the beginning, God said, "Light and dark shall be separated and that's good." We say, "I'll bet I can get light and dark to dwell together and that'll be even better!" However, any time we have tried to bring light and dark together, we've ended up with the macabre. We have ended up with unholy terrors, with the nightmarish, the grotesque, the sadistic and all the imagery and demonic spirits that emanate from the chamber of horrors. This explains homosexuality, lesbianism, bestiality and sodomy. It explains divorce, spousal and child abuse, rape and sexual molestation. It explains the brutality of slavery, racial prejudice and the Holocaust. It explains 9/11 and the war in Iraq today. This insatiable desire to connect with the unknown or to tap into some greater, higher source of knowledge or power is at the root of all of what is known as the occult. At its deepest core this desire is the sin of covetousness, the craving to possess something that belongs to someone else, or to which one is not entitled.

The word "occult" is a derivate of the Latin word *occultus*, which means "covered over" or "concealed." This Latin word *occultus* also means "knowledge of the secret, hidden, or supernatural." The desire for knowledge, in and of itself, is not evil. Proverbs 10:14 states: "Wise men store up knowledge." This thirst for more knowledge becomes evil only when that which is given to us to know by God is simply not enough for us and we begin to try to uncover what He has hidden from us by some other means. The gates to our ears come down very easily when God "forgets" about us or "withholds" something desired from us. Satan whispers lies into our ears and we quickly lose our grip on the truths about the character of God that we once believed. When we feel forgotten, slighted, or abandoned by God, we will try to wrestle the answers out of His hands by consulting witches and warlocks. We use tarot cards and eight-balls, attend séances, go to palm readers, consult mediums and fortune tellers and read our astrological forecasts, all in an effort to try to get the answers by some other means that God, in His divine sovereignty, has chosen not to reveal to us. All of these methods have their root in Romanticism and the occult, otherwise known as demonic activity.

In 1 Samuel 28 we read the account of Saul's consultation with the witch of Endor. This account of scripture tells us that when Saul saw the Philistine army coming up against him, his heart was filled with terror. He sought the LORD for direction, "but the LORD did not answer him by dreams, or Urim or prophets," the scripture says. God was not talking to Saul because Saul had been a disobedient king. However, Saul was desperate to hear a word of direction from God, so he asked the medium to conjure up the dead prophet Samuel, so that he could inquire of Samuel concerning the Philistines. Saul was well aware that consulting mediums was an abomination before God. In fact, to his credit, he had been responsible for ridding the land of all mediums and spiritists (v. 3). Nevertheless, in his desperation, Saul once again chose to disobey God. The witch did what she was asked to do and conjured up Samuel. However, when Samuel spoke he prophesied doom and gloom for the Israelites, and death for Saul and his sons.

Let me be very clear. Any means of receiving knowledge about a person, place, or thing and even about God Himself by a spiritual means other than that which has been provided to us by God – such as the study of His Word, materials passed on to us as dictated to His servants by the Holy Spirit, prayer, preaching and teaching and even godly counsel and life experiences – is satanic. Deuteronomy 29:29 tells us, "The secret things belong to the LORD, our God, but the things which are revealed belong to us and to our children forever." Therefore, in matters where God has chosen to tell us nothing, we would be wise to honor His right to exercise His sovereignty – good judgment would tell us to leave it alone! On the other hand, those things that He has given us to know, we should make it our passion to pursue, uncover and make ours. He has given us Himself to know.

How often we read in God's Word where He asks us to seek Him, to search for Him, to wait for Him, but then we read other places in His Word where He tells us that He hides Himself (Ps. 10:1; 97:2) and that "His ways are past finding out" (Rom. 11:33). It is precisely this divine paradox of endlessly chasing after a God Who cannot be fully discovered that wears many of us out and sends us down other paths where the catch is quicker, but lead to deception. We have to remain convinced that the Lover of our souls is more than worth the chase and that if we faithfully continue the pursuit we will inherit the reward of the diligent seeker. Though we would still never know all that can be known about Him, it is for sure we would know Him better. He will daily load us with benefits and our love for Him would grow stronger with every mountain that we conquer with Him, every valley that we walk through with Him and with every hill that we climb with our Savior. Oh, how rich we would be! How His glory would rest upon us. As kings and priests, we have yet to come into our full inheritance and we will not until we seek to own, at any cost, this Jewel, this Pearl of great price that is our beautiful Savior and Lord. Unfortunately, we are all too often just like our big sister, Eve, for with all that our generous and loving Creator has given us, it is not enough. If He keeps something secret from us, for Himself, or off limits to us for our protection, we are convinced that He is holding out on us and therefore, we *must* have it!

The following excerpt from Hannah Hurnard's book, *Hinds' Feet on High Places* paints a picture of what that struggle looks like and where it leads, when we set our hearts on pilgrimage without the Savior, convinced that we know what is best for our lives and that we know how to achieve those goals a lot faster without His assistance:

> For one black, awful moment Much-Afraid really considered the possibility of following the Shepherd no longer, or turning back. She need not go on. There was absolutely no compulsion about it. She had been following this strange path... simply because it was the Shepherd's choice for her. It was not the way which she naturally wanted to go. Now she could make her own choice. Her sorrow and suffering could be ended at once and she could plan her life in the way she liked best, without the Shepherd.

> During that awful moment or two it seemed to Much-Afraid that she was actually looking into an abyss of horror, into an existence in which there was no Shepherd to follow or to trust or to love – no Shepherd at all, nothing but her own horrible self. Even after, it seemed that she had looked straight into hell. At the end of that moment Much-Afraid shrieked – there is no other word for it – Hell. [3]

A pilgrimage without the Shepherd is a hike into the chambers of hell itself. To what lengths are we willing to go to possess the forbidden? What have we allowed into our ear gates that has us convinced that God has withheld something from us that we simply must have? Would we fake an illness to take advantage of a young, innocent female or male relative? Would we trade our inheritance for a bowl of beans, or sacrifice our anointing to lie in the lap of a seductress? Would we set up our most valiant warrior to be murdered in battle to have his wife? Would we sell out our Lord for thirty pieces of silver?

These were the sins of the ancients, but they are still being committed today. Fathers, brothers, uncles and cousins are still molesting and raping their own, innocent relatives. Husbands and wives are still sacrificing their precious families on the altar of forbidden sexual pleasures. Every day, another young Christian forfeits their godly inheritance by giving their talents and gifts to Satan because they are convinced that Satan pays better. We daily sell our Lord for thirty pieces of silver by the choices we make that compromise our Christianity and render our gates worthless.

When reason is asleep, there exists the very real and present danger that, not only will every one of our gates be violated, but completely destroyed. When we romance our desires, entertaining thoughts, pleasures and ideas that God tells us are off-limits to us, then we set ourselves up to lose the treasures that God has stored up for us behind those gates. We come dangerously close to operating in disobedience just like Saul, who continued to disobey God right up to the day of his tragic death. He was chosen by God to be king over Israel, but because of his disobedience, his pride, lack of foresight, and faulty mode of reasoning, Saul went to his grave in ruin. Our God has created us with the freedom to make our own choices, but the pull of our flesh keeps us bound in chains of disobedience, compromise and rebellion. We can take a lesson from the life of Saul. God is serious about radical obedience.

Part Three

The Eye Gates

"While we are looking at God, we do not see ourselves – blessed riddance. The man who has struggled to purify himself and has had nothing but repeated failure will experience real relief when he stops tinkering with his soul and looks away to the perfect One."

-A.W Tozer, *The Pursuit of God*

Chapter 4

Do You Wish To See?

"Be Thou my vision, O' Lord of my heart.

Naught be all else to me save that Thou art.

Thou my best thought by day or by night.

Waking or sleeping, Thy Presence, my Light."

-*Be Thou My Vision*, Saint Dallan Forgaill

"If we could only pull out our brains and use only our eyes."
-Pablo Picasso

*P*hysiologists record that the eye is the single most sensitive of all the human sensory organs. Nearly 70% of the body's sense receptors are located in the retina, an intricate light-sensing apparatus, which is only about a tenth of an inch in diameter. [4] What physiologists have discovered serves only to confirm what was recorded in the Word of God some 2,000 years ago in Matthew 6:22-23: "The eye is the lamp of the body. If your eyes are good, your whole body will be full of light. But if your eyes are bad, your whole body will be full of darkness. If then, the light within you is darkness, how great is that darkness."

Both the research of physiologists and the Word of God make it very clear that the eye gates are very important gates to guard. With the eye being the single most sensitive of all the human sensory organs, we get the unmistakable message that what we see, or fail to see, has the ability to significantly impact the entire body! Diane Ackerman notes in her book *A History of the Senses* that it is not the eyes that tell us what we see, but in fact, it is the brain that tells the eyes what they see "and all the eye does is gather light." [5]

Without getting too technical, here's how it works. The action of light on the cells of the retina fires off an impulse to the optic nerve and down to the visual portion of the brain. These impulses are interpreted as shapes and colors. If the contributions from the nerves of both the left and right sides of the retinas are 50/50, then what is communicated to the eyes, via the brain, is pretty clear with no distortions. What is seen, or perceived, is then recorded by the brain, so that every time you look at your dog, for example, good ol' Rover looks the same. Thus, it is important to note that relative to our natural sight, it is always true that we only see what we think we see. This is why optical illusions are such an enigma, because while the eye sees the illusion, the brain is remembering the image as recorded prior to the illusion.

To provide a little more clarity, let's define the word "illusion." According to Webster's Dictionary, an *illusion* is "a false impression, a delusion, a figment of your imagination, a fantasy, or a deception." Children of God, this is where the Adversary sees an opportunity to gain an advantage. He is the master of optical illusions, creating his very first illusion in a garden called Eden. Let's go back there for a moment.

In the beginning, when God created the heavens and the earth, the Bible tells us in Genesis 1:1-4 that "darkness was over the surface of the deep... And God said, 'Let there be light,' and there was light. God saw that the light was good, and He separated the light from the darkness." Genesis 1:31 tells us that after God created all He had made, He saw it was all very good. Then God put Adam and Eve in the Garden, giving them access to everything that was in the Garden, with the exception of one tree. The infraction of that one exception is where the guard to the eye gate was initially let down. The light that hit their spiritual retinas, being from an evil source, Satan, resulted in an act of disobedience that caused a visual distortion, both spiritually and naturally, which still exists today across the body of Christ. That distortion exists in the way we view God, in the way we view ourselves, and in the way we view one another. Pain also has a way of distorting our perception. In his book *The Problem of Pain*, C. S. Lewis very aptly describes the disorienting effects of pain upon the human body and soul:

> When I think of pain – of anxiety that gnaws like fire and loneli-
> ness that spreads out like a desert, and the heartbreaking routine
> of monotonous misery, or again of dull aches that blacken our
> whole landscape, sudden nauseating pains that seem already
> intolerable, and then are suddenly increased, of infuriating
> scorpion-stinging pains that startle into maniacal movement a
> man who seemed half dead with his previous tortures – it quite
> o'ercrows my spirit. If I knew any way of escape, I would crawl
> through sewers to find it.[6]

Because of our various painful life experiences, it is difficult for
us to trust God, in spite of what we know about His character. We
know what we know about Him, but when our lives fall prey to the
ravaging effects of sin and we find ourselves held fast in the grip of
pain, we begin to formulate a false impression about God. It is then
that we mold a god with our own hands. We come to the conclusion
that God is cold, sadistic and merciless. We reason that since He
is not answering us or coming to our rescue, then either He cannot
hear, or He is as powerless as us. Our man-made gods, fashioned
from the deep, dark wells of our pain-stricken, confused and grieving
souls, ironically, have all the faulty characteristics of our own fallen
nature. Like us, they are weak and powerless, unable to provide any
help to us in any way. They are gods that are erected higher and
higher by the many tormenting, unanswered questions posed during
the traumatic assaults upon our lives. These dangling questions now
only serve to bind us up and to hinder us from entering into true intimacy with our loving Lord and Savior, the Redeemer of our souls.

When the Adversary of our souls shouts at us after a brutal rape, "Your Loving God permitted this!" He shouts at us after the senseless, brutally horrific murder of a loved one, "Your Omnipotent God couldn't prevent this!" He shouts at us during and after years of molestation, "He didn't care then, and He doesn't care now!" He shouts at us after a financial crisis, in spite of the fact that you've been a faithful tither and a generous giver, "Jehovah Jireh? Can He even put a meal on your table? Ha!" He shouts at us after a failed marriage, "Where is your Present Helper now?" and we fail to hold fast to the truths that we know about our God in the midst of our unbearable pain; the God that we know crumbles before our very eyes. The god birthed out of our pain that then appears before our eyes will be very, very distorted.

Often, in the midst of our pain, we prefer our blindness because it becomes our justification, or a cover for the irresponsible course of action that we may choose to take, using our pain to excuse inglorious behavior. John 3:19-21 says: "This is the judgment, that the Light has come into the world, and men loved the darkness rather than the Light, for their deeds were evil. For everyone who does evil hates the Light, and does not come to the Light for fear that his deeds will be exposed. But he who practices the truth comes to the Light, so that his deeds may be manifested as having been wrought in God." (NASB) Although Jesus came to give sight to the blind, the blind must want to see. They must also be willing to acknowledge their blindness, because Jesus said, "It is not those who are well who need a physician, but those who are sick" (Luke 5:31, NASB). As long as we keep pretending as if everything is all right and we can manage just fine on our own, the Lord will allow us to remain in a state of infirmity.

In John 5:6, we find a paralyzed man whom the Bible says had been in his condition for a "very long time." Jesus asked him this one pivotal question, "Do you wish to get well?" Time and time again we read where Jesus asked the one who was sick if they wanted to be healed. This may seem like a foolish question to one who is sick or blind, but as John 3:19-21 has pointed out to us, more often than not, we do prefer our blindness and our illness because of the advantages they seem to afford us. Once we have allowed our eye gates to be violated, every principality and power of darkness will work overtime to make sure that what we have let in those gates is so gratifying to our senses that we will have no desire to have our vision restored. This is why Jesus asks us as well, "Do you wish to see?" We must have enough presence of mind, even in the midst of overwhelming pain, to cry out as did the two blind men in Matthew 20, "Lord, have mercy on us, Son of David!" (v. 30, NASB)

The scripture tells us that the crowd told the two blind men to "be quiet" (v. 31). Do you think that those men went and quietly sat back down on the road? Absolutely not! Look at what verse 31 says, "The crowd sternly told them to be quiet, but they cried out all the more, 'Lord, Son of David, have mercy on us!'" They were sick of being blind and unable to see the way God had intended them to see, so they became radical in their quest for restoration. They cried out, "Lord, we want our eyes to be opened!" Their sincere, desperate cry moved the heart of God, and the Bible says, "Moved with compassion, Jesus touched their eyes; and immediately they regained their sight and followed Him" (v. 34, NASB).

When we get good and ready to have our spiritual sight restored, we must be prepared to hear our flesh screaming at us to "shut up!" Our flesh will work hard at reminding us of all the benefits that blindness has achieved for us: sympathy, handouts, government assistance, temper tantrums and the best seats in the house. The Devil will be doing his job tightening that veil of darkness around our eyes, but our radical response should be to cry out all the more – "Jesus, Lord, Son of David, have mercy on me! I want to receive my sight! I want to see through a pure lens again! When God sees that we are serious, He will immediately restore our sight. His zeal is stirred for us when He sees that we are depending upon Him as our Helper.

This is what the LORD says to his anointed, to Cyrus, whose right hand I take hold of to subdue nations before him and to strip kings of their armor, to open doors before him so that gates will not be shut: I will go before you and will level the mountains; I will break down gates of bronze and cut through bars of iron. I will give you treasures of darkness, riches stored in secret places, so that you may know that I

am the LORD, the God of Israel, who summons you by name
(Isa. 45:1-3, NIV).

On our own, we are no match for Satan. We have to ask the Holy
Spirit to help us and to teach us how to effectively use every weapon
in our spiritual arsenal. We must be ever straining to discover those
"treasures of darkness" and those "hidden riches" found only in the
secret places, during the dark nights of the soul. There are lessons
that God wants us to learn as we grope along in the dark, leaning
upon His strong right arm. Beyond the surface of our excruciating
pain are precious, hidden nuggets of truth to be uncovered along the
way as we walk with the Savior, listening to His voice, and learning
from His instructions.

The layers of pain that we have to endure are often so thick that
we have to make up our minds, ahead of time, that we are committed
to the journey. We have got to dig and dig for those truths just as a
man would dig for gold. As we are digging, we might hit a nerve
that pains us so until we are ready to turn back, but the Holy Spirit is
there to help us face our pain and feed us truth as we are able to bear
it. No matter how loud or persistent Satan's knocking – *do not open
that gate!* We must know and follow the voice of the Good Shepherd
and not dare listen to the Thief's accusatory lies. We must slam the
gate shut and lock it, clutching the keys tightly to our bosoms, even
if we feel weak and timid. One such act of deliberate strength that
goes against our divided will in the midst of a brutal attack can

release mighty, divine power! Isaiah 28:6 tells us that God will be "a source of strength to those who turn back the battle at the gate," not after the gate has been opened and the Devil is already in, but before he has even had a chance to pick the lock! You have got to tell your Adversary, "Devil, I said, No! You can't come in!" "No, Devil! I will not have that drink!" "I will not fornicate with him tonight!" "No Devil, I will not indulge in pornography ever again!" "I will not gamble my hard earned money away again!" "I will not cheat on my taxes!" "Devil, I will not tell another lie!" "No Devil! Get away from my door!"

It is important to note that although Satan began his deception with a conversation with Eve, shrewdly unlocking her ear gates, it was not what she heard that caused her to disobey God, although true enough, the fact that her ear gates were left unguarded made it easy for the Serpent to whisper lies in her ears. Faith comes by hearing. The lie whispered in her unguarded ear gate gave her enough faith to go the next step and look at the forbidden fruit. What moved Eve to take action against the command of the LORD God was what she saw. In Genesis 3:5-6, of the forbidden fruit, Satan tells Eve, "God knows that when you eat of it, your eyes will be opened, and you will be like God, knowing good and evil" (v. 5). The scene continues, "When the woman *saw* that the fruit of the tree was good for food and pleasing to the eye, and also desirable for gaining wisdom, she took some and ate it" (v. 6). The optical illusion that Satan created presented the forbidden fruit to Eve as a source of greater power, or a greater light, a deeper realm of knowledge than that which God, her Creator had made available to her. They would become gods in their own rights, was the message that Satan was trying to communicate to both Adam and Eve.

While Eve's brain had a recorded image of herself as a woman, a a created being, the optical illusion, or false impression of the fruit's ability, as craftily presented by the Serpent, coupled with Eve's own lusts, resulted in the fallacy of vision that led her to believe a serpent and to doubt her Creator, God. What was she looking for that she did not already have? What made her feel that she was lacking in some area of her "being"? What made her feel as though God was keeping something from her that she should have been entitled to possess? What made her feel that she was not completely free? Satan, the master of deception, still schemes the same way today as he did back in the genesis of time.

Like Eve, we can easily fall prey to this same enticing spirit when we take our eyes off of our Lord and shift our gaze to the Adversary of our souls. We lock eyes with him and hoist him up to dizzying heights of influence over the decisions concerning our destinies. This enticing spirit makes a happily married man look outside of his marriage for something more, something different. This spirit causes a perfectly healthy young woman to starve herself to death to conform to an unappeasable, distorted and unrealistic media image of the perfect woman. This monster called "the media" has been given the power to dictate to her who and what she "should" look like to be considered acceptable by the world's standards. To a single person, watching all of his/her friends get married, this spirit plants a seed in their minds that manifests as the thought that God is withholding their "good thing" from them. To the little-known pastor who has been entrusted with fifty congregants, seeing mega-churches on The Word Network and TBN causes him to feel dissatisfied with the few sheep God has entrusted to his care.

For each of the above scenarios there is a Word from God, which, if skillfully applied, can seal the gates shut to victoriously ward off Enemy invasion. To the married man, Hebrews 13:4 states, "Marriage should be honored by all, and the marriage bed kept pure, for God will judge the adulterer, and all the sexually immoral." To the anorexic young lady, Psalm 139:13-14 says, "You created me in my inmost being; You knit me together in my mother's womb. I praise you because I am fearfully and wonderfully made." To the dissatisfied single, Psalm 84:11 tells us, "No good thing does He withhold from those whose walk is blameless." To the pastor who thinks that mega is better, "For God is not unjust so as to forget your work and the love which you have shown toward His name, in having ministered and in still ministering to the saints" (Heb. 6:10, NASB).

Since the gates are considered places of authority where one can see and be seen, we have to be very careful about what we continue to center our gaze upon. We must understand that whatever we hoist up at our eye gates is what is going to operate in the position of authority in our lives. We have to ask ourselves if the thing that we are constantly looking at is the thing to which we are willing to submit our lives. It requires a great deal of discernment to rightly distinguish between the truths of God and the optical illusions that the Devil holds up before our eyes. When discernment is operating, we will quickly disengage the Enemy and look to our God for clarity and truth. This means that discernment is a vital building material in the reconstruction of our gates.

Chapter 5

A Holy Gaze

"They shall look upon Him whom they have pierced"
John 19:37 (NKJV).

*R*ecently, I had a vision of the bride of Christ standing before her mirror, completely frustrated with her wedding apparel. She was confused as to what to wear on her wedding day. Her veil was beautiful, but underneath her veil were body piercings on her upper eyelid, nose, and upper lip. She had tattoos on her upper body, which she was having difficulty covering up with her low-cut top. Wearing only the bottom portion of a wedding gown that ended mid-thigh, black spandex slacks and stilettos, she dropped to her knees before her mirror, sobbing bitterly at her appearance. She knew that her Groom would not be pleased with what He saw, but she had been gazing at the world so intently for so long that she knew only how to adorn herself as the world's images adorned themselves.

When we fix our eyes on worthless idols and devote count-less hours to studying their ways and manners, though we may not realize it, we slowly begin to accept their behaviors and ultimately adopt their ways. The Glory of the true God that was once evident upon us begins to fade and the deep veil of darkness that Isaiah says covers the face of the earth now begins to rest upon the children of God as well (Isa. 60:1-3). Soon we will begin to forget whose bride we are. Soon we will forget what we are supposed to look like. The corruption of the world that we have allowed to enter into our eye gates begins to flood our whole being until the difference between the world and us is no longer evident. Paul exhorts us in Colossians 3:1-4 with these words:

> Since then, you have been raised with Christ, set your hearts on things above, where Christ is seated at the right hand of God. Set your minds on things above, not on earthly things. For you died, and your life is now hidden with Christ in God. When Christ who is in you appears, then you also will appear with Him in glory.

The wickedness and immorality of the world that is consid-ered in-vogue should never become acceptable amongst believers. If we take a look around, we will clearly see that we have indeed allowed the world's influences to creep into every facet of our living, including our style of dress, how we spend and invest our money, into the music that we listen to and the music that we create, into our entertainment through the programs that we watch on television and the movies that we pay to see, into our relationships as we yoke ourselves with unbelievers and into our ideas and beliefs concerning morality, sexual intimacy, marriage and the family.

Increasingly, popular female Hollywood celebrities, who have chosen their careers over devoting themselves to their marriages, have opted to have children out of wedlock, boldly claiming that they don't need a husband to have the baby. Their influence over the minds of young, impressionable teen-aged girls is not to be underestimated. In addition, a recent article entitled *Exposing Pornography,* written by Bishop Clifford and Pamela Frazier, was published in *Gospel Today Magazine* January/February 2011. It records the following statistics on Christians who indulge in pornography:

- Although four out of five Christians believe that pornography is a morally unacceptable vice, 47% of Christians acknowledge that pornography is a major problem in their homes.
- In the 2001 Leadership Survey it was discovered that 40% of evangelical Protestant clergy who responded to the survey admitted that they struggle with pornography.
- A survey conducted by Rick Warren of Saddleback Church found that in the previous month, 30% of pastors had viewed pornography.

These statistics are frightening and disturbing. We must do a radical shift and look intently again at the blessed face of our Lord, our Savior, Jesus Christ. When we gaze upon Him, His Word tells us in 2 Corinthians 3:18 that the veil is removed and we, then, "with unveiled faces all reflecting the Lord's glory, are being transformed into His likeness with ever increasing (not decreasing) glory, which comes from the Lord, who is the Spirit," (parenthesis added). When we gaze upon the blessed face of the Savior, light begins to shine out of our darkness. This light, the scripture tells us penetrates and enters into our hearts and "gives us the light of the knowledge of the glory of God" (2 Cor. 4:6). This is all in the face of Jesus Christ, if we will only really look at Him. You see, whatever we fix our gaze upon is what we will ultimately begin to reflect. We must ask ourselves, "What images do we want seared across the lenses of our eyes?" "What do we want to look like?" "Whose image do we want to reflect?" "Whose bride have we become?"

Saints of God, I am sounding the alarm! This is a shake-up, because we, the bride of Christ must wake up! The prophet Jeremiah was appalled at the idea that a nation would ever even consider changing its god. "Have you ever seen anything like this?" he asked. "Has a nation ever changed its gods? (Yet they are not gods at all.) But my people have exchanged their Glory for worthless idols... Shudder with great horror" (Jer. 2:10-12). If ever I were to find myself stranded in the middle of the desert beside a crystal clear stream of water and some lone traveler were to approach me, offering to trade his cracked, leaking bottle of water for my stream, I would be a fool to accept his proposition. Give me something that will satisfy my longing and quench my thirst. However, isn't this in effect what we do when, by turning our gaze from the Lover of our souls to the things of this world, we begin to trade our passions? We buy the cheap thrill goods that the world is holding up before our eyes and we sell our precious Jesus in exchange for these worthless idols. Our thirst remains unquenched – our souls unsatisfied. It's that same thirty pieces of silver type deal that cost Judas Iscariot his life and his soul (Matt. 27:3-10).

In Matthew 4:8-10, we find Jesus battling with the Devil, being tempted by him out in the desert. He had been in a place of serious consecration, having fasted for forty days and forty nights. Satan thought he had the upper hand. He kept making Jesus grandiose propositions to sell out His Father in exchange for worthless things. In verses 8-11 we read: "Again, the devil took him to a very high mountain and showed him all the kingdoms of the world and their splendor. 'All this I will give you,' he said, 'if you will bow down and worship me.' Jesus said to him, 'Away from me, Satan! For it is written: "Worship the Lord your God, and serve him only."' Then the devil left him and angels came and attended him." Jesus had full control of His eye gates and was not able to be tempted to accept any one of Satan's offers. Everything that he held up before Jesus's eyes, Jesus threw back at him, in essence saying, "No, thank you! You can keep your worthless idols. They are of no value to Me!" He loved the Father more, thoroughly understood His mission and was radical in His obedience. Through His obedience He has reversed the curse that was passed down to us through Adam's disobedience and has made it possible for us to inherit eternal life through our obedience and belief in Him (1 Cor. 15:20-23).

One of my favorite books of the Bible is the gospel of John because it is the one book that very clearly shows us how close Jesus was to His Father. It repeats the theme that Jesus so wants us to get. He loves the Father. The Father loves Him. He does nothing without the Father. He speaks no words unless they are the Father's words. If you have seen Him, you have seen the Father. He and the Father are one. Jesus always kept His gaze on His Father. This is the secret He has freely given us to know.

At the writing of this book, my daughter and two granddaughters – Aiyana, who is five years old and Tiasha, who is three years old – are all living under my roof. Very often, I catch my five-year-old granddaughter, Aiyana, staring at me. When we sit down to dinner to eat, she stares at me. When we are driving along in the car, she stares at me. When I am talking to her mother or her little sister; Aiyana stares at me. We could be sitting watching a movie together, one that she likes and rather than her watching the movie, I will catch her in my peripheral vision looking intently at me. Feeling somewhat uncomfortable with this habit of hers, I have often asked her why she stares at me so. Her only response is, "I don't know." However, I have discovered that Aiyana stares at me to study me so that she can mimic me in her own little world. At the tender age of five, she has seen something in me that she likes and respects and this has caused her to want to be like me. If she has a tummy ache and I hug her and pray over her, she will show that same kind of compassion towards her little sister. It may be weeks later that Tiasha may get a tummy ache, or some sort of little "boo-boo," but Aiyana will recall how I treated her and she will respond in kind to Tiasha.

I have learned two very important lessons from Aiyana. The first is that, once I realized she was staring at me because she was looking for clues from which to draw conclusions that would shape her identity as an individual and as a woman, I became even more careful of how I behaved in front of her. I wanted to be able to give her something worthwhile to look at. In this same way, when we set our gaze upon Jesus Christ, we, too are drawing valuable clues from Him that will shape our lives. He, too, wants to give us something to look at. As we gaze upon Him, we see His holiness and we want to be holy as He is holy. We see His compassion and we want to exhibit this same compassion towards others. We see and experience His love and mercy and we want to be loving and merciful towards others. The outward expression of this inward gaze of the soul continues with us as an abiding presence of the Holy One and is readily evidenced in our treatment of others. Second, I realized that every time she set her gaze on me, I saw her. I saw her seeing me. It is strengthening to know that the God we have fixed our gaze upon also sees us. We are not some tiny speck of dust that He has lost track of amongst the other billions and trillions of specks down here on earth. David said in Psalm 139 that there is no place where we can go where the eyes of God do not see us.

A holy gaze upon our Lord will help us to filter out everything from our eye gates that does not reflect Him. We will become sensitive to those things that offend the eyes of God and they will begin to offend our eyes as well. As His bride, we will be confident of our relationship to Him and of our identity in Him. We will come to know the kind of attire that our Groom likes and dislikes on us and we will understand that holiness must be woven throughout the fabric of our gates if we are to have gates of substance. When we stand before that mirror, reflecting His image, we will know exactly what to wear on that glorious day when He returns for us=a gown without spot or wrinkle.

"Let us be glad and rejoice and give honor to him: for the marriage of the Lamb is come, and his wife hath made herself ready. And to her was granted that she should be arrayed in fine linen, clean and white: for the fine linen is the righteousness of saints" Rev. 19:7, 8 (KJV).

<u>Men as Trees</u>

When they arrived at Bethsaida, some people brought a blind man to Jesus, and they begged him to touch the man and heal him. Jesus took the blind man by the hand and led him out of the village. Then, spitting on the man's eyes, he laid his hands on him and asked, "Can you see anything now?" The man looked around. "Yes," he said, "I see people, but I can't see them very clearly. They look like trees walking around." Then Jesus placed his hands on the man's eyes again, and his eyes were opened. His sight was completely restored, and he could see everything clearly (Mark 8:22-25, NLT).

Upon reading the story of the blind man from Mark 8:22-25, one of the very first questions that came to my mind was, *Why did not Jesus heal this man the first time He laid hands on him?* Surely, He could have. As I began to study and pray about this, the Holy Spirit revealed to me that seeing clearly – both natural truths and spiritual truths – does not come easily. Sometimes we have to work at seeing clearly. Sometimes we need the Holy Spirit to bring truth to us in stages, in much the same way as a camera allows us to see clearly objects that are far away as we turn the lens to bring them sharply into focus. Sometimes we need our lenses cleaned to see clearly. Always we need the Savior's touch upon our eyes so that when we look at men, we see men as men and not as trees. In my own walk with Jesus, I have found that often He will touch me the first time to get my attention so that I will posture myself for the second touch, which comes to bring deeper insights.

If we listen in on the Genesis conversation between Eve and the Serpent, we witness an attempt by God to tug at Eve to bring a truth sharply into focus for her; to make it sit down in her spirit like concrete, unmovable. As the Serpent twists the words of God in Eve's ears, Eve initially puts up a good fight – much like Jesus did in His battle with Satan in the desert in the gospel of Mark 4. As Jesus said to Satan, "It is written," likewise Eve squared off on the lie of the Serpent by reminding him in Genesis 3:2-3 that God did not say that they could not eat from *any* of the trees in the Garden. What He did say was that they could eat from *every* tree except the one tree that sat in the middle of the Garden, or they would surely die. Score one for Eve! She threw the first blow, landing squarely on the Serpent's lying lips. The very fact that Eve declared truth over the Serpent's lie was evidence that God was there with Eve, helping her fight this battle. He was trying to get Eve's attention; trying to keep her eyes locked in with His.

Unfortunately, Eve never made it to that second tug on her spirit from God. She had quickly shifted her gaze from her God and had, instead, locked eyes with the Serpent that was holding up the optical illusion before her face. The Lover of her soul, her Creator God, no longer had His creation's attention; therefore the battle of Eden was lost to the Serpent on that woeful day in the genesis of time. No, Eve never got the chance to receive the deeper revelation – that she was created by God and for God. She was His special treasure, made for His delight to bring Him great glory all the days of her life. Had Eve kept her eyes fixed on her God, she would have discovered that nothing in all creation could ever have brought her more delight and satisfaction than Him. He was and is more than enough.

Eve was a woman who had it all and yet she allowed herself to be deceived into thinking that something was missing. What was at the core of her deception? The passage of scripture found in James 1:13-15 gives us some insight into this. According to James, we sin when we are enticed and then allow ourselves to be dragged away by our own particular, unholy desires. The desire conceived births sin and the full-grown sin then gives birth to death. It is indeed a tragedy that one little desire can result in death—the death of a marriage or other relationship, a lifelong dream, the death of a church, a nation, a world. From the moment that Eve gave birth to her desire and ceased to guard her eye gates, the darkness began to flood her whole body. Though she could eat of any of the other trees in the Garden, she reasoned that *this* fruit was "good for eating" (representative of the lust of the flesh), "pleasing to the eye" (representative of the lust of the eye) and "desirable for gaining wisdom" (representative of the pride of life). After thus reasoning, she cast care to the wind, flung the gates open wide and in a blatant act of rebellion and disobedience to her God, she ate the fruit and then gave some to her husband. As a result of this one act of disobedience, she forfeited the good land that God had given to her, to her husband and to their descendants. Her destiny was determined not only by what she saw as presented to her by Satan, but also (very tragically) by what she failed to see.

Eve saw a piece of fruit disguised as something that could give her a new level of freedom and promote her to the status of being equal with God. She failed to see the provision of a loving God in all that comprised her world. She failed to see the freedom that she already enjoyed, the peace and the comfort that God had given to her. She failed to see the Serpent for what he was, but by far, her greatest indiscretion was in her failure to see God for who He is. Thus, Eve missed her opportunity to deal the Devil that knockout punch! Every gate was violated on that dreadful day and we have been struggling to reconstruct the gates to the kingdom of God within us ever since. Perhaps if we would just consider ourselves legally blind when it comes to perceiving the things of God, we would be forced into leaning entirely upon the Lord to help us understand the things that we see, or think we see.

On our own, we see only illusions. With our best sight, 20/20 vision, we still can only see what we think we see. However, because we have an inclination to be carnal-minded, far too often what we think we see is what we latch onto as reality. This method of drawing conclusions can be very costly to our interpersonal relationships. It can be costly to our marriages and our families in how we relate to our spouses and our children. It can be costly in how we respond to things that we think we see at our jobs and in the church.

Joe and Susan had been dating for about three months. They really enjoyed each other's company and each thought they had found their soul-mate in life. After a romantic dinner out one evening, Susan excused herself to go to the ladies room. When she came out of the ladies room, she looked around for Joe, but did not see him. She waited for what seemed like ten minutes. Finally, she flipped open her cell phone to call him. Just then, Joe exited the men's room and hastily and angrily walked past Susan as though he did not even see her, almost brushing up against her. He walked straight to the exit door, then stopped just short of walking out of the door, turned back and motioned to her to accompany him. Susan was shaken, confused and humiliated. The silence between them was thick.

Once they got in the car, Susan broke the silence by asking Joe if he was all right. Joe was tight-lipped, but responded that he was okay. A few minutes into the drive home, Joe suddenly asked Susan if she was talking to another man. Susan was completely caught off guard by the question, but answered honestly that she was not. She then asked Joe what would make him think such a thing about her? Joe responded by telling her that almost since their first date, he had noticed that every time he left the room, upon his return she seemed to have been checking her phone, but would quickly close it and put it away, as though she had been texting or receiving a text from another man. Now Susan's head was spinning and she was hurt that Joe would accuse her of having an unfaithful heart towards him.

Joe was right about the fact that Susan always seemed to be checking her phone whenever he left the room. He was also correct in observing that she would always close it and quickly put it away upon his return, but he was wrong about her motive. The truth of the matter was that Susan was very much the introvert. Joe was very much the extrovert. When they were together, Joe's outgoing nature always made Sue feel comfortable and at ease, but when Joe left her all by herself, she became anxious and self-conscious. To be at home alone by choice was safe and in fact, comforting for an introvert such as herself, but to be out in public with another and then suddenly left on her own, was a problem to be solved. Sue solved the problem of being left alone by temporarily replacing Joe with her phone. It was something to keep her company while he was gone. Her fiddling with her phone was nothing more than a nervous habit. She quickly closed it upon his return because she was happy that Joe was back and she no longer needed her phone to keep her company.

Joe was completely wrong about Susan's faithfulness to him and in the course of time, his unfounded suspicions cost him the relationship, all because he quickly and erroneously judged a situation based solely upon what he saw with his eyes. It has been said that "What you see depends on what you are looking for." Oftentimes, when the lamp of our body is bad, what we see outwardly in others or in situations outside of ourselves is filtered by what we project from within. Titus 1:15 says, "To the pure all things are pure, but to those who are corrupted... nothing is pure." If you look for dirt hard enough, you will find it, even if there is none there.

When the lens of a slide projector is dirty, everything projected on the screen filtered through that lens is also dirty and muddy. We expect others to respond, to act or react to others or situations in the same way that we would if we were in their shoes. Herein is evidence that a gate was violated and then rebuilt by the hands of man, a shabby gate at best. This is where we err and why we so desperately need the Lord's hand upon our eyes. Thus did David petition his God, "Save us and help us with your right hand, that those you love may be delivered …Give us aid against the enemy, for the help of man is worthless. With God we will gain the victory" (Ps. 60:5, 11-12).

The method we use to assess natural things, frequently drawing conclusions hastily and without careful thought, is unfortunately the same way that we will often approach spiritual matters. Take prayer, for instance. How many times do we hastily run into our prayer closets and try to pray down fire and brimstone over a situation that is, at best, seen through a cloudy lens? We come out of the prayer closet sweaty, exhausted, dry-mouthed and hoarse from crying out to the Lord. We eagerly look for God to move on behalf of our prayers, watching and waiting in expectation. Time passes by slowly and we wonder what is wrong with God; we wonder where God is, why the answers have not come and why the matters undertaken in prayer remain unchanged.

It is so important for us to take what we see with our natural eyes into the light of God's presence. Sitting in His presence we wait, we listen, we hear and there we receive council from the Spirit of the Lord in discerning with the spiritual eye what He has allowed us to see with the natural eye. This is how we gain spiritual insight into the matters for prayer. When we come to hasty conclusions based solely upon what we see with the naked eye, we will almost always come to the wrong conclusion. Standing in the council of the Most High God, we are privileged to gain His perspective on the issues. Jeremiah 23:18, 22 says, "But which of them has stood in the council of the LORD to see or to hear his word? Who has listened and heard his word? But if they had stood in my council, they would have proclaimed my words to my people..." Jeremiah 33:3 says, "Call to me, and I will answer you and tell you great and unsearchable things you do not know." Did you see that? It's not what you think. It's what God knows and chooses to reveal to you.

When we are conscientious to stand in the council of the all-seeing, all-knowing, all-wise God, it is not an exercise in futility. It is not a time waster. On the contrary, we are wasting our time trying to conduct kingdom business in the place of prayer when we neglect to take the time to stand in His council. This means that we must choose to *sit* and *wait* for Him to speak to us. We must wait for a holy unction from Him, an unmistakable movement upon our hearts, a sensing of His presence in the place of prayer and that it has left a deposit upon our spirits. Standing in the Lord's council, we sense His heart, receive His mind and hear His voice over every other voice.

Praying over disturbing or pressing matters that we see or hear about, in a manner that assumes that we know what God is up to, without seeking God's council, reveals an arrogance that pushes God away from us. This defeats the whole purpose of prayer, which is to move God to bend His ear to us, hear our cry and answer us. If Jesus, the Son of God and God incarnate, could do nothing without the Father, what makes us think that we can? Jesus said, in John 5:19, "I tell you the truth, the Son can do nothing by himself; he can only do what he sees his Father doing, because whatever the Father does, the Son also does." It must resound in our spirits that we can do *absolutely nothing* without the Father! It is the Spirit of the Holy One that quickens our mortal flesh and gives us fervency in prayer. His wisdom gives us accuracy and makes our prayers effectual and it is only by doing it His way that we are considered "righteous" in our doing. Then and only then, will our prayers avail much (James 5:16). You see, it is not merely the praying of prayers that makes one effective in prayer, but it is the right praying of prayers that gives one power in the halls of heaven and causes the very foundations of hell to crumble.

Consider this scripture taken from Isaiah 11:3-4. Speaking of Jesus, it reads, "He will not judge by what he sees with his eyes, or decide by what he hears with his ears; but with righteousness he will judge the needy, with justice he will give decisions for the poor of the earth." Now surely one would think that Jesus Christ could trust what He saw with His eyes and render judgments based on the same, but why didn't He? It is because He rendered judgment based on His character. The very character of God is just. I believe that

Jesus was always thinking about us in all of His actions. Therefore, it was important to Him to leave us an example, a method, if you will, of judging matters and coming to righteous conclusions. His example cautions us not to make hasty decisions based exclusively upon what we see and certainly not based upon what we project from the inside out. Our Lord is righteous in all of His ways. Lest we be tempted to judge a matter solely based upon what we see, God has given us a standard to follow and uphold. We allow so much impurity to flood our eye gates that we must be ever conscious to keep looking to Jesus. We must keep returning to the true standard, giving Him permission to tear down our faulty gates and rebuild our gates in righteousness.

I, myself, have found in the most painful of ways that God deals with the sin in the life of the intercessor first, that individual who feels called to stand in the gap for others, before He allows the intercessor to deal with sin on any other front. We must be willing to allow Him to reveal areas of unfaithfulness, rebellion, disobedience, untruth and compromise in our own lives and we must labor alongside the precious Holy Spirit to rid our lives of such transgressions.

> ...and we lead every thought and purpose away captive into the obedience of Christ (the Messiah, the, Anointed One). Being in readiness to punish every [insubordinate for his] disobedience, when your own submission and obedience are fully secured and complete (2 Cor. 10:5-6, AMP).

If you are reading this book and you believe that you have been called to the ministry of intercessor for your family, your community, your coworkers, or your local church, you should know that such a call is more than a notion. It is not a call to be taken lightly. You will never see your family, your coworkers, your neighbors, or your pastor and first lady the way that God would have you to see them; you will never see your God-appointed leadership the way that God wants you to see them; you will never see the body of Christ in your local assembly in the way that God wants you to see them until you first get before God and allow Him to let you see yourself for who you really are in the light of His holiness.

I want to caution you that you are not the standard! As an intercessor, it gets tempting to judge things by what you would like to see God do, rather than by what God knows needs to happen in the lives of the ones for whom we are praying. You cannot judge merely by what you see, or by what you think you see. Everything must be sifted through the eyes of God and the Spirit of God.

Should you dare to answer the call to the ministry of intercession, you will find yourself on a journey the likes of which you have not taken before. You will come to understand the importance of guarding every gate to the kingdom of God within. Under the mighty hand of God, as you yield to Him in humility, reverent submission and obedience, He will wisely and lovingly send difficult and challenging situations into your life that will serve to break you, cleanse you and make you into the anointed vessel that you must be to achieve efficacy and fervency as an intercessor. In His infinite wisdom and under His watchful eye, God will allow you to undergo trials fashioned by the Devil himself. God may let the trials come your way, but He will not allow them to have their intended effect upon your life (Isa. 54:17). What Satan means for evil, God can and will turn around for your good if you will embrace His Sovereignty, submit to Him, continue to earnestly seek Him and steadfastly trust Him (Rom. 8:28). I am a firm believer that God can use any and every trial, just and unjust, to mold us into the vessels of His intention if we will simply yield our whole selves to Him. Eventually, we come to realize the inescapable, yet wonderful truth that we are all mere tools in the Master's hands that He skillfully uses to accomplish His will upon the earth.

If we are going to be advocates of our Lord's standard for judging matters rightly, then we will need a strategy for maintaining the purity of the lamp of our whole body. Our failure to guard our eye gates can certainly wreck our truth compass and dim our lamps. We have just such a strategy found in Psalm 19:8 which states: "The law of the LORD is pure, enlightening the eyes." This tells us that if we keep looking into God's pure Word and if we keep walking in God's pure Word, the light of our eyes will become purer and more glorious. With that greater glory come greater revelations into the perfect will of God. Psalm 119:105 tells us that God's Word is a lamp unto our feet, and a light unto our paths. His Word will lead us and guide us into all truth.

On the other hand, if our eyes are focused on the wrong things, our sight becomes bad. The lamp of our whole body becomes a filter for evil, a wide open gate, an entrance for darkness to come in and flood our entire being, mind, body and soul. When this happens, everything that we see or think we see will be seen through a filthy lens. How does one pray for himself or for others, when he can only see men as trees? How does one "stand in the gap" while looking through a dirty lens? When the lenses of my eyeglasses are dirty, I become frustrated because, first of all, it is extremely difficult to see and second, what I do see is greatly distorted. I can't find a tissue fast enough to clean off my lenses because I want to see everything as it is supposed to be, without any distortions. Shouldn't we be at least this eager to see clearly in the spirit? We ought to be running into the presence of God, asking Him to restore our vision and to forgive the sins of our eyes that have caused our spiritual lenses to become cloudy and to repair our eye gates. We ought to be asking Him to restore our gaze upon Him.

Jesus longs for us to look upon Him. John 19:37 says, "They shall look upon Him whom they have pierced" (NKJV). In Greek, this "look" is *optanomai* (op-tan'-om-ahee).[7] It means "to gaze; i.e. with wide-open eyes, as at something remarkable..." It is a derivative of another Greek word *horao* (hor-ah'-o),[8] which means "to discern clearly... behold, perceive... and to take heed." This is how our Lord wants us to look at Him. He wants to flood our eye gates with His beauty, His radiance, His love and His glory. He wants every part of our eyes to see every part of Him as the Beautiful One, the Remarkable One who loves us with a jealous love, so much that He gave up His own life for us (John 3:16). If I could describe this desire of our Lord in everyday terms, I would liken it to that of a jealous husband who desires his wife to have eyes for him only and who is deeply offended when she sees another man as more remarkable than him – it's just like that, only much, much purer.

When we turn our eyes to another lover, the heart of God is grieved because He already knows that no other lover can satisfy us like He can. He sees the intense sorrow that awaits us and He makes many attempts to win back our gaze. While we spend our time and our energy drinking from fountains that continuously run dry, He patiently waits for us. He broods over us. He misses us. Although He has millions and trillions of other children, His love for each of us is so intense and unique that it is as if we were the only object of His affection. His love for me takes nothing away from His love for you.

It would seem that it takes great faith to maintain a steady gaze upon something or someone who, to the naked eye is completely invisible, but this is not the case. With each new day, we place our faith in countless things that we cannot see and of which we have only a finite understanding of how they exist and operate. We are able to walk with our feet planted firmly on the ground because of gravity, unseen with the naked eye. We live on a planet that travels in its orbit at 66,700 miles an hour, or 18.5 miles a second and yet I have never heard anyone say that they were afraid that they might fly off the earth's surface.[9] We breathe in air every day that we cannot see. Jesus said that if we have only mustard seed faith, we can move mountains (Matt. 17:20). If we will only exercise our little mustard seed faith, we will experience the Holy Spirit's help empowering us to do what we never imagined possible. We can fix our gaze upon the unseen God. God places His supernatural ability upon our weakest "yes." All we need is the desire to look upon Him and to seek His face continually. Hence, without faith as a building material of our gates, we can expect they will be torn down again.

Chapter 6

A Faulty Lamp

"The lamp of the wicked will be put out" Prov. 13:9 (NKJV).

olomon records in Ecclesiastes 3:2 and 6, "There is a time to plant and a time to uproot; a time to keep and a time to throw away." Jesus said in Matthew 5:13, "You are the salt of the earth. But if the salt loses its saltiness, how can it be made salty again? It is no longer good for anything except to be thrown out and trampled by men." As Christians, God has entrusted us with His light. We are to let it shine in our homes, in our communities and to the nations. If we are not careful to guard our eye gates, what pulses through the currents of our temples – that is, our bodies – will ultimately cause our lamps to go completely out. We will be unable to see the needs of the lost all around us and we will definitely be unable to meet those needs. Let us take a look at some of those influences that have the power to make the lamp of our bodies go bad. Among them are the spirits of compromise, lust, envy, hatred, rebellion, pride, jealousy and fear.

<u>Compromise</u>

Wisdom from the Word of God, in Deuteronomy 16:19-20 warns us, "Do not accept a bribe, for a bribe blinds the eyes of the wise and twists the words of the righteous. Follow justice and justice alone, so that you may live and possess the land the LORD your God is giving you." The spirit of compromise will distort our vision and persuade us to see only what the one for whom we are compromising wants us to see. If the bribe is sweet enough, this spirit will even prostitute us like dummies and make us say what it wants us to say. The prophet Samuel asked the Israelites in 1 Samuel 12:3, "From whose hand have I received any bribe to blind my eyes?" Samuel was a true prophet of God, used greatly of God in his day. His refusal to compromise was, in large part, why God was able to use him so mightily. The integrity of these prophets ensured that their gates could not be violated.

However, many of the prophets of old were rendered useless to God because they walked in agreement with the spirit of compromise. These prophets would speak whatever the king or the people wanted to hear, rather than what God wanted and needed them to say. Those true prophets – such as Moses, Elijah, Jeremiah, Isaiah, Ezekiel, Micaiah, Samuel, the minor prophets of old and last but not least, Jesus the

Christ – who allowed God to speak to them and through them, paid a high price for walking in the Spirit's boldness and power. They were mocked, ridiculed, misunderstood, undermined, cursed and held in stocks and prisons. They were loners and by the world's standards, they appeared to be losers, preferring the will of God over and above the things of this world. Others were slapped, beaten, spit upon and ultimately hung on a wooden cross. Their unwillingness to compromise put them in position for God to use them mightily as prophets to the nations and to kingdoms, to tear down, uproot, destroy and overthrow satanic ideologies, traditions, doctrines and even establishments, then to rebuild and to plant (Jer. 1:10).

In our pilgrimage, many of us have walked in agreement with this spirit of compromise at one time or another and in so doing we have caused the plumb-line of God's righteous standard to be lowered. This spirit of compromise is dangerous, not only to the believer, but also to the watching world of unbelievers who are secretly looking for authenticity in the Christian community. Christians are called to be light shining in the midst of darkness, illuminating the path for those who are lost, but if we walk in agreement with the spirit of compromise in the face of a watching world, we lead the lost further astray and God will hold us accountable. God's standard of righteousness is the same today as it was in the beginning. He has not changed. At times, the challenges of our lone pilgrimage can cause *us* to change, but God still sees sin as sin and holiness as holiness. As it relates to the Christian's call to holy living, Jesus still commands us to separate ourselves from sin. Make no mistake about it – compromise is a terrible sin.

Compromise, however, is a powerful motivator. The spirit behind it will have us believing that we can get what we have our eyes set on if we will only walk in agreement with it. In truth, compromise will set off a trigger within us that will result in an action birthed from a hidden motive. The spirit of compromise causes us to ignore boundaries that we have established and will result in the loss of our integrity. Compromise will have us forgetting that God is holy, sovereign, just and faithful. It will deceive us into believing that He is just like us. The spirit of compromise will have us take our eyes off of God and put our hope in man. It will have us seeking lofty positions on our jobs and in the church and doing whatever we have to do to attain those positions. This grieves the heart of God because He so desires that His children come to Him and ask for what they need. His heart delights in giving good things to His little children who wait in hope for Him. He is our heavenly Daddy, our Abba Father and just like any good father, He rejoices to see us come into our own (Matt.7:7-11). He says to us, lovingly: "Just ask Me." David said in Psalm 62 that he would wait on and hope in God and God alone and in the waiting, he would not be moved (vv. 5-6). He would not be moved to compromise. He would not be moved to fear. He would not be moved to take matters into his own hands. This heart attitude is especially pleasing to God and it is an attitude that He rewards.

It is a fearful thing to be placed in a position of leadership for which we are not equipped. Every day we are filled with horror that someone will find out that we have no idea what we are doing. We feel insecure and threatened that our replacement is right on our heels, but oh, the liberty and joy when the promotion comes from God! God's Word tells us that He "sets the times and the seasons" (Dan. 2:20-21). Psalm 75:6 says, "No one from the east or the west or from the desert can exalt a man. But it is God who judges: He brings one down, and he exalts another." We can rest assured that by the time God promotes us, He has put us through every test necessary to form His character in us and make us ready for that high place. Bless His name, for He will continue to prepare new tests for us that will help us to maintain that position and to move on to even higher places. His Word tells us that He will give us "hinds' feet" to walk with ease "upon every high place of trouble, suffering and responsibility" (Hab. 3:19, AMP). It is to His glory that we bear much fruit, fruit that will remain (John 15:2, 16). Knowing these things is enough to pull us from behind the Enemy's gates and deliver us into freedom with God as we realize that we do not have to compromise.

We do not have to walk in fear of man. Proverbs 29:25 tells us that "the fear of man will prove to be a snare." Another word for "snare" is "trap" or "a counterfeit or deception." Promotion coming any way other than by the hand, wisdom and timing of God is a set-up. Turn it down! The w*hat*, *when* and *how* of what God does for us is not dictated by the w*hat*, w*hen* and *how* of what He is doing in the lives of others. We learn to rejoice with those who rejoice and we take a deep breath and relax as we wait patiently for God to send us the real thing. We can rejoice in knowing that the "blessing of the LORD brings wealth and he adds no trouble to it" (Prov. 10:22). No, we do not have to compromise. We can rest confidently in our Abba Father. We can trust Him completely with our past, our present and our future.

> "An appeaser is one who feeds a crocodile,
> hoping it will eat him last."
>
> -Winston Churchill

Lust of the Eyes

The lamp of our body is dimmed by the lust for things that flood our eyes. When our eyes become covetous, we will compromise the truth in exchange for monetary gain, as in the story of Balaam, a sorcerer whom God allowed to enter into the prophetic office to deliver a message to the Moabites. His story is found in Numbers 22-25. Though the Spirit of God filled him so mightily that, in spite of himself, he had to speak what God commanded him to speak to the Moabites (24:1-13), eventually his ungodly character led him and many of the Israelites into pagan worship, sexual sins and greed. Balaam saw himself as being in the employ of man, rather than as a tool in the hand of his Creator, God. Proverbs 28:21 says, "To show partiality is not good, yet a man will do wrong for a piece of bread."

What of Esau (Gen. 25:29-34), who sold his godly birthright for a bowl of stew? Certainly, what his eyes saw and his belly craved at that moment outweighed his good judgment, for when the time came for Isaac to confer the blessing upon Jacob and Esau, only then did Esau realize what a fool he had been to give his birthright away for a bowl of stew (Gen. 27). We have to be very careful not to misinterpret the Gospel of Jesus Christ. Although He tells us that He came that we might have abundant life, He also tells us that He came to suffer and to die for us, "leaving you an example, that you should follow in His steps" (1 Pet. 2:21). "Then Jesus said to his disciples, 'If anyone would come after me, he must deny himself and take up his cross and follow me. For whoever wants to save his life will lose it, but whoever loses his life for me will find it. What good will it be for a man if he gains the whole world, yet forfeits his soul? Or what can a man give in exchange for his soul?'" Matt. 16:24-26

When we fully understand the true message and heart of the Gospel of Jesus Christ, the light will come on in our heads that we were created for the glory of God and not for self-indulgence. Our lives are not our own. Paul said that he had been crucified with Christ and the life that he lived was not his own, but he lived it by faith in the Son of God who loved and gave Himself for him (Gal. 2:20). Jesus said that as suffering and death awaited Him, so it awaits us. If we are to follow in His steps, then we must prepare ourselves to lose some things that we have gained, to suffer some things that are painful and that seem unfair and to deny ourselves some things that we think would be good for us. If we could get this understanding of the gospel, it would change everything. It would change our desires and our passions for certain things that we think we must have or "we will die." It will take the pressure off of us that we have to get or achieve certain things because someone else has it or feels that we, too, should have it by now. This prompts us to ask the question, "Then what is in this for us, if we are called to such radical self-denial and suffering?" Peter, one of Jesus's disciples, asked the same question of him. "'We have left everything to follow you. What then will there be for us?' Jesus said to them, 'And everyone who has left houses or brothers or sisters or father or mother or children or fields for my sake will receive a hundred times as much and will inherit eternal life. But many who are first will be last, and many who are last will be first'" Matt. 19:27-30.

For many who cling to their lives in this present age, who simply must have their things right now, they have already received their reward in full. To many of these Jesus will say on that day, "Depart from Me, I never knew you," but to those who gave up their lives for Him will He say, "Enter into the joy of your Lord!" "No eye has seen, no ear has heard, no mind has conceived what God has prepared for those who love him" 1 Cor. 2:9.

Envy, Anger and Rage

The spirits of envy, anger and rage were all operative in Cain when he killed his brother, Abel, because Abel had offered unto God a more acceptable sacrifice than he did. God asked Cain, "Why are you angry? If you do what is right, will you not be accepted? But if you do not do what is right, sin is crouching at your door. It desires to have you, but you must master it" (Gen. 4:6-7). Those spirits that fuel and drive our envy, anger and rage lead us to commit irrational, blatant acts of rebellion and disobedience against God and man. They make the lamp of our bodies go completely dark. Reason is not only asleep, it is non-existent. The results are sad, horrific and often tragic, often ending in suicide and often leading to the deaths of many other innocent victims. These spirits have been unleashed over the face of the earth and while no one is exempt from their reign of unholy terror, we consistently see their shocking effects in the slaughter of women and children in epidemic proportions. Statistics on domestic violence are staggering and bear witness to the accuracy of this statement.

- One woman is beaten by her husband or partner every fifteen seconds in the United States.[10]
- In England and Wales, two women a week are killed as a result of domestic violence.[11]
- 85% of domestic violence victims are women, 15% are men.[12]

- In a national survey of American families, 50% of men who frequently assaulted their wives also frequently abused their children.[13]
- Witnessing violence between one's parents or caretakers is the strongest risk factor of transmitting violent behavior from one generation to the next.[14]
- 25% - 45% of all women who are battered are battered during pregnancy.[15]

The demons of rage, envy, jealousy and anger that fuel these unspeakable domestic violence crimes have completely eliminated entire families. We dress up all of this murderous activity by referring to them as crimes of passion, but they are, in actuality, crimes committed by Satan and his posse of demons. It's the Devil doing what he does best, stealing, killing and destroying. Revelation 12:12 says, "But woe to you, O earth and sea, for the Devil has come down to you in great wrath, because he knows that his time is short!"

Though death began with the first act of disobedience in the garden of Eden, we have Cain to thank for the first physical murder ever committed and we have been taking each other's lives ever since. When we become consumed with envy, like Cain, we will seek to rid the world of our competition by any means necessary. God exhorts us to just do the right thing according to His laws and He will empower us to overcome. Obedience will give us power to master the raging, out of control passions that Satan delights in fueling to destroy us and the ones we love.

The testimony of Hannah is a perfect example of one who seemingly had every right, by human, worldly standards to lash out in a jealous rage against her adversary, Peninnah. Her story is told in 1 Samuel 1. Hannah was one of the wives of Elkanah. The Bible tells us that the LORD had closed her womb so that she could not bear children, but Peninnah, Elkanah's other wife and Hannah's rival, was quite fertile. "And because the LORD had closed her womb, her rival kept provoking her in order to irritate her. This went on year after year. Whenever Hannah went up to the house of the LORD, her rival provoked her till she wept and would not eat" 1 Sam. 1:6-7.

Hannah's story is a story of victory and triumph, because in the midst of years and years of discouragement, sorrow, disappointment, shame, and deep grief, she kept her composure. In the midst of Peninnah's evil assaults upon her to provoke her to jealousy, though Hannah wept bitterly, she maintained her focus on the God who was able to avenge her. "In bitterness of soul," the Bible tells us that she "wept much and prayed to the LORD," asking Him to "look at her;" look at her as His servant and look at her misery. Hannah had enough faith to believe that if she could only get the God who is just, merciful and compassionate to lock His eyes upon her that He would see and understand her misery, suffering and longing of soul and be moved to remember her and grant her heart's desire. It was the sovereign plan of God all along to grant Hannah her desire, but He had to first get Hannah to see Him – really see Him – and she did.

Hannah understood the power of an intense and purposeful gaze. Her supplication was not that God would just look at her, but look at her to see her and to know her intimately. Her prayer moved the heart of God. His Spirit became intimate with her spirit and the spiritual intercourse that took place that day – Hannah locking her gaze upon her God, knowing His justice, mercy, compassion and intimate knowledge of her pain, suffering, grief, longing and faith – caused a seed to be planted in Hannah's womb that day that produced the prophet Samuel. Despite the many years of grief and barrenness that Hannah endured, we can see that she had great faith in God and that she possessed an unusual awareness of her value and worth in God. Her belief that she was no less loved by God than Peninnah was what kept her free from envy and looking to God to do for her, not what He had done for her rival, but simply what her own heart desired.

Rebellion, Pride, Jealousy and Fear

In the story of Saul and David, we witness the spirits of rebellion, pride, jealousy and fear active in the life of King Saul. His story is sad and tragic. Like so many other similar accounts in biblical history, the lost inheritance was the result of a bad lamp in the body and the failure to, not only guard his heart, but to also diligently guard his eye gates.

We first encounter Saul in 1 Samuel 9, looking for some lost donkeys that belonged to his father. After searching for them for some time and not finding them, Saul's servant suggests that they go to the "seer," the prophet Samuel, to inquire as to the whereabouts of the lost donkeys. Meanwhile, the LORD has already instructed Samuel to anoint Saul as Israel's next king. When Saul and Samuel finally meet at the gateway, Samuel invites Saul to come dine with him and to stay the night. Here is where we catch a glimpse of the one character flaw in Saul that would lead to his downfall. That flaw was fear.

The spirit of fear often operates in conjunction with other spirits, such as low self-esteem and rejection. In the life of Saul, the spirit of fear was often also accompanied by the spirit of pride. The first thing that Saul does after Samuel's invitation is to point out to the prophet how incredibly insignificant he and his family are. "I'm a Benjamite, from the smallest tribe of Israel, and is not my clan the least of all the clans of the tribe of Benjamin? Why do you say such a thing to me?" 1 Sam. 9:21. Then, in 1 Samuel 10:14-16, just after Samuel had anointed him king over Israel, we witness that spirit of fear operating in Saul once again. After Samuel told Saul that he would be the next king, Saul met with his uncle to report to him on the whereabouts of the lost donkeys. He told his uncle that when they could not find the donkeys, they went to the prophet Samuel. When his uncle asked him what the prophet said, Saul only told him that Samuel said not to worry about the donkeys; they had been found. He said nothing to his uncle about the fact that he had just been anointed king over Israel (v. 16).

The question arises as to the reason why Saul never mentioned to his uncle something as important as the fact that he had just been anointed king over Israel. Could it be that he was overwhelmed by the idea of just having been anointed the king over Israel and was therefore afraid that he would not be able to handle the responsibility? After all, the Bible does not say that Saul went to war to be the next king. He did not run for the office. Being king over Israel was not his idea. He was chosen to be king. Later in this same chapter, as Samuel is trying to present Saul to the Israelites as their new king, he looked for him, but Saul was nowhere to be found. The people inquired of the LORD and the LORD revealed to them that Saul "was hiding amongst the baggage," afraid (v. 22). What was Saul afraid of? What had so clouded the lamp of his body that he felt so utterly incapable of fulfilling the call of God on his life? Where was his confidence in his God?

We need only to ask ourselves these same questions as they relate to the call of God on our own lives to understand what demons Saul must have been wrestling with. What causes us to hide from responsibility? Did someone tell us that we were less than, incapable of, not too smart, or not as smart as someone else? Why is it that when we get blessed in some area of our lives, we are afraid to tell others about how God has blessed us? Could it be that those with whom we have kept company are the kind of company that love misery and who, in all truth, would not be able to stand to see us truly blessed? Why do we feel that we have to hide our blessings? Why are we afraid to rejoice and celebrate the goodness and the favor of God manifested in our lives?

We have to wonder if there was someone in Saul's life, perhaps an authority figure he looked up to, who could have possibly instilled a deep sense of inadequacy in him by making him feel that he was not as capable as some other child. Maybe he allowed his lowly origin to dictate his self-esteem, or possibly he witnessed someone close to him fail miserably and shamefully at some great undertaking and this caused him to be deathly afraid of failure. Whatever the reasons were, Saul's fears led him to operate in rebellion and disobedience to God, which resulted in him being rejected by God as king over Israel (1 Sam. 13:1-14). When David, Saul's replacement, came on the scene in 1 Samuel 18 and valiantly killed the Philistines,

> The women began to frolic and laugh and sing, "Saul has slain his thousands, and David his ten thousands." Saul was very angry, for the saying displeased him; And Saul jealously eyed David from that day forward. The next day an evil spirit from God came mightily upon Saul, and he raved madly in his house, while David played the lyre with his hand, as at other times; and there was a javelin in Saul's hand. And Saul cast the javelin, for he thought, "I will pin David to the wall." And David escaped twice. Saul was afraid

of David, because the LORD was with him but had departed from Saul (vv. 7-12).

In our walk with God, radical obedience is a must. When God chooses to exalt us, we must humbly submit to His instructions, or else we can be sure that our replacement is on the way. We will find ourselves in the same predicament as Saul, jealously eyeing every person who is new on the scene, viewing them as potential rivals. Our pride will not accept the fact that someone else can be as gifted or more gifted than ourselves. We will begin to look at them through eyes of suspicion, wondering where they are, what meetings they are attending that we were not asked to attend, who they are hanging out with, what they are being asked to do in the church that we have not been asked to do. We will find ourselves being unloving towards them and refusing to encourage them in their area of giftedness, especially if they are gifted in the same area in which we are gifted. We may even find ourselves trying to get them to leave the church in an attempt to rid our immediate environment of all potential rivals. This is a scheme that will backfire, just as it did with Saul. In the church, this type of individual and corporate pride and jealousy entering the gates can mean death to that assembly. As God removed His Spirit from Saul and sent a tormenting spirit upon him to trouble him (1 Sam. 16:14), so this spirit of jealousy in the church will cause the Spirit of God to depart from our worship and the spirits of contention and strife to enter and trouble our churches.

David, the same man to whom Saul lost his inheritance, said in Psalm 101:3, "I will set no vile thing before my eyes." Instead, he said, "My eyes are ever towards the LORD" (Ps. 25:15). Jesus said, "And if your right eye causes you to sin, gouge it out and throw it away. It is better for you to lose part of your body than for your whole body to be thrown into hell" (Matt. 5:29). As we shift our gaze to our God, we must ask Him to show us how to appreciate the beauty in the giftedness of others and help us to understand that their beauty takes nothing away from our own. As we walk in obedience and humility, God will also begin to open our eyes so that we can see and appreciate the beauty in our own uniqueness and gifting, even if that gift is similar to another's who shares the same space with us. When we adopt this attitude about our brothers and sisters in Christ, then we can serve the Savior with joy and contentment.

Part **Four**

The **Heart Gate**

"The more we meditate on what prayer is and the wonderful power with God which it has, the more we feel constrained to ask who is and what man is that such a place in God's counsels should have been allotted to him. Sin has so degraded him, that from what he is now we can form no conception what he was meant to be."

-Andrew Murray, *With Christ in the School of Prayer*

Chapter 7

Bring Him the Broken Pieces

Spirit of God, descend upon my heart;

Wean it from earth; through all its pulses move;

Stoop to my weakness, mighty as Thou art;

And make me love Thee as I ought to love.

Hast Thou not bid me love Thee, God and King?

All, all Thine own, soul, heart and strength and mind.

I see Thy cross; there teach my heart to cling:

O let me seek Thee, and O let me find!

Teach me to feel that Thou art always nigh;

Teach me the struggles of the soul to bear.

To check the rising doubt, the rebel sigh,

Teach me the patience of unanswered prayer.

Teach me to love Thee as Thine angels love,

One holy passion filling all my frame;

The kindling of the heaven descended Dove,

My heart an altar, and Thy love the flame.

Spirit of God Descend Upon My Heart, George Croly

"God can heal a broken heart, but He has to have all the pieces."

-Unknown

*I*t was around midnight on a Saturday evening when the trumpet of my desperate prayers resounded to heaven's gates. I believed that my melodic prayer, in the form of this inimitable hymn, had ultimately ascended to the very heart of my heavenly Father. That evening, as I first began to sing the prayer to the Lord, I was standing up. As I stood singing the first thirty-three words of this old hymn over and over like a broken record, I could feel His Spirit descending into my room. It was as though He had come and laid His warm and tender hand right there upon my heart. His touch had caused me to become so unmistakably aware of the utter hopelessness of my condition. My fretful, anxious heart was so shattered and torn apart by people, by life; so broken, bruised, abused, scarred, and marred by grief, disappointment, rejection, and shame. "Surely, Jehovah Rapha," I prayed, "if Your Spirit does not move through the pulses of my heart, perfecting Your strength in my weakness, I will never love Thee as I ought, neither will I have the capacity to love Your people as You have commanded."

As the tears flooded my eyes, the Spirit of the Lord moved my heart to repentance. No longer standing, but now kneeling in the presence of Almighty God, I continued my petition in song. His heart of pure love for me had moved my depraved heart to repentance. I don't even recall how long I sang to the Lord that night. Eventually, I crawled into bed and closed my eyes, yet petitioning Jehovah Rapha in my heart with this melody.

In the morning when I awoke, there was that same melody still ringing in my heart. I got dressed and headed off to church. When I walked into the sanctuary, there it was again. The choir was singing my midnight plea during the morning devotion, *Spirit of God Descend Upon My Heart*. "My God," I said, falling to my knees. "It is as if You are singing this song back to me." It was as though He was saying to me, "Yes, Nancy, I want your heart. And I am going to do just as you petitioned Me to do, but you must be willing to bring to Me every broken, scarred, marred, and shattered piece. You must be willing to lay every part of it on the altar. If you gather up the fragments and bring them to Me, I will see to it that you have no lack. I am Sar-Shalom, the God in whom there is nothing missing, nothing lacking and nothing broken." I suddenly became even more convinced that it is the heartfelt, simple, yet desperate prayer, prayed in brokenness of spirit and lining up with the revealed will of God that moves the heart of God to respond so definitively.

The Word of God admonishes us, "Keep and guard your heart with all vigilance, and above all that you guard, for out of it flow the springs [issues] of life" (Prov. 4:23, AMP). In its biblical context, the Hebrew definition of the word *issues* is "boundaries" or "borders." These boundaries are defined by the virtues that we cultivate, such as, honor, love, courage and integrity. When we establish our boundaries based upon biblical principles, we can be confident that they are sound. To the extent that we have failed to guard these boundaries, we will experience a diminishing degree of the fruits of these virtues. The overflow of these fruits into the lives of others will be equally diminished, detrimentally impacting the effectiveness of our ministry to others, whatever that ministry may be.

Unfortunately, we err when we question our virtues and begin to redefine good and sound boundaries simply because the Adversary of our souls has trespassed over them and disregarded them. We begin to think that maybe we should lower our standards a bit. We rationalize that perhaps our expectations are too high and maybe, if we are willing to compromise our virtues, we will not get hurt so often. May God, who is rich in mercy, forgive us all for our failure to diligently guard the most important of all gates, the heart gate. For as the scripture says, not only do all the issues of life flow forth from it, but it also admonishes us that our mouths speak out of what is stored up in our hearts (Matt. 12:34). God has given us the ability to declare and decree things in and out of existence. If our hearts are marred and scarred, torn, broken, shattered and fragmented, what kind of speech do you think will proceed out of our mouths? We will touch on this question somewhat in this chapter but more in

Part Five – The Mouth Gate. Perhaps if we look at the heart from a natural aspect, we can get a better understanding as to why it is so very important to guard the gates to our hearts.

The ancient Chinese and Egyptian physicians stood in awe of the human heart and considered it to be the "seat of intelligence and emotion."[16] The 17th century physician William Harvey regarded the heart as "the sovereign of the body... the center of life."[17] For Harvey and his fellow contemporaries, they judged that by its positioning in the chest – encased in the ribs, and fortified front and back by the sternum and the spinal column – nature did not intend for the living heart to be seen, let alone cut open, sewn up and restored. To operate on the heart was strictly forbidden; therefore, if a person sustained an injury to the heart, it meant certain death.[18] There was no cure for a "broken or wounded heart." They were awed by the fact that the disembodied heart had the ability to continue to beat, and that even when it was cut into pieces, the fragmented pieces still pulsated with life.[19] Later discoveries showed that the mind – considered the intellect to the soul – still functioned, even though the heart had sustained serious injury.[20] Don't ever let anyone tell you that you are not fearfully and wonderfully made!

The heart, thought to be the sovereign of the body by 17th century physicians, is still the sovereign of the body today. It is the master, ruler and the king of the physical body. From the heart of a king come decrees that impact the entire realm of his jurisdiction. If the heart of the king is pure, then the effect of his decrees upon those who fall under his rule will be positive. His subjects will be prosperous, healthy, whole and secure. His kingdom will be established in righteousness. Conversely, if the king's heart is corrupt, the effect of his decrees will have corrupting repercussions upon his kingdom. His subjects will be oppressed, weak, unstable, poor and even themselves corrupt. Proverbs 29:12 states, "If a ruler pays attention to falsehood, all his ministers become wicked." What is true of an earthly king is also true of this ruler, this sovereign of the body that beats beneath the breasts of mankind: the heart. If our hearts are pure, then what comes out of our mouths will also be pure. In matters of prayer, effectual and fervent prayers proceeding from a pure heart will ultimately line up with the will of God and the Word of God. Then we will see the sick healed, the impoverished made rich, the weak made strong, the blind receive their sight and the bound set free. Right praying can cause even the dead to live again.

The Word of God tells us that "the tongue has the power of life and death" (Prov. 18:21) and that "A wholesome tongue is a tree of life" (Prov. 15:4, NKJV). James 3:6 warns us that "the tongue also is a fire, a world of evil among the parts of the body. It corrupts the whole person." Let me say it again, if the heart is corrupt, what is brought forth from our lips will also be corrupt: slander, back-biting, gossip, dissension, corrupt communication and the like. The mouth has no choice but to declare that which resides in the heart. If there is bitterness in your heart, then your words will be bitter. You will find yourself constantly saying negative, hateful things about people. If you find that you are always spewing forth negativity, know that Jesus Christ wants to deliver you, not only from the spirit of negativity, but also from the accompanying spirits: namely, rejection and anger. If you are operating under a spirit of negativity, I want to ask you to pause right now, put the book down and ask the Holy Spirit to search your heart so that you can get to the root of the bitterness. Ask Him to deliver you from the spirit of negativity and to reveal to you the source of the negativity that has taken up residency within your heart. Once you pray this prayer, you had better brace yourself, because when the Holy Spirit turns on the searchlight and lets it hover over your heart He will uncover some things concerning you that you will not want to see.

No one can search a man's heart like the Holy Spirit. Says Watchman Nee in his book *The Release of the Spirit*, "Under the light of God you will see in a very little time your true condition and how useless you are."[21] He will reveal the anger, the bitterness, the rage, the lack of forgiveness, the lustful thoughts, the covetousness and so on. After the Holy Spirit allows you to see some of the ugliness that is residing in your heart, you may say, "Well, Lord, I didn't ask You to show me my ex's heart, I asked You to show me what's in *my* heart." The Lord will calmly say, "My child, that's exactly what I've done."

When God reveals to you that you are harboring anger and lacking forgiveness, He may do it by showing you that you have never forgiven a former employer for firing you, or that you have never forgiven your father for not being there for you during your childhood. He may show you that you have never forgiven your ex-wife for committing adultery during your marriage. Then He will take you deeper by letting you see how your inability to forgive her may lead you to believe that not only can she never be trusted again, but that all women are given to harlotry. You may foolishly vow never to open your heart gate to another woman. You may even go so far as to tell anyone who asks you that no woman can be trusted. You have nothing good to say about any woman, not even your mother! You are speaking out of the overflow of your heart.

The trials of life can cause these types of emotional and spiritual setbacks and they happen to us all at one point or another in our lives. Not to worry! God can handle our setbacks. "And we know that all things work together for good to those who love God, to those who are the called according to His purpose" Rom. 8:28 (NKJV). Isn't it good to know that God can make it all work together for our good and for His glory, both the good and the bad things that we encounter in life? If we want to see Him work the bad things together for our good, then we must be willing to repent of our distrust of God and of our negativity towards others. We must learn to cultivate a thankful heart even when we do not understand the plan that God has laid out for us. 1 Thessalonians 5:18 says, "In everything give thanks for this is the will of God, in Christ Jesus, concerning you" (NKJV). This is easier said than done, but we must learn how to embrace the trials while trusting God to make them work in our favor. There is a grace for such seasons in our lives, but we must take hold of it.

During a season of setback, it is so very vital to access the grace supplied by God. If we fail to appropriate God's grace during the crises of our lives, we leave every gate wide open for satanic attack and infiltration. Here come the clever, demonic spirits of frustration, anxiety, bitterness, doubt, fear, depression, rage and anger. You name them, they're coming! Those infiltrating spirits are not coming just to pass through. They are coming to make certain that you will be overwhelmed by the crisis to the point of alienation from God. They are coming to set up permanent housing, with a mortgage so high that you will end up paying with your life. Those unclean spirits move in, bringing loads of garbage bags with them. Inside of those garbage bags are the trash they push on us, hoping that we will use their trash to patch the holes in our souls that, in truth, only Jesus's love can fill. This is why we drink until we are sloppy drunk, smoke marijuana until our minds and thoughts come under the control of demons, pop pills, pierce our bodies, dye our hair purple and green, cut ourselves, and look like walking billboards for tattoo shops.

In our emotionally weakened condition, we are foolishly following the commands of the "garbage man" – Satan. We pull from his foul-smelling bag of trash until its empty and then we go back to him to have him fill it up again. Make no mistake, the unclean spirits are coming to build powerful strongholds to keep you unlawfully imprisoned for years, when the intent of God for you in the crisis was that this merely be a season that you would pass through, learning valuable life lessons along the way, had you taken hold of and appropriated His grace. "When you pass through the waters, I will be with you: and through the rivers, they will not overwhelm you. When you walk through the fire, you will not be burned *or* scorched, and the flame will not kindle upon you. For I am the LORD your God, The Holy One of Israel, your Savior" Isa. 43:2-3 (AMP). God is trying to tell us to get away from the garbage man! He is trying to get a message to us that we are only walking through the mist. It's not what it seems. This trial is coming to pass.

Bobby is a very gifted hip-hop artist. He was raised in a Christian home and was practically born on the pews of the church. When I first witnessed him perform, he was performing in the church, rapping for Jesus. His poems were powerful and anointed. He skillfully wove scripture throughout his poetry and as a Christian rapper/poet, he was very much in demand to perform in his home town. Bobby met and married Christie, a young lady who sang in the choir at the church that he attended. Not even a year into the marriage, Christie wanted out. She abandoned Bobby, who thought that he had married the woman who would be by his side until the end. Bobby loved Christie more than his own life and would have given his life for her in a heartbeat. Although Bobby tried to repair his marriage, Christie was a very confused and self-centered woman. After three years of following after the woman he so desperately loved, Bobby finally faced the reality that Christie was never coming back to him. They officially divorced.

Today, Bobby is a very wounded, angry, bitter and resentful young man. He has completely abandoned the church and now only performs secular hip-hop music in nightclubs. Although he is still a young man, he has completely given up on love, marriage and the church. He is angry with God because he cannot understand why God would have allowed his marriage to fall apart. Why, he asks, when he was never a womanizer, when he waited for the woman he prayed over and believed was the one that God wanted him to marry – a Christian woman, and one who was serving the Lord in the church – why would God just sit on His hands and let her walk out on him? Why would God allow so much emotional and mental devastation to enter into his life? Why would God break his heart so drastically beyond repair?

Bobby was completely overwhelmed by the biggest trial to hit his life at the tender age of twenty-two. He was never able to grab hold of the grace that God was extending to him, but had he been able to, that grace would have carried him through the trial to a victorious end. That grace would have given him a peace that would have surpassed any lack of understanding with which he had been wrestling. That grace would have washed over his heart and washed out any bitterness, preventing any bitter roots from being established there. The grace of God would have allowed him to know the Savior and Redeemer of his soul on a far richer and deeper level.

Bobby never brought the broken pieces of his heart to the only One who could have made him whole. Instead, in self-righteousness, he stood with his broken heart hanging out of his chest, shaking his fists in the face of God, demanding to know why He'd seen fit to take away what he felt he was entitled to have. After all, hadn't he been a pretty good boy? Hadn't he played by God's rules? With tears streaming down his face and bitterness taking root in the broken pieces of his heart, Bobby stormed out of the presence of God, stuffing his fragmented heart back into his chest as best he could. With one final act of rage against redemption and grace, he then locked his heart up as tight as he could, and hurled the key into the dark abyss of pain where all other such keys are pitched and left to rust and rot. In confusion, deep anguish and bitterness of soul, he walked away from the God whose love for him ran so deep that even as Bobby stormed away from Him, his Savior followed right on his heels. Bobby never realized that the God he scorned would never let him leave without Him, his only hope for restoration. Bobby is still a young man, and I continue to pray for his deliverance, complete healing, and restoration because I know that nothing is impossible with God.

Amongst the things that we are promised in this life are suffering, persecution and tribulation. We only overcome these trials through Jesus Christ, not apart from Him. Jesus said in John 16:33, "In the world you will have trouble. But take heart! I have overcome the world." Here, Jesus is telling us that we, too, can overcome, but we often fail to overcome a broken heart because we wonder if we can entrust it to the One who allowed it to get broken in the first place. When I think of the pain that this young man has endured, I am reminded of my failure as a parent to guard the gates of my children's hearts when, in rebellion, I married a man who was an agnostic, some twenty-nine years ago. A few years into the marriage, he fathered my daughter and four years later, he was gone, leaving the heart of a once confident little girl, who was convinced that she was the apple of her daddy's eyes, completely shattered. With my own hands, I helped to tear her gates down before I could ever help her build strong ones.

On many occasions, I watched helplessly, my own heart breaking, as she sat by the phone for hours on end, waiting for the phone call from her daddy – the phone call that would never come. I would rub her tiny little back, wipe her tears and try to coax her to bed. Always, she would refuse to abandon her lonely vigil by the phone, confident that her daddy would call, as he'd promised her he would. Eventually, her tired little body just gave out; her spirit was willing, but her flesh was weak and I would find her fast asleep, lying on the floor by the phone that never rang. Picking up her little body up, I carried her to her room. As I laid her on her bed, covered her up and bent to kiss her sweet little face, I couldn't help but notice the tears that stained her precious cheeks. I couldn't help but notice the shattering of her little heart. I couldn't help but wonder about the extent of the damage she would suffer later in life and of how much

I had contributed to that damage by failing to guard the gates to my own heart in my choice of a husband and father of my little girl.

I have worked hard to rebuild her gates by instilling good Christian values into her and modeling those values in my own life in front of her. I have always praised her for both her inner and outer beauty and strength and have loved her unconditionally. Although I have done all that I have known to do to rebuild her gates, I have come to realize that there is nothing like the presence of a godly daddy in a child's life, be it a girl or a boy, to foster strong gates. I have also come to realize that God is a loving and forgiving God. He does not hold our past against us. He does not leave us stuck in the valley of regret and lack. To our little strength He graciously and faithfully adds His strength. He makes up for where we have fallen short. I am grateful for grace. "His Grace is sufficient" for us: for *all* of us (2 Cor. 12:9-10).

According to *"Father Facts" Fourth Edition (2002),* from the National Fatherhood Initiative, approximately 80% of African-American children can expect to spend a significant portion of their childhood living without their biological fathers. It is devastating to think of what this statistic and very real social condition, means for the structure of these children's gates. My precious daughter is now twenty-six years old; however, as recent as last year she tearfully expressed to me that she has longed to hear her daddy tell her that she is beautiful. It does not matter how many times I tell her that she is beautiful, she will not really believe it until she hears it from daddy. As recently as last year, she tearfully expressed to me that she longs for her daddy to pursue her.

I can tell her that her real Daddy, her Abba Father calls her beautiful and that her beauty enthralls Him. I can tell her that her real Daddy pursues her all day long, but because the gates to her heart have been shattered by her earthly daddy, she is skeptical and unconvinced about her heavenly Daddy and His pursuit of her does not register. It does not compute. Therefore, like young Bobby and so many other young men and women who have experienced similar wounds to their hearts, my daughter, who once served faithfully in the church, has also stepped away from both God and the church. She, too, sits in time-out in the Outer Court, (see Chapter 8) nursing a shattered heart. However, rather than being outwardly angry with God, she chooses to stand aloof from Him, as her earthly daddy has done with her. In both her relationships with her earthly, biological daddy and with her heavenly Daddy, at the writing of this book, she is not on speaking terms with either of them. However, my faith in God's relentless love encourages me that one day I will see her wrapped in Abba's arms, in a mutual embrace.

Our Lord does not intend for us to keep finding ourselves in setback or time-out mode, sitting angrily in some seemingly God-forsaken corner in the Outer Court. His will for us is that we enter into His presence by way of the Outer Court and make our way through the Holy Place and ultimately into the Holy of Holies, beyond the veil. This is where we must purpose to dwell, directly at the feet of

Jesus. I am not saying that we are to always be on our knees, twenty-four hours a day, seven days a week. What I am saying is that we are to live out our lives in the presence of God, acknowledging Him, including Him and seeking Him in our everyday existence. We must be not just conscious of His presence, but invoking and inviting His presence into our daily activities, into the joys and pleasures of life as well as into the hurts and pains that we encounter. God sees all and knows all about us. Hebrews 4:13 reminds us that "nothing in all creation is hidden from God's sight. Everything is uncovered and lies bare before the eyes of Him to whom we must give account." If we make it our goal to live this way, when seasons of setback come and we find ourselves nursing a wounded heart, we can have the assurance that God sees us. With the understanding that nothing about us is hidden from our Lord, we can rest assured that in the divine providence of His Sovereignty, He has a specific purpose for allowing the pain that we experience in our lives to visit with us for a season.

If we allow Him, He will use our pain and hurt to mature us and to teach us more about who He is and wants to be to us. Our pain and hurt can be used by God to get glory out of our lives, but we must fully trust Him with our broken pieces. He will equip us and give us hinds' feet so that we can "continue to walk, not stand still in terror and be afraid, but to walk and make spiritual progress upon every high place of trouble, of pain and suffering and responsibility" (Hab. 3:17-19, AMP). We will discover that trust is a substance of building material that we cannot afford to leave out in the rebuilding of our gates.

Chapter 8

A Holy House

"There must be a work of God in destruction before we are free. We must invite the cross to do its deadly work within us."

-A.W Tozer, *The Pursuit of God*

The Apostle Paul asks the question, "Do you not know that your body is a temple of the Holy Spirit, who is in you, whom you have received from God? You are not your own, you were bought at a price. Therefore honor God with your body" (1 Cor. 6:19-20). As God's children, we must realize that our bodies have a higher purpose and value than what we may have considered. In her book *Beyond the Veil*, Alice Smith makes the observation that the human body was designed to be more than simply a pleasing aesthetic. God has designed our bodies, the spiritual tabernacle, after the pattern of the physical tabernacle of the Old Testament, she observes. The physical tabernacle has an Outer Court, a Holy Place and a Holy of

Holies. Our spiritual tabernacle also has an Outer Court, which is our *body*, or our fleshy covering, a Holy Place, which is our *soul* (the mind, will, and emotions) and a Holy of Holies, which is our *spirit*.[22]

We know that we are maturing in our relationship with God when we freely allow His Spirit to move upon our hearts to reveal its true condition; when we are stirred from our complacency and are no longer satisfied with the status quo; when we burn with an unquenchable desire to move from *where* we are to become more than *what* we are; when we will not be happy with less than God's highest goal for us and when we yearn and hunger for holiness more than we labor for temporary happiness. When this describes our state of existence, we know then that we have moved from the superficiality of the Outer Court as it relates to the physical tabernacle, which is our flesh and into the Holy Place, which is our souls. This is where the work of sanctification begins, in the Holy Place. The more devoted we become to Jesus Christ, the deeper the level of sanctification we will experience. We will desire more of the holiness and purity of God to be reflected in our own lives. We will discover that we are progressively becoming a set-apart vessel through which the Spirit of God can move to accomplish His work upon the earth (2 Tim. 2:20-21). As our level of devotion to the Lord increases, we begin to enter into the very Holy of Holies, where we experience the joy of communing with the Holy Spirit. We talk to Him and He speaks to us as He did with Moses, face to face, as a man speaks with his friend (Ex. 33:11).

In Leviticus 10:3, Moses reminds Aaron of the words of God when He said to the people of Israel, "Among those who approach me I will show myself holy." The closer we get to God, the more He allows us to see of His holiness and of the worthlessness of our own righteousness. He makes us see the futility of our own weak efforts to clean ourselves up. But, the closer we get to God, the greater the benefits are for us, too. His presence near to us means that He will love us enough to chastise us, convict us, prune us, refine us, forgive us, wash us, heal us, sanctify us and glorify us. His nearness to us results in a work of destruction within us if we will only yield to Him and raise up the white flag of surrender to Him. If we will ask Him and submit to Him, He will destroy every worthless thing in us that stands in opposition to the riches of His grace that were won for us at Calvary. He will destroy our disobedient and rebellious ways – they are useless to Him. He will destroy our bitterness – it is useless to Him. He will destroy our gossipy tongues – they are useless to Him. He will destroy our rage, our jealousy, our greed, and covet-ousness – they are all useless to Him and they are obstacles to His perfecting work in us. Isaiah 4:4 says that He will come as a "spirit of burning" to burn the filth off of us (NKJV). He is jealous for us, and His desire for us is that we will be like Him – holy.

Within the body of Christ, God's children have been called to function in many capacities: as priests, prophets, teachers, elders, pastors, evangelists, healers, encouragers and exhorters. However, if we have not allowed the Spirit of God to descend upon our hearts and deal with whatever corruption is residing there, we will be powerless to operate successfully in our divine callings. We will not fulfill our purpose in the kingdom of God. We will not have a crown to place at the feet of our King and we will not hear our Lord utter the six most rewarding and powerful words that we are all living to hear, "Well done, good and faithful servant" (Matt. 25:21).

One of the most sensitive ministries within the body of Christ is the ministry of the intercessor, to which we have all been called, according to 1 Timothy 2:1-8, from the top to the bottom, from pastor to parishioner. While not everyone has answered the call to intercession, those who have must certainly make it a priority to stand in that place in the gap with a pure heart. Am I implying that one who has heart issues has not been called of God to the ministry of intercession? The answer is no. Were that the case, not only would there be no intercession, but there would be no ministry going forth in any part of the body of Christ, because we all have heart issues. At one time or another, we have all failed to guard the gates to our hearts. As Philip Yancey points out in his book, *Prayer, Does it Make Any Difference?*: "A sense of unworthiness hardly disqualifies me from prayer; rather it serves as a necessary starting point… Unworthiness establishes the ground rules, setting the proper alignment between broken human beings and a perfect God."[23] Though Yancey's topic is prayer, the principle is the same and can be applied to any area of service in which we enlist in the kingdom of God for the purpose of serving God and His people. It has often been said, "God doesn't call the qualified, but rather, He qualifies the called." It is the blood of the spotless Lamb of God and the righteousness of Christ that allows us to boldly enter into the Holy of Holies and make our petitions known.

> Therefore, brethren, having boldness to enter the Holiest of Holies by the blood of Jesus, by a new and living way which He consecrated for us, through the veil, that is, His flesh, and having a High Priest over the house of God, let us draw near with a true heart in full assurance of faith, and having our hearts sprinkled from an evil conscience and our bodies washed with pure water (Heb. 10:19-22, NKJV).

The right to access God's presence and attention has never been based upon our righteousness or upon our perfection. God is not looking for perfection, but for the one whose hearts are "perfect towards Him" (2 Chron. 16:9). This *perfection*, in its biblical context is *shalem* (shaw-lame') and is defined as "made ready, peaceable... quiet."[24] The heart that is perfect towards God is the heart that chooses to trust God without having yet laid hold of His promises or having received the answers to the things that we have petitioned Him for in the place of prayer. It is even the heart that is fearful, yet willing, willing to be made quiet before God. It is the heart of the child of God who is pressing on to God, perhaps making mistakes along the way, but getting up and getting back in the press towards God.

I can recall the one time that I ran away from home as a young girl. Not brave enough to go very far, I knew right where I was headed when I ran away – to the little white church building that was approximately ten to fifteen miles from my home. I had passed the little church many times on my walk home from school and recalled that it always looked so peaceful, its small white peaks pointing up to a God many galaxies away. In my contemplative moments, I often wondered if He knew that I even existed. I walked up the steps of the little church and slowly opened the door and peered into its sanctuary. It was empty, but the emptiness was warm, inviting and so soothing to a sad and troubled little girl. Over the sanctuary was a holy quietness, a blessed peace. I wanted to stay there forever in God's Holy House and tell Him everything that no one else cared to know about my sorrow, my pain and my fears. Perhaps this was what David felt when he penned the words to Psalm 27:4-5: "One thing have I desired of the LORD, this is what I seek: that I may dwell in the house of the LORD all the days of my life, to gaze upon the beauty of the LORD, and to seek Him in His temple. For in the day of trouble He will keep me safe in His dwelling; He will hide me in the shelter of His tabernacle."

In a culture that is conditioned to having everything quick, fast and in a hurry, God yet requires us to be still and quiet before Him and to wait on Him. A heart that is tranquil and at rest, not fretful and anxious, is a heart that can commune effectively with God. A.W. Tozer says in his book, *The Pursuit of God*: "A spiritual kingdom lies all about us, enclosing us, embracing us, altogether within reach of our inner selves, waiting for us to recognize it. God himself is here waiting our response to His presence. Where faith is defective the result will be inward insensibility and numbness towards spiritual things."[25]

Indeed, God is waiting for us to take the posture of faith in waiting upon Him that He might do His strange and wonderful work in us and through us. He has much to say to us and much to impart to us. Without this faith to wait in holy quietness, we will not recognize His voice or see His hand moving in our lives to perfect that which concerns us. The Holy Spirit needs our undivided attention so that He may leave a deposit in us that will change our lives and the lives of those He has called us to impact. He does not impart the deeper insights and revelations to our flesh, nor to our emotions. While He may use creative ways to interrupt our pity parties, at such times, in order to get our attention as He did with the prophet Elijah in 1 Kings 19, the deeper impartation comes after our spirits have been quieted.

You may recall those times when you have laid out before God just crying, weeping, and wailing, "How long, oh Lord? How, God? Why, God? Why me? Why now? Why this? Why that? Why him? Why her? Why not him? Why not her?" Let me ask you, "Has God ever spoken to you in the midst of your emotional breakdown?" It has been my experience that God will choose to speak to us after our emotional ranting and ravings have subsided and our spirits are postured to receive His impartation. The next time you have a ranting and raving session, take note of the fact that the only voice that you will hear loud and clear is your own. We must "be still before the LORD and wait patiently for him" (Ps. 37:7). "Be still and know that I am God," He says to our anxious hearts (Ps. 46:10). "Deep calls to deep" (Ps. 42:7).

The Spirit of God desires to communicate with us by way of His Spirit living inside of us. The Lord discloses His ways, His will and His words to our spirits, yet so often we miss His visitation either because of the noisiness that we allow to take over so much of our lives, or because we have not taken Him seriously. Something is wrong with our faith. We idly squander precious time in the Outer Court, content to waste our lives frolicking about in the superficiality of our fleshly nature because we really do not believe that there is a great reward for those who diligently seek Him (Heb. 11:6).

God wants to make us a holy habitation for His Spirit to indwell, a Holy House for His presence. In Isaiah 66:1 God says, "Heaven is my throne and the earth is my footstool. Where is the house that you would build for me? Where will my resting place be?" It is utterly amazing that our God, so grand and glorious, so holy, so fair and so noble, who has the highest heavens as His throne and the earth as the place where He rests His feet, would seek to place His Spirit in something as small and fragile as the hearts of men. His Spirit finds a resting place in a heart that is holy, in one who is "humble and contrite in spirit and who trembles at His Word" (v. 2). He is committed to helping us establish our hearts as holy habitations for the indwelling of His Spirit. In Malachi 3, we see His zeal for us in coming near to us "as a refiner's fire or a launderer's soap. He will sit as a refiner and purifier of silver; he will purify the Levites and refine them like gold and silver. Then the Lord will have men who will bring offerings in righteousness... acceptable to the Lord, as in days gone by" (vv. 2-4). Truly, it is good for us to draw near to God and for God to be near to us (Ps. 73:28).

We often say that we want more of Jesus, but our actions too often say otherwise. This is a common area of struggle throughout the body of Christ from the greatest to the least of us and this is why we have our Savior to help us. With the Holy Spirit's help, we can move from superficiality to authenticity in our faith and in our works. We can become that holy house for the indwelling of His Spirit.

Chapter 9

Let's Play Dress-Up!

"Surely what a man does when he is taken off guard is the best
evidence for what sort of a man he is. What pops out before
the man has time to put on a disguise is the truth. If there are
rats in a cellar you are most likely to see them if you go in very
suddenly. But the suddenness does not create the rats: it only
prevents them from hiding."

-C.S. Lewis, *Mere Christianity*

Most little girls play dress-up in their mother's closets.
I certainly did. I recall her having a little dusty brown
shoulder mink that I would put on along with a set of her gloves
that ran up to the elbow. I would don one of her little black hats that
looked much like an upside down bowl with a black mesh veil that
came down just low enough to cover my eyes. I think I loved the
gloves most of all. They were so elegant to me. Although the mink

was soft and furry, I didn't care too much for it. Perhaps it was those tiny little black, glass eyes on that poor little creature, staring at me from off my right shoulder, that made me feel so uncomfortable wearing it. At any rate, I loved playing dress-up in my mother's closet. She was fair, petite and beautiful and I wanted to look like her. However, when playtime was over, I had to take off her garments, put away the pretense and return to being the little girl that I was and the person that God created me to be. I wanted to look like my mother, but I did not want to live her life. She had paid some dues that I could never pay. I decided that I would settle for simply looking like her.

In our walk with God, many of us want to be like Jesus in our hearts, but are not willing to pay the high price of following in His steps. We play in His closet and put on His apparel from time to time, but when it comes time to make sacrifices for the sake of holiness, we quickly disrobe, neatly hang Jesus's garments back on the rack, put our old clothes back on and hasten on our way. The price to be like Jesus is simply too high. We'll settle for just looking like Him. After all, His closet door is always open...

The very first piece of furniture that we encounter in the Outer Court is the brazen altar. Now, we know that in the Old Testament an altar always symbolized the death of something living: a lamb, a bull, a goat, etc. Jesus was that perfect spotless sacrifice, the Holy Lamb of God, slain for the sins of the world. Crucified on a cross, He died a shameful, horrific public death for all of our sins. His very public death reminds us that the Outer Court demands a sacrificial, public death from each of us. We see the brazen altar, but pretend not to. We see the brazen altar, but we ignore it and step over, or walk around it. We see the brazen altar and are moved by it, but then we quickly move away from it. Many of us are genuinely terrified by it, so we do nothing about what we see.

For so many, the Outer Court is viewed as a permanent residence, when in actuality the Outer Court is God's invitation to us to enter into the Holy of Holies. However, look around and you will see God's little children trying to decorate it with extravagant plants, pretty flowers, wall hangings and new carpet, as if God intended for us to stay there. Think about this for a moment: that's like accepting an invitation to dine with an honored dignitary, showing up at his mansion and when the door is opened for you to enter, you choose to sit on the front steps.

Our very conduct, primarily displayed in the manner in which we tirelessly attend to our flesh, bears witness to this Outer Court mentality. We treat it with collagen, botox it, suck it out, slice it, lift it, nip it and tuck it. We will buy a new suit, a new pair of shoes, a new dress, a new purse, or a new shade of lipstick every week. We color our hair so much that we cannot even remember what color God made it originally. We wear false eyelashes and colored contacts, an assortment of wigs and weaves, dreads today and bald tomorrow! This is all Outer Court activity that consumes most of our time and money and God is not pleased. We have made idols of our own bodies. We are playing dress-up with our exterior – looking good on the outside, while drying up and dying on the inside.

The very brazenness of the altar, the positioning of the laver and bronze basin, cry out to us to cease with our frivolity, take a good look at ourselves and see the stains that the problem of our sins has left on us, then make the choice to die a public death! The process of rebuilding the heart gates will begin with our complete surrender and brokenness before God. The first step is to lay all of our heart on the altar – every broken, fractured, shattered, hardened, cold, grief-stricken or numb piece of it! God wants it all. He wants to heal it all.

We are hindered from drawing closer to God because we have had a chance to get too comfortable in the Outer Court, especially since there is no one there to present us with the challenge to move, to change or to grow. God forbid that some spiritually motivated individual – one who is sick and tired of sin having dominion over them, sick and tired of having no purpose, no anointing, and no power – would shake up hell to advance the kingdom of God, choose to break free from the bondages of Outer Court mentality and dare to go deeper into the Holy of Holies. That individual will encounter the forces of darkness that will pull out the big guns to stop them from going after more of God.

God chasers always make the people around them who have no desire to go deeper with God feel most uncomfortable with them, because they have the audacity to accept the invitation to press in to God. This holy hunger within our hearts was given to us by God and is extremely intimidating to those around us who have gotten comfortable with the status quo. The Devil will use those people to try to hinder us from pressing past them, but we have got to be determined to press on. They will try to discourage us from moving from every direction. Press on! They will try to block our path, hold us back, step on our toes, but we must maintain a righteous determination to press on into the more of Jesus! The Devil will appoint people to lie on God chasers, slander them and make many demonically inspired attempts to discredit their ministries. Keep pressing on! Pray for your enemies as you press on. God will strengthen the one who is determined to know Him better.

Much of what motivates and sustains all of the ungodly Outer Court activity is the spirit of fear. We run from what we do not understand, but always, as we run away from one thing we run towards something else. The thing that we choose to run to, we think will give us comfort and make us feel good about the particular escape route that we have chosen to take. The immediate truth is that a new pair of shoes *will* make you feel better, as will a new hairdo, a new shade of lipstick, a pint of butter pecan ice-cream and those Oreo cookies and milk. That new suit and tie, shiny new car, or diamond and gold watch can sure make a man feel good too, but the liberating, sobering and deeper truth is that those good feelings brought about by worldly things are only temporary. The human heart is easily deceived. Satan knows that, so he uses those *things* as distractions to keep the people of God blinded and blissfully content right where they are, secretly afraid to venture past the superficiality of the Outer Court.

If Satan can keep us primping in front of the mirror, fiddling around with our stuff, toys and trinkets long enough, then he can keep us in ignorance of our true purpose. If he can keep people around us in the Outer Court whose assignment it is to constantly speak flattering words into our ears, telling us how good we look in all of our worldly trappings, then he can keep us in bondage to our flesh. If he can convince us to make simply playing dress-up and looking good our main focus in life, then he has done his job. For what else is Satan's job but to rob, kill and destroy? If we, in ignorance allow him, Satan will steal precious years from our lives by causing us to waste time tending to the mountain of self-preservation and self-indulgence that we have been busy building.

If we allow him, Satan will manipulate time to destroy opportunities that God gives us to significantly impact His kingdom and to weaken his already doomed kingdom. He will try to keep possession of our gates as long as he can. You see, the Devil knows scripture and he knows what God's Word tells us in Galatians 6:8 (NKJV), "He who sows to his flesh of the flesh shall he reap corruption, but he who sows to the Spirit will of the Spirit reap everlasting life." The Word of God urges us to be quick-witted when we encounter the schemes of Satan so that he will never be able to get the upper hand (2 Cor. 2:11). Why should we rot and die in the Outer Court? This is not God's will for His little children in whom He delights.

The Outer Court was never built for the children of God to live in. We see evidence of this in Revelation 11:1-2. John records: "I was given a reed like a measuring rod and was told, 'Go and measure the temple of God and the altar, and count the worshipers there. But exclude the outer court; do not measure it, because it has been given to the Gentiles. They will trample the holy city for forty-two months.'" Look carefully at this scripture. The only ones who God has placed favor upon and will honor are those who have moved beyond the Outer Court and into the very presence of God, into the Holy of Holies. Those who choose to remain in the Outer Court do not count. They do nothing to point unbelievers to Christ. They do nothing to glorify God. They do nothing to prepare their own hearts to be a resting place in which the Spirit of God can abide. They do nothing to advance the kingdom of God. They do not consider drawing near to God with their bodies, much less their hearts. According to this scripture, the Outer Court has been given to unbelievers who have no regard for or understanding of holy, sacred and precious things.

We seem to have let the Devil deceive us into believing it is okay for us to just continue to "hang out" in the Outer Court as lukewarm Christians for as long as we want, no harm done. Many of us have read the fictional story of the three apprentice devils on a mission to planet Earth to corrupt mankind. One by one they report to Satan to tell him of their plans. The first one says, "I will tell the humans that there is no God." Satan replies, "That will never work," and sends him from his presence. The second apprentice says, "I will tell them that there is no heaven and no hell." "Won't work," Satan says, "Humans know better." The third apprentice says, "I will tell them that nothing is urgent." To this, Satan urges him, "Go now! Go quickly! You will ruin them by the thousands."

The Outer Court may indeed be that place where everyone is welcome, but it does not belong to us to simply do with it as we wish. It all belongs to God. We do not call the shots, as the Devil would have us believe. God finds this type of religious activity repulsive. He is watching and He requires that we make a decision. Either come closer, advance from the Outer Court into the Holy Place, or back all the way out of the Sanctuary. Make your position sure. He said to the Laodiceans: "I know your deeds, that you are neither cold nor hot. I wish you were either one or the other! So, because you are lukewarm – neither hot nor cold – I am about to spit you out of my mouth" (Rev. 3:15-16). We must not attempt to play with God, or with the people of God. We cannot straddle the fence: "But if serving the LORD seems undesirable to you, then choose for your-selves this day whom you will serve..." (Josh. 24:15). What profit is there in trying to convince others that we are something we are not? In 2 Timothy 2:19 we read, "The Lord knows those who are his" and "everyone who confesses the name of the Lord must turn away from wickedness." We may succeed in fooling those around us for a time into believing that we are authentic in our Christianity, but eventually the pretense before people will come unraveled. God, on the other hand, cannot be fooled.

We said earlier that people fear what they do not fully comprehend, but we also fear what we do know and the one thing that we do know about altars is that they require that a sacrifice be made. That is what we fear, the sacrifice. Who is going to have to die and what kind of death will it be, we wonder. If it is me, what kind of pain will I have to endure? What will the sacrifice cost me? You see, we recall all too well the sacrifice that God demanded of Abraham in Genesis 22; that of his only son. We remember the price that Jesus paid for the sins of the world when He laid down His life for our redemption and we become so overwhelmed by the spirit of fear. The Devil uses that fear to chase us into a safe corner in the Outer Court where he makes us sit in the "time-out" chair for years and years, doing absolutely nothing for Jesus. Jesus said that if we are not for Him, then we are against Him (Matt. 12:30).

The brazen altar sits in plain view of all. It calls out to us that a sacrifice is required of us if we are to be called by His name. That decision to lay one's life down on the altar is every man's individual choice. No one is going to force us to lay our lives down. Jesus said, "The reason my Father loves me is that I lay down my life – only to take it up again. No one takes it from me, but I lay it down of my own accord" (John 10:17-18). We must be willing to do the same for His sake, to offer our bodies as "living sacrifices, holy and pleasing to God – this is your spiritual act of worship" (Rom. 12:1).

The next time you are in the Outer Court, just take a few moments to actually notice who is around you. What you discern in the Spirit and what you see in the natural may break your heart. You will see saints and sinners alike who are laughing on the outside, but crying on the inside. Some want to move closer to God, but are lacking the zeal and love for Jesus that is necessary to put motion behind the desire. Some are shedding tears over what appears to be remorse over sin when there is not even an inclination to repent. Others are mere charlatans, donning the mask of holiness and clothed in the handmade, poorly stitched, tainted garments of self-righteousness.

How often do those of us who wrestle with going deeper with God say that we want to be sanctified vessels of God, yet in and out of the Holy Place we go, as through a revolving door, always ending up back in the Outer Court? Some days we really want to live holy, but most days we live like a child of the Devil. At church, we are the perfect Christian, but on the streets, at home and in the workplace, when faced with adverse situations, the person that we really are comes to the surface. The sudden appearance of adversity upon the already fragile scene of our lives, lived in quiet desperation, have a way of forcing the rats out of hiding. We know that we are maturing in our walk with God when we cease to blame the adversity for our fits of rage, our unkind and profane words, our failure to show compassion, mercy and love, and our willingness to indulge in unrighteous behaviors and simply agree with God that we are not who and what we have pretended to be. This is yet another reason why we need the closeness of God in our lives. He is our Helper. He anchors us in turbulent times so that we do not become completely unraveled at the seams, so that we do not cast away our confidence in Him. When we are weak, He makes us strong. When we are afraid, He gives us courage. He helps us to become more than what we are and yet we keep Him at a safe distance.

Much of the time we choose to run from the presence of God. Without the understanding of the power of the special graces that Jesus won for us at Calvary, we unfortunately reduce sanctification to nothing more than another fifty-cent word in our vocabularies. We fail to recognize and embrace it as a deeper work of grace of the Spirit of God upon our hearts. When, as Christians, we attempt to keep God at a safe distance, we move into religiosity. Though we say with our mouths that we want more of God, in truth, our hearts are far from genuinely desiring the kind of intimacy of which our mouths speak. Jesus said, "These people come near to me with their mouth and honor me with their lips, but their hearts are far from me" (Isa. 29:13).

Intimacy with God means that as we draw close to Him, our Abba Father will see and point out the dirt that He sees on us. Being the good Daddy that He is, He is going to want to give His children a good scrubbing. He will require that we take off our costumes and stand before Him as our authentic selves, naked, bare and totally dependent upon Him. As He did in the genesis of time, God special-izes in creating something beautiful and glorious out of nothing. In love, He will wash us and then cover us, clothing us with His robes of righteousness, but this must also be our heart's desire. It must be our heart's cry, to stand before Him stripped down to our humility so that He can lift us up, whole and healed. May we become sensitive to the Holy Spirit's tug at our hearts to come closer to God. May we desire deliverance from hindrances and bondages that alienate us from our heavenly Father. May our prayer be as David's, "Cleanse me with hyssop, and I will be clean; wash me and I will be whiter than snow... Create in me a clean heart, O God..." (Ps. 51:7-10).

Yes, Daddy's closet is always open to us, but Daddy wants to strip us down before He will allow us to dress ourselves up in His regal robes. He wants us to be able to keep the garments that we find in His closet. To Him, they look good on us after we have been washed in the blood of the Lamb. In our most authentic apparel, our hearts are clean and we are covered in Jesus's blood, clothed in His righteousness, consecrated, set apart for His service and proud to be called by His name. We won't have to *play* dress-up. The fabric of our Christianity will be woven throughout our being: heart, mind, body and soul.

Chapter 10

Good Tree – Good Fruit!
Bad Tree – Bad Fruit!

"If conversion to Christianity makes no improvement in a man's outward actions – if he continues to be just as snobbish or spiteful or envious or ambitious as he was before – then I think we must suspect his 'conversion' was largely imaginary."

-C.S. Lewis, *Mere Christianity*

*A*s a young woman, after having received the call to minister to the body of Christ with my gifts and talents, I entered the church world like a kid in a candy store. While I was not new to the church itself, being a minister in the church was new to me. Although I was a musician, I was drawn to the ministry of intercession, habitually spending countless hours on my knees in prayer for others, especially for my pastor and first family. The first church that I served in as a minister was a relatively small church on the east coast, about 700 miles from my hometown in the Midwest. We averaged about 150 to 200 members on a good Sunday. Everyone knew everyone. We were like a close-knit family. We all even knew each other's children's names. Most Sundays, dinner was at the pastor's house, or at one of the saints' homes.

Often, visiting preachers were invited to preach at our church and, occasionally, they would stay at our pastor's house for days, weeks and sometimes months. One such preacher came to stay with our pastor for quite a long time. I was asked to assist him with some of his needs, such as helping him package the tapes of his sermons and driving him around to take care of some of his personal business, since he did not know how to drive. Over time, he and I became friends.

One Saturday I received a call from him. He was at the church packaging some of his taped sermons and needed me to come down and type up some labels for the tapes. I drove to the church and when I walked in, there he was, looking helpless with a mound of tapes surrounding him. I started right in typing up the labels and sticking them on the tapes. After some time, I ran out of tapes and got up to get more. As I was pulling more tapes, I turned around and there he was right upon me. He grabbed me and tried to kiss me. In horror, I pushed him away, grabbed my purse and ran out of the church that I had come to love so dearly, and had served in so joyfully.

Driving home, my hands gripped the steering wheel as I wept and wept. I was deeply hurt and confused. Never in a million years would I have expected a holy man of God to behave in such a way. Prior to becoming involved in ministry in the church, I had sung in night clubs and had expected the men that I encountered there to behave unseemly – which, by the way, they never did, at least not with me – but a man of God? I was not expecting this. The deep sense of sadness and grief that gripped my heart and soul was compounded because, almost immediately, I knew that I could never return to serve and worship in that church and amongst the people who had become like family to me as long as he was still there.

Admittedly, I was very naïve to think that everyone in the church had honorable intentions, but was I wrong to expect a man of God to exhibit godly behavior? Was I wrong to expect to be safe in the presence of a man of God? Was I wrong to expect a man of God to cover me and not try to uncover me? Was I foolish to think that I could count on a man of God to exercise integrity around women? I do not think so. Furthermore, I believe that God expected the same noble and holy behavior from one who named himself by the name of Jesus and carried His Gospel.

I spent many nights and days grieving over that awful incident. I asked the Lord, "How could a 'man of God' lay his hands on the people of God and pray for them with the one hand, and then try to take advantage of them with the other hand?" How could he produce both good and bad fruit at the same time? Something was terribly wrong at the root of his tree. I had tasted of his bad fruit firsthand and it caused me to struggle in prayer for pastors for many years following that incident. I began to look at male pastors, preachers, and evangelists with an untrusting heart. I began to wonder if they were all phonies. Were they just in it for the money? Were they in it for the women? Was there even one who had integrity? The Word of God warns us that offenses will come, but, it says, woe to the one by whom comes the offense (Matt. 18:7). It became very clear to me how vitally important it is to have integrity built into the fabric of our gates as we work to reconstruct them.

Men of high, godly integrity, such as the Reverend Billy Graham, will have a posterity that will endure forever. At the writing of this book, he is celebrating his 93rd birthday and amongst men of this generation, there has not been another used so mightily by God to save so many souls through the preaching of the Gospel of Jesus Christ. As a result of the remarkable level of integrity that he has walked in, in ministry as well as in his personal life, Rev. Billy Graham's name has never been linked with scandal – financially, morally, in dissipation, or in the way that he has handled the Gospel message. He served one God – Jehovah; loved one woman – Ruth Graham; had one mission – to preach salvation to the lost, and he preached one simple, clear, unambiguous message – "Jesus loves the sinner. He died for sinners. You can be saved today by repenting of your sins and believing in His name. His blood can wash away your sins. Come to Jesus, *just as you are*." It is astounding what God can and will do in and through the life of one who has His integrity built solidly within the structure of their gates. Without integrity, a man walks a crooked and obscure path.

As a result of the experience that I suffered at the hands of one who lacked such integrity, I was deeply offended for many years and the offense found a home in my heart until I learned how to forgive that preacher. Jesus said in Luke 6:28, "Bless those who curse you, pray for those who mistreat you." One of my first assignments on the road to healing was to pray for the very one who had horribly mistreated and greatly offended me. Oh, the wisdom of God. If we will only obey His instructions, we will enjoy the abundant life and liberty that God promises to His obedient children. The matter of heart issues is a very sensitive one for the children of God and even more so for those who have a desire to intercede on behalf of others. We need pure hearts and clean spirits as we pray.

As an intercessor, I had to be willing to lay my heart on the altar and insist that God remove every hindrance that prevented me from being able to effectively co-labor with Him in this vital and delicate area of ministry. All that resided in my heart that was diseased, corrupted and infected had to be gutted out at the very root, lest the fruit of my labor also be diseased, corrupted and infected. Jesus said, "Make a tree good, and its fruit will be good, or else make a tree bad and its fruit will be bad. For a tree is known by its fruit. You brood of vipers, how can you who are evil say anything good? For out of the overflow of the heart the mouth speaks. The good man brings good out of the good stored up in him, and the evil man brings evil out of the evil stored up in him" (Matt. 12:33-35). The Holy Spirit effectively used this scripture to purify my tainted heart. We must all take inventory of what is *stored up* in our hearts. As we pray, if we want the ear and arm of God, we must literally take Jesus's words to heart. If Jesus is saying in Matthew 12 that a person who has an evil heart cannot even speak anything good, then we must know that it is impossible for a person with an evil heart to tear down strongholds, destroy arguments and pretensions and take every disobedient thought captive to make it obey Christ, as it states in 2 Corinthians 10:3-6.

When trying to explain the reason for the plight of those who had been taken prisoner by the Nazis, Holocaust survivor Corrie ten Boom simplistically and eloquently sums it up in the movie *The Hiding Place* with this profound statement: "We are who and what we are and cannot be any more or less than what we are."[26] The reason why a man can tell a woman that he loves her more than he has ever loved any other woman, buy her expensive gifts, whisper sweet nothings in her ears, then turn around and slap her in the face, or verbally put her down when things don't go his way in the relationship, is because his tree has bad roots. For the same reason, a mother will exhibit warm and loving behavior towards her child while she is in public places, but behind closed doors she terrorizes that same child with abusive words and violent actions. Something unclean is troubling the roots of her tree.

The true Christian must always be in a state of becoming more and more like Christ, but Corrie ten Boom is correct in stating that what we are at the present moment is exactly what we are. The Spirit of Truth will have us deal truthfully with the *who* and *what* of our essence at the present moment so that we are certain to stay in the place of evolving more and more into the image and likeness of our Savior. "Dear friends, now we are the children of God, and what we will be has not yet been made known. But we know that when he appears, we shall be like him, for we shall see him as he is. Everyone who has this hope in him purifies himself, just as he is pure" 1John 3:2-3. If we have been truly born of the Spirit, then we will not be satisfied to remain who we are if that *who* is any less than what God intends for us to be. We will make it our goal to destroy the rotten roots that have fed our trees and caused us to bear rotten fruit.

"The heart is deceitful above all things and desperately wicked. Who can know it?" This asks Jeremiah, the prophet. God is the only One who knows our hearts inside and out and the only One who can cleanse our hearts. He is sovereign over this heart that seeks to rule our destinies. We should be glad about that! God knows what is stored up in our hearts. He knows the beginning of the story. He knows exactly how our hearts have deteriorated into the sick condition in which they are and praise His name – He knows exactly what it will take to fix our hearts. However, the restoration of a marred and infirm heart entails a process that seems almost as painful as the reality of living with a marred and infirm heart. The marked difference is that when we choose to live with a marred heart, we also choose to live in defeat. However, if, in faith, we surrender our hearts to God and commit to the process of restoration, we have the blessed hope and promise of victory!

Just think about it. In the natural, the thought of undergoing open-heart surgery is frightening. For that matter, having any surgery is frightening. Slap a bandage on me, give me a pill, fix me some chicken soup – change the diagnosis! Anything but surgery! Who wants to be cut wide open to have his damaged heart totally exposed? Any number of adverse conditions can threaten the success of the operation. What of those people in the operating theater who are just watching the whole medical procedure? There are those who are excited by blood and gore, so they observe for the shock value. Some just watch to see what the process looks like. Others observe to see how *we* go through the surgery, knowing that the same surgery awaits them. They will gain strength from our strength. Still others watch with wide open eyes for the sheer knowledge. One can only hope that they are all pulling for a successful surgery!

*H*upomeno!

(Greek: *to endure, stay under, submit to the process*)

"Bitterness was next to speak, and sneered from behind another tree. 'He would do this. It's just as I told you. After you have dutifully gone through one terrifying experience he's always got something still worse lying ahead of you.' Then Pride said, 'You know, he won't be able to rest content until he has put you to complete shame. Because that's the way he produces that precious humility he's so crazy about. He'll humble you to the dust, Much-Afraid, and leave you a groveling idiot in front of everyone.'" [27]

-Hinds' Feet on High Places, Hannah Hurnard

For anyone who has had to undergo surgery, you know that just having to go under the anesthesia alone is scary. How many horror stories have we all heard of patients who have been anesthetized in preparation for surgery, but never wake up again? Once a patient is under the effects of the anesthesia, he is completely helpless and at the mercy of the physician. He has no power to come out from under its effect of his own will. He has to wait for the anesthesia to wear off. Then, too, he must completely trust in the ability of the physician to both properly diagnose his condition and to successfully administer a cure for his damaged heart. This is also a good reason why we need to have holy men and women of God standing in the gap in prayer for us whenever we have to undergo any type of surgery. We need God's protection.

Equally as horrendous as what happens in the natural is what occurs in the spiritual when one considers the concept of open-heart surgery. We cringe at the idea of having our spiritually damaged hearts exposed. Why on earth would we want anyone else to know what's in there when we don't even know ourselves? There are many demonic forces in the operating theater that stand in opposition to the healing process, blocking the gates to redemption. They fight to keep us weak, bound, defeated and sin-sick. They are akin to spiritual antibodies fighting to break us down to the point where we have no chance of surviving the surgery. This is where and when our faith in Jehovah Rapha must kick in. We must trust Him even more than we trust the power and skill of human doctors.

I remember some years ago when I underwent a major surgery. It was a dreadful experience. I was completely and utterly overcome from head to toe with a fear such as I had never ever experienced in my entire life. As I lay on the gurney in the hallway waiting to be wheeled into the operating room, I could feel my whole body starting to chill. I began to shake uncontrollably, both from the chill and the fear. In fact, it was the fear that made my body temperature drop to what seemed like below freezing. Certain family members were standing by my bedside, trying to comfort me. I was embarrassed by the fear that made my body shake so terribly. I was embarrassed by the very real fact that for the next three days I would be totally dependent upon strangers for all my physical needs. The next thing I knew, there were tears rolling down the side of my face, yet another body function over which I had no control at that vulnerable moment. I did not even realize that I had been crying until I felt the moisture from the tear on the side of my face. I began to pray for the Holy Spirit to comfort me and give me His peace.

As I prayed, I noticed a nurse walking over to me. Seeing how frightened I was, she came over to my gurney. Taking my hand and caressing it, she smiled tenderly at me and said something to the effect of, "Honey, you're going to be all right. It will all be over before you know it. Just relax." Just then, I began to feel the peace of God engulf me and she was right. The anesthesiologist asked me to count backwards from ten to one. I had only reached nine when I opened my eyes to discover that I was already in the recovery room with an IV in my hand and an oxygen tube in my throat. All I could think to myself was, "When did all of this happen? Is the surgery over already?" God had given me His peace. He had sent His angel to shut the lion's mouth and take away my fear. His peace enabled me to be calm in the midst of a fearful situation. His peace enabled me to stay on that table, go through the surgery and come out happier, healthier and made whole. All we need is a resolution within that we will endure whatever we have to endure to be all that God intends for us to be.

From the moment that we realize the sin-sick state of our hearts and decide to let Jesus, the Great Physician make us whole, the spiritual battle begins. It's that radical decision that we make to *go with God* in the face of our greatest opposition and our deepest pain that gets the battle raging. Matthew 11:12 tells us, "The kingdom of heaven has endured violent assault, and violent men seize it by force" (AMP). Romans 7:21-23 tells us that there is a constant war in our members whenever we purpose to do right: "evil is right there with me... waging war against the law of my mind and making me a prisoner of the law of sin at work within my members."

In Hebrews we are admonished, "But be ever mindful of the days gone by in which, after you were first spiritually enlightened, you endured a great and painful struggle. Sometimes being yourselves a gazing-stock, publicly exposed to insults and abuse and distress" (Heb. 10:32, 33 AMP). Again, we read of the intensity of the battle in Luke 11:22, "When a strong man, fully armed, guards his own house, his possessions are safe. But when someone stronger attacks and overpowers him, he takes away the armor in which the man trusted and divides up the spoils." Clearly, the battle rages on and the levels of warfare intensify whenever spiritual transformation is underway. We must anticipate the tension between where we are and where it is that we are trying to go. If we understand that simply by virtue of the fact that when light appears in the midst of darkness, darkness is overpowered and so must flee, then we will have rightly anticipated the battle (John 1:4-5). Darkness does not want to flee and so there *will* be a battle, because daylight *is* coming!

We must presume that our spiritual house is going to be in disarray while the battle rages violently between Satan and our Lord. Satan wars to hold onto what his wicked heart desires to be his for eternity, but God knows what is His from before the foundation of the earth. It is indeed a time of great distress upon the soul. The Lord gives us great grace to endure the struggle and reminds us that until we have resisted and sweat blood, we cannot say that sin cannot be overcome. For this reason, we do not lose heart (Heb. 12:3-12). We must pray for strength and for the peace of God to keep us and hold us together until the battle has subsided and the victory has been won.

In the struggle for transformation the spiritual battle is so intense that we cry out even as Paul did, "O wretched man that I am! Who will deliver me from this body of death?" It is so intense that often your whole body, soul and spirit seems to be held in an indefinite state of trauma as there you lay on the operating table with everyone watching you in all your glorious nakedness. Your soul is in distress and there they are gazing at you. At times, you agonize as the battle between flesh and spirit rages on, so desperately desiring to be free from the powerful grip of sin in your life and its shameful effects that you feel you *would* soon sweat great drops of blood. You know you need the surgery, but can you endure so much exposure in the face of so many onlookers? You feel humiliated! You want to jump off of the table, totally exposed and just dash out of the operating room, shouting back at the heart surgeon, "Just forget it! I can't go through with it! Let me stay just like I am and if I perish, I perish!" However, the Spirit of the Lord God is speaking to you right now that you have come to the kingdom of God for such a time as this... to be healed! God wants to help you rebuild your heart gate.

How often have we all been guilty of dressing up and covering over our infirmities, so certain that no one will notice that we are sick. We fool ourselves into believing that a spritz of expensive per-fume will mask the odor of an old, festering, gangrenous wound to the heart. We drag our tattered heart gates around, hoping that no one will notice that they are only slightly held together with thumb tacks and push-pins – you know, those catchy, cliché phrases like: "Time heals all wounds," and "This too shall pass." These are both passive conclusions to a desperate situation that requires our aggressive involvement. As long as our hearts are badly damaged, our lives will continue to spin out of control. We will just barely know how to maneuver our own lives on a daily basis, much less consider ourselves capable to guide anyone else along their journey.

As wounded physicians, we extend our hands in an attempt to tend to the wounds of others, only to have the puss, poison and stench of our own unattended wounds spill onto and further infect the ones to whom we are attempting to administer healing. It is not that we do not desire healing for ourselves, but that we have not yet allowed ourselves to be genuinely broken before the one true Source from whence our healing must come. We must come to Him and cry out for healing. The LORD says in Jeremiah 17:10, "I, the LORD search the heart and examine the mind, to reward a man according to his conduct, according to what his deeds deserve." The prophet Jeremiah then cries, "Heal me, O' LORD, and I shall be healed; save me, and I shall be saved, for you are my praise" (v. 14). O' thou tempest tossed and not as yet comforted soul, there *is* a Balm in Gilead! His name is Jesus, the Christ.

In Ezekiel 36:24-31, we see a picture of God as Chief Surgeon amongst His people, Israel. He lets them know that He is about to perform open heart surgery upon them and just as any good doctor would do, He gives them a blow by blow account of what the surgery will entail. He says, "For I will take you from among the nations and gather you out of all the countries and bring you into your own land" (v. 24, NKJV). You see, sometimes God has to take us out of a sin-infested, contaminated environment and just flat out quarantine us. This means that He has to separate us from toxic people, places and things that are hindering our walk with Him and ruining our testimony. He has to put us in sterile surroundings so that when He opens us up to clean us out there will be no risk of infection coming in from the outside.

God then preps us for surgery by giving us a good Holy Ghost scrubbing and detoxing. He says:

Then I will sprinkle clean water on you, and you will be clean; I will cleanse you from all your impurities, and from all your idols. I will give you a new heart, and put a new spirit in you; I will remove from you your heart of stone and give you a heart of flesh. And I will put my Spirit in you and move you to follow my decrees and be careful to keep my laws. You will live in the land I gave your forefathers; you will be my people, and I will be your God. I will save you from all your uncleanness (vv. 25-29a).

When we have suffered a wound to the heart, it is easy to begin to adopt the negative and accusatory thoughts and attitudes of unbelievers, especially when we feel that the wound is undeserved. This is why God has to airlift us, if you will, out of an infected environment, and place us around people of great faith. Often, you will hear of Christians who have fallen prey to serious illness giving explicit instructions to only allow visitors in the room who love them and are faith-filled. They want only those around them who can stand in faith with them and believe God for their healing. They will demand that negative people be kept away from them. They understand the concept of quarantine and how vital it is to the healing process.

What would a quarantine from God necessitate? Well, it may demand that you skip this year's Christmas party with the mixed crowd where they will be decking the halls with more than just boughs of holly. A quarantine from God would mean that Friday nights with the girls is off if all the girls end up doing every time they fellowship is having gossipy "prayer sessions." It means that you cannot watch "R" rated movies and think that the sex, violence and profanity will have no effect upon your spirit. These days, where technology has rapidly increased, Babylon is often located on a stroll through the Internet, a visit to a chat room, or on Facebook or Twitter. God commands us to "Come out from among them, and be ye separate! Touch no unclean thing! Come out from it, and be ye pure" (Isa. 52:11). Quarantine from God would require that you stay off the computer if surfing the net means that you might fall off your surfboard and into the murky, dark and slimy waters of Internet pornography. For sure, it means that man or that woman you are living with, but not yet married to, has to go! "If your right eye causes you to sin, gouge it out, and throw it away," said Jesus in Matthew 5:29.

Paul said, among believers "there must not even be a hint of sexual immorality, or any kind of impurity or of greed, because these are improper for God's holy people" (Eph. 5:3). Even though we are God's children, still we behave in ungodly ways at times and there was a reason why Paul felt the need to say what he said to the believers at Ephesus. Paul clearly understood the battle between the flesh and the spirit. He understood that all it takes is a little leaven and it would not be long before it worked its way all through the lump of dough (Gal. 5:9). This is why he urges us in Ephesians 6:10-18 to make ourselves battle-ready, having on the full armor of God when we go to war against the strategies of our Adversary.

If you are considering jumping off of the operating table, afraid to endure the pain, afraid of the unknown, afraid of becoming a gazing-stock, I want to encourage you to *hupomeno*. Go through what you have to go through that God may receive glory out of your life and you may be an encouragement to someone else. If we will only make up our minds to submit to the process, we will discover that the end result of the process will translate into something beautiful. "Did not the Christ have to suffer these things and then enter into his glory?" (Luke 24:26) It is His glory that we want to put on display for the watching world. The love of Christ and the brilliance of the glory of God shining upon us and through us is what will draw unbelievers into the gates of the Good Shepherd (John 13:35; Isa. 60:1-3).

My daughter has a funny habit of opening up her bills and then either throwing them in the garbage or hiding them in a drawer. Her theory is that if she just ignores them, they will magically go away and she will never have to pay them. She received a rude awakening once, when a sizable income tax refund that she was eagerly awaiting never arrived. It had been intercepted by the IRS and applied to her outstanding college loan.

Once the Holy Spirit shows us the x-rays of our damaged hearts, we are responsible for what we do with those x-rays. If we choose to ignore them or discard them, the results of the x-rays will not change. Payday is coming sooner or later. If we decide to try to squirm off of the operating table once the doctor has opened us up, we will only remain an exposed, open wound in the body of Christ. What happens to an open wound? The same thing that happens to rotten fruit – it stinks. It stinks of rebellion, disobedience and ulti-mately, it becomes the tragic stench of death! As believers, we are to spread the fragrant aroma of Christ everywhere we go. That aroma is the fragrance of life to those who believe and death to those who are perishing (2 Cor. 2:16).

To the saint of God whose heart is perfect towards God and who has decided to endure the pain, trust God, and ignore the shame, let me offer you these encouraging words found in Hebrews 12:1-3:

Therefore, since we are surrounded by such a great cloud of witnesses, let us throw off everything that hinders and the sin that so easily entangles, and let us run with perseverance the race marked out for us. Let us fix our eyes on Jesus, the author and perfecter of our faith, who for the joy set before him endured the cross, scorning its shame, and sat down at the right hand of the throne of God. Consider him who endured such opposition from sinful men, so that you will not grow weary and lose heart.

Let nothing stop you from going through with your decision to be made right before God. There is a joy set before you, too. Jesus said to Peter, "…and when you yourself have turned again, strengthen and establish your brethren" (Luke 22:32, AMP). How do we strengthen our brothers and sisters in Christ? We do this by feeding them good, healthy fruit from off of our carefully cultivated branches. Jesus's desire for us is that, as His children, we will bear fruit that remains, fruit that is useful and beneficial to someone else (John 15:1-17).

We enter this world with a heart that is already infested with a sinful nature. Simply living life exposed to the evils of this world compounds the sinful condition of our hearts. In addition, our failure to obey God by diligently guarding the gates to our hearts has left the spiritual condition of our hearts in a far worse state than we could have ever imagined. However, we do not have to be afraid of the exposure. We do not have to fear what the exploratory surgery will reveal about our heart's condition. We do not have to fear what the Great Physician will "put us through" or require of us. He will not put more on us than we can bear and He will never abandon us to shame. Romans 5:2-5 gives strength to our gates with these words: "And not only so, but we glory in tribulations also: knowing that tribulation worketh patience; and patience, experience; and experience, hope. And hope maketh not ashamed; because the love of God is shed abroad in our hearts by the Holy Ghost which is given unto us." (KJV)

These are some of the necessary building materials for strong gates: endurance, patience and hope. The prophet Jeremiah said in Lamentations 3 that though God had pierced his heart with arrows from His quiver so that he became the laughingstock of all the people, yet he had hope in his God. He encourages himself and us with these words, "Because of the LORD's great love we are not consumed, for his compassions never fail. They are new every morning; great is your faithfulness" (vv.13, 14, 21-23).

We can take hope and praise God because He is the Vinedresser. John 15 lets us know that God will cut off every branch in Christ that has ceased to produce good fruit and that He will prune every branch that bears good fruit so that it will keep on bearing even more fruit.

Good tree – good fruit. That's His goal for us and we can be rightly encouraged, for we know that He has promised to perfect those things that concern us (Ps. 138:8). James, Jesus's brother, encouraged the believers in his letter to the church to strive towards the goal in the midst of trials and suffering, to *hupomeno*, that is, to endure, stay on the table, so that they would be made mature and complete, lacking nothing (Jas. 1:4). God is committed to helping us bear good fruit, even if it means that He has to radically cut off every branch that threatens to spoil our testimony and our witness for Him.

Chapter 11

Thy Will Be Done

"Nothing in all creation is hidden from God's sight. Everything is uncovered and laid bare before the eyes of Him to whom we must give account." Heb. 4:13

"There are two kinds of people: those who say to God, 'Thy will be done,' and those to whom God says, 'All right, then, have it your way.'"
-C.S. Lewis, *Mere Christianity*

*J*esus, our Great High Priest, is ever interceding for us. He is praying for the day when we will rise up and tell the Devil, "Enough is enough!" He is praying for the day when we will walk in our jurisdictional authority at the gates. You see, like the fierce warrior David (1 Sam. 17), we need to get to the place where we boldly run towards the Philistines in our lives long before they even reach our gates, slay them on the spot and without thinking twice, cut off their heads and give glory to God! This is possible for those who are willing to surrender the reigns of their heart to God and allow the Great Physician to repair the years of damage. Our willingness and readiness are the qualifiers that untie the hands of God, allowing Him to release power and strength to us to carry out our heart's desire to be made whole. Once the Lord has performed the necessary surgery, your formerly weak and timid heart will heal with new courage and a renewed zeal and love for God and man.

In my own life as an intercessor, my travels through the corridors of heaven had brought me to the valley of decision. I had to decide to come out of hiding and just allow the Holy Spirit to really have His way with me. You see, when we begin to get serious about regaining possession of our gates and drawing near to God, then we begin to discern the Holy Spirit moving upon our hearts, searching out the dark places of our souls and our spirits to uncover any lies that the Devil has planted there.

The Holy Spirit works to reveal to us the truth that God wants us to know about anything that hinders our lives and our relationship with Him; this includes the ugly truth about ourselves that we have been trying to ignore. That's our way, you know. At least, it was my way – ignore truth, stand aloof from it and just keep on trucking along a twisted path that leads to a tragic demise. Solomon said, "There is a way that seems right to a man, but in the end it leads to death" (Prov. 14:12). When we begin to see how filthy we really are before our Holy God, it becomes a bitter pill to swallow. It is at this moment of truth that we have to decide just how much of God we really want.

When I first answered the call to the ministry of intercession, it had never occurred to me that each time I entered the Outer Court and stood at the laver to wash, the blood of the Lamb of God was washing off layer after layer of sin, going deeper and deeper to the root causes of the sin-sickness that filled my heart. Each time that I gazed intently into the bronze basin, the reflection that I saw revealed an image that was so unlike the reflection I had been accustomed to seeing in the mirror into which I gazed at home. From my mirror at home, surrounded by flattering lighting, I was only able to see my dressed up externals. I could leave this mirror feeling pretty good about myself. A little concealer and foundation and *voila* – all flaws had been covered over, all blemishes hidden. However, in this mirror in the Outer Court, this bronze basin positioned in the stark light of the holy presence of this holy God, I was forced to see all the things that I did not want to see. This mirror had the ability to reveal my ugly insides. I learned then and there that the eyes of God run deeper than I ever imagined. No amount of layers of foundation can hide our sins or flaws from Him. No concealer can camouflage them from His sight. No eye shadow or false eyelashes can disguise my flaws enough so that His eyes are deceived. The eyes of God see everything. His eyes know us in all of our glorious nakedness. While looking at my flesh in this mirror, I saw no good thing – no, not one – and the things that I did see about me in this most holy place, made me want to run in the opposite direction and abandon my pursuit of God altogether. Fixing so many flaws and imperfections seemed to be an impossible feat. However, in spite of the ugliness that I saw of myself in the Outer Court, the light from the Holy Place kept bidding me to go deeper, to draw nearer to this holy God.

As I entered into the Holy Place, the light of God's presence gave me revelation into His Word, His ways and His purpose for my life. His Spirit began to reveal things to me that I needed to know about myself. He showed me the hindrances that were keeping me out of the Holy of Holies. These hindrances were literally blocking the gates so that I could not dwell in the presence of the Most High God. He revealed to me that if I did not deal violently with these roadblocks, they would ultimately rob my life of His divine purpose for me, thereby stealing the glory that God intended to get out of my life (See Deut. 7; Judg. 1:19-36; Judg. 2:1-4).

Had I petitioned God to search and cleanse my heart every time that I knelt in prayer? Absolutely! Was I sincere in my daily requests? Most definitely! Did I really know what I was asking for? Not entirely, for who amongst us can really know this enigma that beats within the breast of man? Who can know this heart? However, on this particular day, I had passed that mirror for the last time, seeing and yet not really seeing. I had dipped into that bronze basin for the last time thinking that I was *nearly* clean, *almost* done. I had sat in the glorious light of His beautiful, yet consuming presence, seeing only clouded shadows of my own heart.

On many other occasions, as I sat quietly at the feet of my Lord, He would choose to reveal things to me concerning others' lives. Sometimes, as directed by the Spirit of the Lord, I was just to pray over the secrets that He would reveal to me. On other occasions, the Holy Spirit would direct me to go to the individual and share with them what He had revealed to me. Sometimes what I would give to the individual would be a word of wisdom, a word of knowledge, or a word of prophecy. Sometimes it was a word of encouragement; other times, a word of warning or rebuke. This has been a consistent part of the ministry that God has placed in my hands for many years now. However, on this day, sitting in His presence, the only revelation that He was speaking to me was for me, about me and only me! He was showing me the condition of my own heart. Let me tell you, it was not pretty.

The Lord said to me that it was always possible for me to see the condition of my heart. The only thing that had prevented me from seeing was my own unwillingness to surrender my whole heart to Him. I was still hanging on to my own will, to my own ways. I was still benefiting from having and doing things my own way. I had not allowed myself to be brought to the place where I was willing to not only see the truth, but to also embrace the hard truth revealed. However, there is something powerfully motivating and strategically compelling about having an insatiable desire to dwell in the center of God's will that draws the true seeker to the place of total surrender. This desire will make us climb over walls, push down gates and plow through every barrier that hinders us from getting to that place where God has reserved His greatest blessings for our lives. The Holy Spirit escorted me to that place by way of the spirit of conviction and the gift of repentance.

As I stood before Him, raising the white flag of surrender with tears streaming down, I slowly lifted my head to look to Him for the next instruction. The next thing I knew, the Spirit of Truth hit me right between the eyes. The bitter truth that the Holy Spirit revealed to me caused me to fall on my face in utter disbelief and in true brokenness. The flow of my tears was uncontrollable. In my great dismay, I cried out to the Lord, "Oh God, how did my heart get so messed up?" The answer from the Lord was immediate and what He revealed to me applies to many of the saints of God. Let me just say right here that during this season in my life, I discovered another thing about God: His confrontational truth has no mercy. It has one purpose and that is to liberate us from the grip of Satan's lies. People have lied to us time after time, telling us that we are okay just the way we are. They fail us because they see the things that hinder us from growing and maturing in Christ, yet they are afraid to challenge us to change. They see us standing behind rickety gates, but fail to warn us that our gates are in disrepair and offer no hedge against an Enemy invasion. They have the mistaken idea that they are being kind and merciful to us by not offending us with the truth. David said, "Let a righteous man strike me – it is a kindness; let him rebuke me – it is oil on my head. My head will not refuse it"

(Ps. 141:5). David's son, Solomon, echoes his father's sentiments when he says in Proverbs 27:17, "As iron sharpens iron, so one man sharpens another."

Currently, I work for a printing company. We produce orders for stationery products, such as business cards, letterhead, business reply envelopes, and so on. Several years back, one of my responsibilities was that of physically locating every order throughout the plant that did not get printed and shipped on time. To do this, I had to walk through the entire plant of mostly male workers and search every single place where a late order might be "hiding." One morning I took a quick bathroom break and like most women who are forced to use public restrooms, I neatly covered the toilet seat with bathroom tissue prior to sitting down. Unbeknownst to me, a long strip of the tissue paper had gotten caught in the back of my slacks as I stood up, making me look like I had a long, white, floating tail trailing behind me.

As I went out into the plant to commence the grueling task of searching for late orders, I noticed the guys looking at me, but not one of them had said a word to me about my "tail." Just then, Monique, who was one of the few women working out in the plant, came up close behind me and whispered in my ear that I had a long trail of toilet paper hanging out of the back of my slacks. I gasped in horror! She then moved in closer behind me, covering me long enough for me to remove my embarrassing tail. I thanked her profusely for not joining the ranks of others who had allowed me to walk around with something glaringly wrong with me, but had said nothing. From that day on, a special bond was formed between me and Monique. I thought it was especially kind of her to cover me, both with a physical gesture and by opening her mouth to make me aware of a little issue that I had goin' on. I was not as together as I thought I was and Monique covered me by letting me know that.

As Christians, we also fail to confront others because we don't want to come across as hypocritical, knowing that we are struggling with the same or worse issues. We think about the plank in our own eyes and suddenly the courage to confront withers away (Matt. 7:3-5). "Why tell someone else about their unsightly tail, when I have a pretty hideous one of my own?" we reason. However, this reasoning should give us even more motivation to become desperate for authentic transformation in our own lives. Paul reminds us in Romans 11:32, "for God has bound all men over to disobedience so that he may have mercy on them all." Yes, the ways of God are difficult to comprehend, says Paul. "Who can know the mind of the Lord?" Still, our God is to be glorified (vv. 33-36). Our loving and compassionate Lord understands our fragile frame. He calls broken and imperfect people to do the work of His kingdom and He expects us to rely on His mercy and grace as we do. Read through the Psalms and you will see how heavily David, a broken and imperfect man, relied on the mercies of God in his day-to-day challenges as he sought to fulfill his purpose in God.

The disobedience that has us bound demands the great, unfailing mercies of God to be poured out upon us and it is also why we must insist that the Holy Spirit have His way in our hearts. We must be willing to offer our lives to God as a drink offering, as Paul aptly said in 2 Timothy 4:6, not kicking and screaming. We have the authority, by the power of the Holy Spirit dwelling within us, to command our flesh to become subject to the Lordship of Christ. David said, "Do not be like the horse or the mule, which have no understanding, but must be controlled by bit and bridle" (Ps. 32:9). No, we are not Paul, neither do we have his assignment, but the willingness that Paul displayed to be near to God, to know God and to be used of God must be the same willingness that we embrace to be healed by God. Our testimony must be, "God, I am yours; do with me as You will."

Yes, we are our brother's keeper in the sense that we are called to hold each other accountable to one another and to God. We are called to spur one another on to love and good deeds. When we allow the Holy Spirit to clean up our lives and make us holy, consecrated and loving vessels, then we have earned the right to confront our brothers and sisters in Christ in love. Our motivation must be love, coupled with a pure desire to see them overcome evil in their lives and grow to be all that God intends for them to be.

This enormous project of rebuilding our gates is not just for us alone. In every blessing that comes into our lives, we are blessed to be a blessing. God must be able to have His way with us. He must be able to trust us to reach out, to reach back, or to reach down and help our brothers and sisters to also get free from behind the Enemy's gates. As we confront, we trust God to release His grace that will enable them to handle the ugly truth and to break free from hindrances and bondages to sin. This He did for me when He showed me the sick condition of my own heart. He graced me and then He schooled me.

God reminded me about what I had gleaned from my studies on the heart. My studies revealed to me that the 17th century physicians discovered that "even when the heart sustained serious injury, the mind still functioned." There was the answer to my question to God concerning the condition of my heart! Each time my heart had sustained a serious injury, my mind kicked into high gear, searching out a plan, a method of survival, that would not only help me to survive the present wound, but that would also help me to prevent any future injury. Let me put a pin here. Every time we choose to depend solely upon our mental skills, rather than on the help of the Holy Spirit, we are putting our confidence in the flesh when we should be placing our confidence in the God of all flesh. Philippians 3:3 reminds us that we are to "put no confidence in the flesh."

When we depend entirely upon our mental coping skills to sustain us and to deliver us in the wake of emotional trauma, all we do is open up the gates to our minds to unwittingly allow Satan to begin establishing powerful strongholds that will then take us years to tear down. And once we have spent all those years tearing down those debilitating, satanic strongholds, we will then have to spend more years reconstructing the gates to our minds and allowing the Lord to renew our minds to a state of mental soundness. Anyone who has been through this process knows that it can take a lifetime to regain soundness of mind once we have given Satan access to come in and build those strongholds. Just consider how much time and energy we spend doing corrective surgery on ourselves, when we could have been effectively serving God and others, making a dynamic impact on the kingdom of God, had we learned early on to depend upon God, rather than on our own unreliable flesh. That realization alone should put us all in high gear to get about rebuilding our gates.

Exalting the mind as lord has a corrupting influence upon the heart that occurs very subtly, much like the physical malady of the heart called arteriosclerosis, commonly known as hardening of the arteries. With arteriosclerosis, a heavy film of fat builds along the interior of vessel walls in areas where the smooth arterial lining has been torn or injured. The fatty deposits calcify into a chalky substance, transforming the elastic wall into dead and unresponsive scar tissue.[28] If the condition continues to exist undiagnosed, the result is the development of a bulge, or aneurysm that eventually ruptures, and is more often than not fatal.

The spiritual parallel to arteriosclerosis occurs each time we suffer an injury to our hearts, such as a betrayal, a broken friendship, the death of a loved one, a failed marriage, etc., and we neglect to take the time to properly work through the various stages of grief. Those stages of grief include: disbelief or denial, hurt, anger, rage, numbness, sorrow and depression. In both the spiritual and the physical realms, the damage done by these conditions is very well concealed, hidden from view until years down the line when it is either almost or ultimately too late to reverse the damage.

When we fail to present our damaged hearts to the Lord for cleansing and for healing, the calcification process begins. Those areas surrounding our hearts, once smooth and soft, accepting, loving, merciful and kind, now become hardened scar tissue, unloving, bitter, cold and aloof. We find ourselves unable to empathize with the suffering of others, when in actuality, having suffered so much ourselves, we should be the very ones who have the ability to bear the compassion of Christ in the face of others' suffering, comforting "those in any trouble with the comfort that we ourselves have received from God" (2 Cor. 1:3-7). However, because our own wounds have not been healed, we stand detached, unmoved by and indifferent to the pain and the needs of others, unable to properly respond to the prompting of the Holy Spirit. If we allow the condition of our hearts to remain hardened, we can easily experience a spiritual death. When the Spirit of the Lord revealed this to me concerning the condition of my own heart, I cried out to the Lord a prayer that I had cried out to Him so many times before, "Create in me a clean heart, O God, and renew a steadfast spirit within me" (Ps. 51:10). The difference in my prayer this time was that it emanated from a place of sheer desperation that the ears of God had not heard before from this intercessor. Without further delay and with very little courage, I made an appointment to undergo spiritual open heart surgery that very day.

The Holy Spirit revealed to me that I would never experience the true life of the Spirit until I allowed Him to go deep into my darkened heart to perform that much-needed radical surgery. You see, the life of the Spirit surpasses the heart and the mind. Galatians 5 exhorts us to "live by the Spirit, be led by the Spirit, and to keep in step with the Spirit." We are told to *love* the LORD with all of our heart, mind, soul and strength (Luke 10:27), but to "*live* by the Spirit." This requires a deeper level of surrender and we will not surrender our minds until we first surrender our hearts. Do you need proof of this fact?

Consider this: why would an otherwise intelligent man or woman allow their lives to be consumed by someone who disrespects, uses and abuses them? Why would anyone remain in such an abusive, dysfunctional relationship? Amongst a plethora of reasons, it is primarily because the heart is still the sovereign of the body. It is deceitful and desperately wicked and it carries all the other parts of the body in tow. What the mind or the intellect, identifies as unacceptable, irrational and cruel behavior, the heart's enigmatic passions will make room for, exposing a person to unnecessary pain, sorrow and suffering that an otherwise rationally thinking person would not allow into their lives. Many intelligent women have claimed that love is the reason why they have chosen to stay in abusive relationships. The actor Woody Allen once said, in justifying why he left his wife for her adopted stepdaughter, "The heart wants what it wants." Renowned theologian, Dr. Irwin Lutzer, amended Allen's quote by adding to it: "and the mind had better follow."

When we decide to fully surrender our lives to the Lordship of Jesus Christ, we will experience a richer communion with His Spirit and while this deeper communion certainly includes our emotions and our reason, it goes beyond both the former and the latter. We find ourselves in a place that crosses the path of the eyes of God, a place called "Spirit and Truth." This is the place where God is seeking the "true worshipers." It is here, in His presence, where we experience fullness of joy, and pleasures forevermore. We must get serious about the business of obeying our heavenly Father and rebuilding our gates. "The days are coming," declares the LORD, "when I will punish all who are circumcised only in the flesh – Egypt, Judah, Edom, Amnon, Moab… and even the whole house of Israel is uncircumcised in heart" (Jer. 9:25-26). As God covenanted with Abraham in Genesis 22, so He has made a covenant with us to give us a heart that will love Him and serve Him only. He wants our hearts.

If you are anything like I was, there have been many occasions in your life where you have failed to guard the gate to your heart. Many in the body of Christ, who have experienced this same failure, are now living with the damage and working to get free from the bondages with which this disobedience has held them captive. God's Word warns us that when we choose to follow the stubborn inclinations of our evil hearts, we can only go backward (into captivity) and not forward (Jer. 7:23-24).

Isaiah 61 reminds us that Jesus came to set the captive free. This is great news! Because of Jesus, we don't have to stay the way we are. Praise His holy name! Jesus wants us completely whole. As we endure, we must pray for fortitude and for patience, because it is a process. There must be willingness in us to say, "My Father... not as I will, but as you will" (Matt. 26:39). "I don't want to wear the makeup anymore. I don't want to conceal my flaws. I give up my disguise. I want to be whole. I want what You want for me, Jesus." As we pray this prayer, our Lord will strengthen the bars of our heart gates, bless us, heal us and grant peace to our borders (Ps. 147:13-14).

Part Five

The Mouth Gate

"Silence teaches us to speak. A word that is not rooted in silence is a weak and powerless word that sounds like a 'clashing cymbal or a booming gong' (1 Cor. 13:1)."

-Henri Nouwen, *The Way of the Heart*

Chapter 12

The Words We Speak

"Set a guard over my mouth, O Lᴏʀᴅ; keep watch over the door
of my lips." Ps. 141:3

*R*ecent studies have debunked the myth that women talk
much more than men. In actuality, both men and women
speak about the same amount of words per day – 16,000. That is a
whole lot of words. Enough to ask ourselves, "Just exactly what are
we talking about?"

Years ago, I had this recurring dream where I would be talking
to someone, but I was doing most of the talking. The more I talked,
I noticed that my teeth were turning into mush, kind of like grits. I
would finally stop talking when I could talk no more, because my
teeth had completely dissolved into hominy grits. At that point, continuing conversation was impossible. I put my hand over my mouth
in horror and ran out of the room, always resolving to speak less

and listen more. That dream was always so real that when I awoke, I would run to the bathroom mirror to see if I still had all my pearly whites intact. Whew! It was only a dream, but from that dream I knew that God was telling me to take care with my words, to value the words I speak and that there is no such thing as a spoken word that does not have some effect, whether good or evil.

Solomon, recorded as the wisest man to have ever lived, said in Proverbs 10:19, "In the multitude of words, sin is not lacking. But he who restrains his lips is wise" (NKJV). David, Solomon's father, must have also understood this dynamic of the unbridled tongue as he prayed to the LORD to "set a guard over" his mouth. David was a just king who certainly recognized the significance and the power of a spoken word, decree, or an edict. One word from his mouth could have meant the difference between life or death for anyone who fell under his jurisdiction. Thus David also prayed, "Let the words of my mouth and the meditations of my heart be acceptable in Your sight, O LORD, my Strength, and my Redeemer" (Ps. 19:14, NKJV). David wanted to be certain that his words were sanctioned by God.

In Psalm 141, David prayed that God would not allow his heart to "be drawn away to what is evil" (v. 4). He understood the connection between the heart and the mouth (as we discussed in the previous section), that what proceeds from the mouth comes from what is flowing out of the heart. During the years that David was being persecuted, God was teaching him how to separate the issues. Let me explain.

Though King Saul meant only evil for David, God placed within David's heart the wisdom to know that his response to wicked King Saul would set a precedent for his own kingly reign. David had several opportunities presented to him where he could have taken the life of Saul, or where he could have given instruction to one of his mighty men to kill Saul. One word from his lips could have meant the death of Saul. In wisdom, he would not touch God's anointed, because he knew that God had not yet removed Saul from the throne. David resisted being led by his wounded heart to make a decision on Saul's life. He prudently opted to be led by the wisdom of the Spirit of God and by his love for Saul, in spite of the fact that Saul was trying to murder him. David loved Saul unto death. Here we see that because David separated the issues of a broken and wounded heart from what he understood to be God's divine order and sovereign will, he did not sin with his words by ordering his enemy to be killed. David was diligent to guard the gate to his mouth, for in his heart he desired to do God's will.

The Bible tells us that David was a man after God's own heart. David's relationship with Saul has similarities to our relationship with Jesus Christ. David loved a man who had no love for him, but only wanted to murder him. Jesus loved a people that not only wanted to, but did, in fact crucify Him. David stood in the gap between life and death for Saul. Jesus stands in the gap between life and death for us and He is the resurrection and the life. What does all of this mean for the children of God as it relates to the reconstruction of the gates to our mouths?

Most certainly we can take a lesson from David, but Jesus, our Great High Priest, established a standard for us all when He said, with your mouth: "Bless those who persecute you; bless and do not curse" (Rom. 12:14). "Well," you say, "I would never curse anyone!" That may be true, but Jesus did not just say, "Don't curse those who persecute you." He commands us to go a step further and actually pronounce a blessing upon those whose hearts are bent towards evil concerning us. You see, Jesus Christ always challenges us in the toughest legs of our spiritual journey, to go beyond that which can simply be accomplished by our flesh to that which can only be accomplished by the help of the Holy Spirit residing within us. His goal is always to reveal to us how much we need Him and how that apart from Him we can accomplish absolutely nothing (John 15:5). Jesus said, "Without me, you can do nothing." You won't be reconciled to that cold-hearted, inconsiderate spouse without the help of the Holy Spirit. You won't forgive and treat that backstabbing coworker to lunch without the help of the Holy Spirit. You will not have a vision to see yourself loving your rebellious child back to obedience and back to righteousness without the assistance of the Holy Spirit.

As children of God, we must learn how to keep short accounts. If we are angry about being treated unfairly at work, or angry about not being appreciated by our family members, it is not a sin to acknowledge those feelings of anger. If we say that we are not angry when in fact we really are, then not only are we angry, but by denying it we are also lying. Instead, we should confess it, repent of it, deal with our anger and move on. This is one of the many reasons why David's ministry to us through the Psalms is such a blessing. He openly expressed his anger, hurt, disappointments, sorrows and fears to God. He let these expressions out of the gate to his mouth so that they would not take up residence in his heart. At the end of such Psalms, David always spoke well of God, expressing his hope, faith and confidence in the God who, in spite of the trials that he was facing, David knew to be a just, holy and righteous God. His knowledge of the character of God gave him the boldness to speak honestly and freely to God about his true feelings. David's reverent candor delivered him from the gates of deception.

In Proverbs 10:18 we read, "He who conceals his hatred has lying lips." Pretending that we are not sad, hurt, offended, or angry when we know that we really are only allows Satan to establish strongholds in our minds. We do not have time to waste undoing such self-inflicted strongholds with which we have allowed ourselves to become bound through our own lies and deception, deceiving others, deceiving ourselves and trying to deceive God.

Fortune magazine published an article entitled *The Art of Lying: Can It Be a Good Thing?* It states, "To win at business, you need to practice gaming ethics, which allows for tactics such as bluffing and artful negotiating that would be considered dishonest anywhere else." Notice that when it is considered necessary for success, it is no longer called lying, but "gaming ethics," "bluffing" and "artful negotiating."[29]

In Jeremiah 9:4-6, 9, we read these words: "Beware of your friends; do not trust your brothers. For every brother is a deceiver, and every friend a slanderer. Friend deceives friend, and no one speaks the truth. They have taught their tongues to lie; they weary themselves with sinning. You live in the midst of deception; in their deceit they refuse to acknowledge me, declares the LORD... Should I not punish them for this?" When addressing the Christians in Rome and believers everywhere, Paul said that when we "suppress the truth by wickedness" we will experience the "wrath of God." Eventually, he says, God will allow us to be "held captive to our own sinful ways," namely: "sexual immorality, wickedness, covetousness, maliciousness, envy, murder, strife and deceit," to name a few (Rom. 1:18-30). As Christians, we must be cautious not to prefer worldly wisdom over God's wisdom when we find ourselves backed up against the wall. Rather than resorting to the world's "gaming ethics," "bluffing," and/or "artful negotiating" methods, which are all colorful words for lying, deceiving and manipulating, we must always opt for truth. Our "gaming ethic" should be nothing less than truth at all costs. As we operate in truth, we will find no cause to bluff, con or deceive. Our "artful negotiating" must be scaled down to the simple truth according to God's holy standards. This is how we escape the Devil's traps.

The ethics of a kingdom people must never be dictated by a world system that revolves on an axis of deception. The world's gaming ethic is to motivate people to make decisions from the platform of a lie. We buy because of a lie that has been fed to us. We sell because of a lie that has been fed to us. We involve ourselves in toxic relationships because of some convincing ad on television or in a magazine, some sensual, mellifluous lyrics from our favorite CD, or some scene from a romantic movie that fed us lies. Marriages are destroyed because somewhere, someone told a lie. Many become addicted to alcohol and drugs because of lies. We kill each other because of lies. Our world is spinning out of control because, as the Word of God says, men prefer the lie over the truth. Are these the types of words we want to speak?

When we engage in enough lying we will eventually begin to believe our own manipulations and deceptions. This leads us to a place where we are no longer able to discern truth for ourselves, so our families, our businesses and eventually our lives are destroyed by the poor decisions that we make because we have bought into the Devil's lies – hook, line and sinker. We run the risk of watching all that is precious to us flow right out of our grasp and out of our gates on account of the lies that we conceive and believe. God's Word admonishes us in 1 Corinthians 3:19, revealing that "the wisdom of this world is foolishness in God's sight. As it is written; He catches the wise in their own craftiness." It is better to prefer truth. Isaiah 59:12-16 stands in defense of truth with these words:

Our offenses are ever with us, and we acknowledge our iniquities: rebellion and treachery against the LORD, turning our
backs on our God, fomenting oppression and revolt, uttering
lies our hearts have conceived. So justice is driven back, and
righteousness stands at a distance; truth has stumbled in the
streets, honesty cannot enter. Truth is nowhere to be found,
and whoever shuns evil becomes a prey. The LORD saw it,
and was displeased that there was no justice. He saw that
there was no one, he was appalled that there was no one to
intervene.

When the world becomes saturated with lies and deceit, God
is looking for a people who will raise the plumb line, open their
mouths and cry out on behalf of righteousness to undo the works of
Satan by declaring His truth wherever the seeds of deception have
been sown. How do we come to declare God's truth over a situation
where Satan has sown a lie? To the degree that we are committed to
abiding in the Word of God, obeying His voice, embracing His truth,
walking in truth and telling the truth when our backs are up against
the wall, we will be empowered though the Holy Spirit to declare
and decree God's truth over the lies sown by Satan, the father of
all lies. We will be empowered not only to undo his evil works, but
like our Big Brother in the faith, Jesus the Christ, we will also be
empowered to completely abolish his works and take possession of
his gates.

An added benefit for us, as we abide in God's Word, is that the Holy Spirit comes to illuminate the Word of God to us. He makes the Word of God alive to us and as we appropriate the Spirit's power, He makes God's words live in us. The Holy Spirit navigates us to and through God's truth and reminds us that God's truth will be a shield and a buckler to us when our lives come under attack. The Word of God exhorts us to "buy the truth and do not sell it" (Prov. 23:23), for truth is an investment into eternity that will never decrease in value, because God's truth endures forever. Our God is Truth. He dwells in truth. His Word is Truth (John 17:17). He is not able to tell a lie.

As we walk in the Spirit, we walk in truth and thereby fortify our gates against deception and error. God will outfit our feet to crush and destroy every lie of the Enemy. We will decree God's truth over broken marriages and see those marriages restored (Mark 10:2-9). We will decree God's truth over rebellious children and see them surrender and return to Jesus Christ, taking possession of the Enemy's gates (Luke 15:24). We will decree God's truth over crack addicts and alcoholics and see them delivered and made whole as we possess the Adversary's gates (Isa. 61:1). We will decree God's truth over homosexuality and lesbianism and see the veil of darkness begin to lift from the eyes of those affected by these particular struggles (Gen. 2:22-25; Rom. 1:18-32; John 8:32). We will decree God's truth over our finances and see the wealth of the wicked turned over to the just (Prov. 13:22; Eccl. 2:26). We will decree God's truth over our churches and our governments and we will witness the rebuilding of the kingdom of God, the overthrow of corrupt laws and policies and the demolition of the kingdom of darkness (Prov. 14:34). We have His promise that the gates of hell will not prevail against us as we exercise our God-given authority (Matt. 16:18-19). In all these areas and more, as we decree God's truth, we will see God hasten to perform His Word and to set His people free from behind the Enemy's gates. We will discover that "truth" is another durable building material for our gates that will stand against the assaults of the Devil.

With the kingdom keys secured by our Lord, Jesus Christ and subsequently given to us, we now hold the power to bind with our tongues and loose with our tongues. With these keys we have the authority, by way of an anointed, strategically spoken Word from God, to cut bars asunder, to open gates that the Enemy had sealed off to us, or that we had locked ourselves out of due to our own disobedience. Jesus said, "I will give you the keys of the kingdom of heaven; whatever you bind on earth will be bound in heaven, and whatever you loose on earth will be loosed in heaven" (Matt. 16:18-19).

There is a fierce spiritual war going on in which we are all engaged, whether we choose to acknowledge it or not. We are all walking on the same battlefield and we are all needed on the battlefield. There is no time to get entangled in needless strongholds, lying, deceiving, bitterness, holding onto anger and harboring grudges. Paul said, "But we have this treasure in earthen vessels, that the excellence of the power may be of God and not of us" (2 Cor. 4:7

NKJV). Everything that God places within us is treasure. We must see it as such because anything good in us is God in us. If the Lord has placed words in us, then we must honor that gift, that treasure, and we must use it to speak words of power, words that encourage, words that will heal, words that will build faith. When we fail to guard the words that we speak, then we become nothing more than mush mouths. We are in danger of flinging wide the gates to our mouths and doing more damage than we can correct in a lifetime. Our unbridled words can negatively impact the lives of generations yet to come. As David prayed, we too must ask the Lord to "set a guard" over our mouths and "keep watch at the door to our lips."

After it became clear to me that the Holy Spirit was convicting me to guard my words, I went out and bought a roll of clear scotch tape that I carried around in my purse with me. Whenever I found myself talking too much, or on the verge of saying something that I would regret, I would go in my purse, take out that tape, tear off a strip and place it directly over my lips. It didn't matter to me if I was in a public place or not, I would wear that tape until I felt I was out of danger of saying too much or saying the wrong thing. I did not care what people thought about me. I was looking to God. I was listening to God. I was accountable to God and I wanted desperately to be used by God.

The people thought the prophet Isaiah was crazy to go about naked and barefoot for three years, at the word of the LORD (Isa. 20). The people thought Ezekiel was crazy when, at the word of the

219

LORD, he obediently lay on his left side for 390 days and then on his right side for another 390 days (Ezek. 4). The people thought the Son of Man crazy when He allowed Himself to be lifted up on a cross to die for a people who despised Him (Isa. 53; Matt. 27:41-44; John 10:17-18). What do the people know? I will say again: God requires our radical obedience to do radical works in us and through us. He is not concerned about our comfort and ease when it comes to His requirements and assignments to us. One of God's primary purposes in giving us words to speak is this: God gave His words to Jesus to give to us. Jesus has given God's words to us so that we can, in turn, give those words to others that they might believe that God is in Jesus, Jesus is in God and that we all may be one in Them (John 17:8, 20). To be "one in Them" is most assuredly a secure fortress and an impenetrable hedge against theft and Enemy invasion.

We have to be willing to exercise radical behavior if we are ever to regain possession of our gates. Put your hand over your mouth, zip your lips, duct tape them; do whatever you must do to walk in obedience to God. We forget how much power is contained in the words that we speak. Like a heat-seeking missile unleashed towards a designated target, undeterred, that missile has but one goal for its target – to blow it to bits! In this same way, a negative word released from the gate of our mouths has the power to do that same kind of colossal damage. An unguarded mouth can lead us straight to our own graves, or can result in the death of someone else who may fall under the influence of our words. Proverbs 13:3 warns us, "He who guards his mouth preserves his life, but he who opens wide his lips shall have destruction" (NKJV). As Paul exhorted the Ephesians in the book of Ephesians 4:22-32, we must heed that same exhortation:

...put off your old self, which is being corrupted by its deceitful desires; ...and to put on the new self, created to be like God in true righteousness and holiness" (vv. 22-24). "Do not let any unwholesome talk come out of your mouths, but only what is helpful for building others up according to their needs" (v. 29). "Get rid of all bitterness, rage and anger, brawling and slander, along with every form of malice. Be kind and compassionate to one another, forgiving each other, just as in Christ God forgave you (vv. 31-32).

Let us be silent for a few moments, in sanctification and in reverence for God, without fear. Amen.

Chapter 13

Bent By A Word

"A single sentence can be a life sentence."
-Unknown

God put much power in man's mouth, but that power was given to man by God so that he could declare and decree that which was good. Man was originally given such power to speak life. After the fall, God intended for us to use our tongues to restore, repair, redeem, resurrect and to destroy the works of Satan.

We see in Genesis 2:19-20 where God first gave man the authority to decree a thing and it was so. Here, God presents each beast of the field and every bird of the air to Adam. God lets Adam name them and the scripture says, "Whatever the man called each living creature, that was its name." Along with everything else good that God was doing in the Garden during this time, this too was good. However, then came the fall of man and now man assigns names to living things in a manner symbolic of a fallen, broken and transitory world. Adam names his firstborn son Cain, which means, "to provoke to jealousy, chant or wail at a funeral, lament, and mourning mother." His second son he names Abel, which means, "emptiness, vanity, transitory and unsatisfactory." Both the names Cain and Abel signify sorrow, grief and tragedy. As were their names, so were their lives. Abel, murdered by his brother Cain; Cain destined to be a drifter, a restless wanderer over the face of the earth, a man for whom the ground would no longer yield its crops.

After the fall, man began to decree in such a manner as to validate the fact that the world was now bent towards sin. From the time of the fall until today, we are still guilty of using our words to bend each other in ways that God never intended. Children look to their parents for validation, but when a mother calls her child "stupid," "lazy," or "good for nothing," she bends that child's spirit and makes her an emotional and mental cripple. When a father tells his son that he will never amount to anything, or calls his daughter a "tramp," he has successfully bent his children towards truancy, depravity and failure. When an angry, disappointed wife fails to guard the gate to her mouth, she will spew forth words that will emasculate and crucify her husband. When an angry husband fails to guard the gate to his mouth, the words from his lips will proceed as well aimed daggers to his spouse's heart, destroying her confidence in him and destroying her respect for the man who promised to love and cherish her until death. We find these words in Proverbs

12:18, "Reckless words pierce like a sword, but the tongue of the wise brings healing." Again in Proverbs 25:15, "Through patience a ruler can be persuaded, and a gentle tongue can break a bone."

As anointed children of God, prophets, priests, kings and queens, our words and our prayers should possess the power to break the back of the oppressor, pierce the darkness of those held in bondage by demonic strongholds and set the captive free. This can and will happen once we surrender our tongues to the Lordship of Jesus Christ and cry out as did Isaiah, "'Woe to me!' I cried. 'I am ruined! For I am a man of unclean lips, and I live among a people of unclean lips, and my eyes have seen the King, the LORD Almighty'" (Isa. 6:5).

Like the prophet Isaiah, we must come to the place where we become undone when we realize that the gates to our mouths are in serious need of repair. Isaiah was gazing upon the King and the more intent his gaze upon holiness, the clearer he began to see his own filthiness. God told the Israelites that if they dared to draw near to Him, He would show Himself to be a holy God (Lev. 10:1-3). A true glimpse of the holiness of God should render us speechless. Before God could use Isaiah to speak for Him, He had to purify him. In the same manner, before we can be used of God in dynamic ways, we must be washed. We must be purified, passing through the fires of sanctification. We must get desperate for the work of reconstruction to get underway with God as the Overseer of the rebuilding project.

What use is there to argue with God? Only a fool would do so and yet often we are guilty of doing just that – debating with the Almighty as though we could convince Him that our sin is not sin. This is precisely what we do when we make foolish attempts at trying to persuade God to see where He might have overlooked something worthwhile or redemptive in our ungodly choices and resultant behavior. This only serves to prolong the purification process and greatly limits our ability to be used mightily of God. When Job tried to argue with God, this was God's reply: "Will the one who contends with the Almighty correct Him? Would you discredit my justice? Would you condemn me to justify yourself?" (Job 40:2, 8)

We must be willing to submit to the painful but necessary process of purification. A live coal must touch our lips, purging from us the iniquities that we have committed as a result of our failure to guard the gates to our mouths. Our tongues must be cleansed from lies, from deceptive and manipulative words. We must have our tongues cleansed from slanderous words, hateful words, words that have spread gossip and words that have carried a curse.

When we slander a brother or a sister in Christ, God is not pleased. Solomon's wisdom, which is really the wisdom of God, warns us "…whoever spreads slander is a fool" (Prov. 10:18). When we stab a coworker in the back, or speak against them in such a way as to use the subtlety of evil words with the intention of harming them, or making them out to be a bad person in the eyes of others, God is not pleased. David asks in Psalm 15:1-5, "LORD, who may dwell in your sanctuary? Who may live on your holy hill? He whose walk is blameless, and who does what is righteous, who speaks the truth from his heart and has no slander on his tongue, who does his neighbor no wrong, and casts no slur on his fellowman... He who does these things will never be shaken." We, however, are quite shaken when we say hurtful things to others in the heat of the moment, only to regret them the split second after they have escaped our lips. It is too late to take them back. The damage has already been done, but we just could not resist the urge to say what we felt "needed to be said." "Somebody had to say it," we tell ourselves.

We have all heard of or have known someone who reportedly had angry words with a loved one, then stormed away from them in a fit of rage, only to receive a phone call later that their loved one was killed in some dreadful accident. How sad and tragic to live with the knowledge that the last words that we might have spoken to someone were vicious words that doubled their spirit over. We arrogantly refuse to make that phone call, or pay that visit to them to tell them how sorry we are and to ask for forgiveness and seek reconciliation while we still have the opportunity. We forget that tomorrow is not promised and that God will call us to accountability for those poisonous words. We forget that life is fleeting and very, very fragile.

We bend our own communities by continuing to speak negative words over them. I live in the state of Ohio and we are constantly bombarded with negative press concerning the financial duress of our state. However, rather than agreeing with the negative press about the state that I live in, I have joined forces with my pastor, Dr. R. A. Vernon and First Lady Victory Vernon, in believing God for the financial, spiritual, mental and emotional healing of our state. Our confidence is in God as we trust and believe Him that these strongholds will be broken off of our state. With our prayers and our faith, we are going to unbend and untwist our state from poverty to wealth, both spiritually and financially. The unofficial motto of our state was once "The Heart of it All," yet we maintain that we desperately want the heart of Ohio to reflect the heart of God. We are crying out for our hearts to burn for Jesus and for God to be glorified in us and in our state. We believe that our prayers are being heard and that through God, they will be answered. The prophet Jeremiah said, "Also, seek the peace and prosperity of the city to which I have carried you into exile. Pray to the LORD for it, because if it prospers, you too will prosper" (Jer. 29:7).

As we, the saints of the Most High God, repent of the sins of our tongues and allow our tongues to be crucified on the altar of God, the Lord will then bathe our tongues in His blood. His blood will cleanse us so that in every city where God has positioned His children, we can stand at the gates fully empowered to bind and to loose, to declare and to decree the will of the Lord for that city. With an anointed, sanctified tongue, the things that we take back from the Devil's hands will cause the kingdom of darkness to go broke!

That's right – the Devil will have to file for bankruptcy because we will leave him empty-handed!

As the saints open their mouths and declare the truth that is revealed to us concerning the riches that Calvary wrought for us and the inheritance that our heavenly Daddy has stored up for us, our discouragement will fade away. As we, through prayer, release such scriptures over our lives as are found in Isaiah 53 and Isaiah 61, we will rise up out of a place of despair. The Word of God will elevate us up and out of depression. God's spoken Word will break strongholds of defeat off of our lives. As we declare the power of the blood of Jesus over our lives and over the lives of the people within our sphere of influence, we will gain new hope and our hope will convert to joy and our joy will result in greater expressions of worship of the One and only true and living God. Satan's power will be greatly diminished, he will be sorely humiliated and we, the saints of the Most High God, will experience a foretaste of glory divine. How sweet!

Jesus said in Matthew 12:36-37, "But I say to you that men will have to give account on the day of judgment for every careless word that they have spoken. For by your words you will be acquitted, and by your words you will be condemned." At the entrance to every gate there are rules that require our obedience if we are to take possession of the gates of our enemies: "Guard your hearts" (Prov. 4:23). "Set no vile thing before your eyes" (Ps 101:3). "Let your ears be attentive to what the Spirit of the Lord is saying" (Rev. 2:7) and in this case…"keep your tongue from evil and your lips from speaking lies" (Ps. 34:13). "Set a guard over my mouth, O' LORD, keep watch over the door to my lips" Ps. 141:3. We must be careful, not only of the things that we say that can bend towards destruction, but also of the things we fail to say that could prevent the bend towards destruction. Let us look first at those idle words that we speak that we feel make no real difference one way or the other, but that in fact possess the power to condemn us to debilitating life sentences.

When the mother of a certain young man named him, we wonder if she realized that the name she pinned on him would cause him to cry out to God in protest of that name. The account in scripture, found in 1 Chronicles 4:9 reads, "Jabez was more honorable than his brothers. His mother named him 'Jabez,' (which means to grieve, and be sorrowful) saying, 'I gave birth to him in pain.'" My pastor preached a sermon out of this scripture and in it he pointed out that this passage of scripture reveals something of the personal struggle that Jabez encountered as he sought to be free from the negative repercussions of his name, for we read in verse 10, "Jabez cried out to the God of Israel, 'Oh, that you would bless me indeed, and enlarge my territory! Let your hand be with me, and keep me from harm so that I will be free from pain.'" The scriptures tell us that "God granted his request." No doubt, Jabez's mother barely considered, if at all, the struggle that she would place on her child by naming him after her own issues. The name "Jabez," was all about her pain, her sorrow and her grief and had nothing whatsoever to do with the little baby she was bringing into the world. However, we see that the young man is left to do spiritual warfare later in his life to liberate himself from his mother's issues.

Many times, the negative, idle words that we speak over another individual have very little to do with the individual, but more likely, reveal the presence of unresolved issues that have produced a negative character trait in the one who speaks the negative words. When a bully picks on an innocent person, pushing them, shoving them, slandering and name-bashing, that bully is really operating from a place of very low self-esteem, self-hatred and cowardice.

Whether they are unrestrained words that spill from our lips as a result of our failure to guard the mouth gate, or anointed words strategically spoken to glorify the kingdom of God and to demolish the works of Satan, our words have tremendous power. Knowing when to speak, what to say when we speak, and when to say nothing at all really requires a great deal of wisdom, and I am always in awe of those who have mastered this discipline. Consider this true story of a woman named Linda. She tells of how an idle word from her dad, spoken in her hearing at the age of 13 would have her battling with self-esteem issues for the next 37 years of her life.

Linda recalls being at home with her mother and father one sunny afternoon in the summer. To Linda, her father was the beat in her heart. She absolutely adored him. On this particular day, the words that her father expressed started out as words of adoration, expressing to her just how sweet and pretty he thought she was. He then gave Linda a warm embrace and Linda turned to leave the room, satisfied that she had her father's affections and affirmation. Linda did not get very far, when she overheard her father say to her mother, "I'm not worried about any boys chasing after her. There's not much to her figure."

Although Linda believes that her father must have hugged her on many other occasions since, the hug that she received from her father that day, prior to her overhearing his hurtful words about her uncomely figure, is the only one that she remembers. So emotionally and spiritually damaging were those few words spoken by the most important man in her world at the delicate age of 13, a time when she was already fighting through confusing adolescent image issues, that the memory of any future words of affirmation or displays of affection from her father had been totally wiped from her remembrance. As soon as she was old enough, Linda confessed that she began wearing full makeup every day of her life for the next 37 years. She even wore her makeup to bed, although she lived alone. Once Linda married, she would leave her makeup on upon retiring to bed, only taking it all off once her husband had drifted off to sleep, and then making sure to get up early enough to reapply her makeup before her husband could see her. If all she was, was a face, then she had better make sure that she had her best face on at all times.

Linda was hopelessly trapped in this bondage to cosmetics and the superficial need to "keep up appearances" far longer than she ever could have imagined those few words could imprison her. However, the bondage went deeper than that of merely a physical bondage for Linda, for she also lost her true identity behind the mask of cosmetics that she donned every day. She believed her father's unflattering and unwise words spoken behind her back about her physical appearance and her belief in her father's spoken words caused her to get stuck, for almost four decades, on concentrating only on trying to look pretty. Those few words and more importantly, the source of those few words, blocked her perception of reality for 37 long years. She was unable to see that she was more than just a "pretty face." It took the redemptive work of the Holy Spirit to finally free her from the bondage of her father's unwise words, but think about the years that she wasted tending to the superficial and the temporary.

Today, I see so many young mothers, 15, 16 and 17 years old, mere children themselves; they have no concept of motherhood. They lack patience, compassion, tenderness, love, and concern for their babies. I shudder every time I hear one of them curse at their children. The poor little baby is looking to its mother for nurturing and some of the first words that its delicate little ears hear are profane, cruel and abusive words spoken directly at them, flowing out of the gate of mommy's mouth. The unwise mother is unwittingly destroying the life of one of God's most precious creations entrusted to her. Little does she know she is molding a monster that may one day become her worst nightmare.

We speak and bend and we fail to speak and unbend, or prevent a bending. Our failure to speak can result in incredible damage to another person's life. Proverbs 3:27 exhorts us with these words,

"Do not withhold good from those who deserve it, when it is in your power to act." As sure as I am writing this, there is an overworked pastor who is waiting for someone to lift up a prayer shield to cover him and the ministry in prayer. You may be that someone who feels the call of God to the ministry of intercession, yet you have failed to say, "Yes, Lord." An overworked and under-prayed-for pastor is sure to bend towards burnout, depression and sin. Some husband or wife who is perhaps weak in their faith, has been waiting on someone to speak life into their dead marriage, over their dead finances, over a rebellious child, over a loved one addicted to drugs and pornography and we have failed to do so. Paul says in Romans 15:1-3, "We who are strong ought to bear the failings of the weak and not to please ourselves. Each of us should please his neighbor for his good, to build him up. For even Christ did not please himself."

God has anointed us to open our mouths wide to declare and decree, to establish and to abolish through prayer, but we have allowed ourselves to be held captive by a spirit of fear or by sheer complacency. In our captivity, we have withheld good from those desperately needing our prayers, our words of encouragement, our words of affirmation and love. In the sight of God this is displeasing, disobedient and rebellious behavior. When, through fear and complacency, we block out the voice of wisdom, love, mercy, compassion and truth, we are ill-equipped to know how to speak a right and timely word when it is desperately needed. Our LORD says in Isaiah 50, "The Lord God has given Me the tongue of the learned, that I should know how to speak a word in season to him who is weary. He awakens Me morning by morning, He awakens My ear to hear as the learned. The Lord God has opened My ear; and I was not rebellious, nor did I turn away" (vv. 4-5, (NKJV).

How often we fail to say, "Thank you," or "I love you," or "I appreciate you" to the people God has placed in our lives for this very short time that we are here on earth. We can be so self-absorbed and prideful that we often only think of our own needs and frequently take each other for granted. If no one is patting us on the back, then we certainly are not going to pat someone else on the back. If no one is encouraging us, then why should we encourage someone else? If no one tells us how much they appreciate us, then we don't feel the need to tell anyone else how much we appreciate them. This is not expressing God's love to our neighbors. It is not the way of Christ who came to serve and not to be served. In the book of Acts, we also read of the renown of a man named Barnabas, whose name meant "Son of Encouragement." He was used mightily of God for his gift of encouragement following the death of Christ and was recorded to have been one of the most quietly influential people in the early days of Christianity (Acts 4:36-37; 9:27).

In giving spiritual guidance to husbands and wives, I noticed that each of them were concentrating so much on what the other was not doing for them, that they failed to see the loving and thoughtful things that their mates were doing for them. Lack of gratitude in a marriage can mean death to that marriage. As parents, we fail to appreciate our children for the little things that they do that bring us joy. We are always quick to point out their rebellion, laziness, or bad habits. This can be exasperating to our children and they will cease trying to please us at all, simply and wholeheartedly giving in to their rebellion. On the other hand, children sometimes neglect to show gratitude to their parents for all they do for them. They often expect to be given everything that their hearts desire without having to work for it and without expressing a word of appreciation.

It is also important to show gratitude in the church. Parishioners volunteer week after week and many work harder and longer hours in the church than they do at their regular nine-to-five jobs. A heart-felt "thank you" is always appreciated and is usually all that is needed to keep them motivated to continue in their good service. Pastors work tirelessly to bring us the Word of God week after week, month after month and year after year; not only do we often neglect to say "thank you," but we blatantly begrudge the tithe because we think that the pastor is going to personally benefit from "our" money in some way. In reality, the tithe belongs to God. Once we give the tithe to the church, what is done with it is out of our hands. The Word of God does say that the servant is worthy of his hire (1Tim. 5:17-18), so why shouldn't the hard working pastor be compensated for his hard work? If we are in a church where we do not believe in the integrity of our pastor or church leadership, perhaps we should resolve to pray for them, and then quietly and quickly move on to another church, where we do trust the leadership and can give freely with an attitude of joy and gratitude. Jesus made a point of showing how important the display of gratitude is in Luke 17:11-19. In this passage of scripture, Jesus had cleansed ten lepers, but only one of them returned with enough presence of mind to say, "thank you." Because of his expression of gratitude, Jesus made him completely whole.

On a deeper level still, our failure to speak a word of correction, warning, or rebuke to the rebellious may very well mean the difference between life and death for that soul and God will not hold us who are appointed to guard the gates – pastors, prophets, teachers, even mothers and fathers – guiltless of the blood of that soul. As God told the prophet Ezekiel, "Son of man, the people that I am sending you to are obstinate and stubborn. Say to them, 'This is what the Sovereign LORD says.' And whether they listen, or fail to listen – for they are a rebellious house – they will know that a prophet has been among them" (Ezek. 2:4-5). Then again, in Ezekiel 33:6-9: "If the watchman sees the sword coming, and does not blow the trumpet to warn the people, and the sword comes and takes the life of one of them, that man will be taken away because of his sin, but I will hold the watchman accountable for his blood... But if you do warn the wicked man to turn from his ways and he does not do so, he will die for his sin, but you will have saved yourself."

Those who proclaim the Word of God have the enormous responsibility of sounding the alarm to warn those who are walking in error to turn from their sins and to righteousness. Prophets cannot be afraid to risk losing their popularity with the people. Pastors cannot be afraid to lose congregants. Teachers must not be afraid to teach, uncompromisingly, according to God's words. Jesus said in John 7:16-18: "My teaching is not my own. It comes from him who sent me... He who speaks on his own does so to gain honor for himself, but he who works for the honor of the one who sent him is a man of truth; there is nothing false about him."

Oh, the power of a spoken word. By a spoken word, God created the heavens and the earth and all that is in them. Think of that. By a spoken word, God created something out of absolutely nothing! He created not just something, but everything that we see in all of creation today, including ourselves, is here and being held together on the strength of a spoken word. Now that's rich! He spoke it and it came to be. "He commanded, and it stood fast" (Ps. 33:9). God has given us that same ability. He tells us in John 15:7, "If you abide in Me, and My words abide in you, you will ask what you desire, and it will be done for you" (NKJV).

We must be careful that when we open our mouths to speak, we are bending our children, our spouses, our communities, our churches and our world in the direction of redemption and not damnation. This takes great wisdom from God and wisdom is a much-needed building material as we work with the Lord to reconstruct our gates. In Proverbs 8:1-4, we read, "Does not wisdom cry out, and understanding lift up her voice? She takes her stand on the top of the hill, beside the way, where the paths meet. She cries out by the city gates, at the entry of the city, at the entrance of the doors: 'To you, O men, I call, and my voice is to the sons of men'" (NKJV). Before we speak, we should ask ourselves, "What will my words cause to be so? What will my words cause to stand fast?" The words we speak should minister grace to the hearer, build others up and glorify God. If this is not the case, we must leave them unsaid.

Chapter 14

Choose Your Battles

"He who lives by fighting with an enemy has an interest in the preservation of the enemy's life."

-Friedrich Wilhelm Nietzsche

*A*s God's administrators of His divine will on Earth, Christians need to be able to envision themselves maneuvering skillfully on the battlefield. We must get a mental picture of the snares, the traps and the landmines that the Enemy has laid out for us. Proverbs 23:7 says, "As a man thinks in his heart, so is he." If we can see ourselves as the warriors that we are, then we will prepare ourselves to do battle as warriors. We will be more likely to respond to the snares of Satan as a warrior would respond, with a well thought out strategy to avoid the pitfalls and to destroy the works of our Enemy and not merely as a naïve Christian who is completely caught off guard by Satan's traps.

A skilled warrior would encounter offenses from a spiritual perspective first, as opposed to a carnal perspective. We elevate ourselves above the mere offense of the action and challenge the spiritual warrior in us to see it as a possible landmine on the spiritual battlefield. From this vantage point, we can gain a spiritual perspective that will empower us to devise a strategy for victory. This will greatly please God as well. As opposed to firing back at the offender in kind, repaying offense for offense, as enlightened warriors we can instead approach our offender quickly in the spirit of love and reconciliation to let them know how what they have done has caused us to feel hurt. This is how we silence our adversary. This is how we take the bullets out of his guns and this is the biblical response according to Matthew 5:23-24.

Always remember, there is no time to waste mulling over who is right and who is wrong. That is how Satan finds time to build strongholds in us and how we step onto landmines. Outsmart the Devil by avoiding the landmines with a counter strategy of quick, loving confrontation and forgiveness. Whether or not the offender acknowledges what they have done to you is completely immaterial to your next move. At the end of the day, we all must give an account to God for the things that we have done or failed to do. This includes the unrepentant, who must give an account to God for their unwillingness to repent. "But because of your stubbornness and unrepentant heart, you are storing up wrath against yourself for the day of God's wrath, when his righteous judgment will be revealed. God will give to each person according to what he has done" Romans 2:5-6. This scripture should help us remember to look well to our ways and to keep short accounts with our offenders. Remember, *you* are the warrior on the battlefield. If you will make room for Him, the Holy Spirit, your Commanding Officer, will give you wisdom and instruction as to how to move about on the battlefield and avoid getting entangled in the Devil's mess. Your one and only next move is to forgive them and to commit them to the Lord.

A few years ago, within a short span of about two weeks, I was offended by my brother and also by a sister in the body of Christ. In both instances, although I was hurt, I wanted to just bury the offense and move on, but God would not allow me to do that. You see, we are given two scenarios in the Bible that counsel us on how to handle offenses – overlook them (Prov. 19:11) or, in love, confront the offender (Matt. 18:15).

Because of offenses that I had silently suffered throughout my childhood, it had become my habit to simply allow the offenses that came into my life to come and go unchallenged, as though I deserved to be offended by anyone and everyone who had a tendency to disregard me as a human being with feelings. I was pathologically non-confrontational, while all the while I was hurting on the inside and becoming an increasingly angry person. Yielding to my Commanding Officer, I clearly heard Him say to me, "Nancy, My daughter, you don't have the liberty to overlook these offenses. My strategy for you is to confront, in love. In the past you have chosen to overlook offenses, not because you had received My grace, but because you were too afraid to confront your offenders. In this season of your life, I am teaching you how to open your mouth and confront your offenders in love." Now, even though I was not excited about confrontation, it certainly sounded like a winning strategy to me.

As I received the instruction from the Holy Spirit and followed through with my assignment using the strategy that He had given to me, in both instances the results were redemptive for all parties. We all gained a better understanding of each other's needs and a deeper respect for each other's boundaries. Leaning on the Holy Spirit helped me to confront in love. I felt empowered and liberated. I knew that I never had to be afraid of confrontation again. The Holy Spirit would always accompany me and empower me to do, through Him, what I would never be able to do in my own limited understanding and strength. He was rebuilding the gate to my mouth. He was giving me utterance in a place where I had been silenced before I ever had the chance to speak. Philippians 4:13 rang true for me: "I *can* do all things through Christ who gives me strength."

"Well," you may ask, "what if the offender strikes again?" Then, you must forgive them again. Jesus said in Matthew 18:21-22 that there is to be no limit on the number of times that we extend forgiveness to an offender. As David did with Saul, we must learn how to separate the issues. There is a real war going on and Satan is only trying to distract us, but not simply to render us ineffective on the battlefield. He is also trying to get us sidetracked long enough to ultimately get us killed on the battlefield. He wants to kill the ministry that God has placed in us. He wants to keep us fighting flesh, fighting our family members and our brothers and sisters in the body of Christ over the superficial non-essentials. He wants to keep our interpersonal relationships so soiled and broken that our witness and our testimony for Christ are stained. He wants to steal the precious and the holy things from us, which are our unique anointing, the effectiveness of our spiritual gifts and our dynamic relationship with our Lord. He wants God's place in our lives. He wants to stop us from opening our mouths to give praise and worship to God by filling us with guilt and condemnation over our choice of actions and words. He wants to suck the life and the *dunamis* (the power of God) out of us so that we will be just like every other walking dead person – looking good, but lacking anointing.

You see, Satan knows that a pure-hearted saint of God can wreak havoc on his kingdom every time they open their mouths to declare and to decree a thing. His goal is to keep us too distracted to engage him in the real war at hand, which is the deeper spiritual warfare. He knows that if he can keep enough of that kind of nonsensical bickering going on, he will soon blind us to the very real fact that according to Ephesians 6:12, "Our struggle is *not* against flesh and blood, but against the rulers, against the authorities, against the powers of this dark world, and against the spiritual forces of evil in the heavenly realms." He wants us to forget who the real battle is against, and what the real purpose of the battle is all about.

We must choose our battles wisely, and wisdom will enlighten us to know when to overlook an offense. We cannot always go fist-i-cuffs with the Devil. There are times when we will have to face an enemy that persistently taunts us like a bully who just will not go away until he feels his fist in our faces. At such times, if we will simply stand back and trust God, He will fight for us and we will not have to lift a finger, but just open our mouths in praise to our God. God will cause our enemies to wreck themselves, as He did for Jehoshaphat in 2 Chronicles 20. All Jehoshaphat and the army of Judah were instructed by God to do was to march out onto the battlefield and face the enemy. God said that is all you have to do, just "face the enemy" and I will do all the fighting for you. The LORD had put it in Jehoshaphat's heart to have all the people of Judah sing praises to God and to give the LORD thanks. As they did so, God caused the armies that had come out against Judah to turn on themselves and they actually slaughtered each other. The army of Judah was completely unharmed in that battle.

When we insist on engaging every enemy in every battle, what we are saying in essence is that our main purpose in life is primarily to argue and fight, because it is a given that the Devil is always going to be standing in the middle of the boxing ring with his dukes up calling us on. You can fight every battle if you want to, but you will certainly find yourself catching some blows that Jesus would have absorbed in your stead had you just backed off and let Him enter the ring.

In the movie *The Book of Eli*, a blind man, Eli, is on a foot journey with a mission to deliver the Holy Bible to a destination out west. On his journey, he must engage in many fierce battles to protect the Holy Bible and prevent it from falling into the hands of immoral men. At one point along his journey, positioned from a mountain above, Eli hears a scuffle below him. A woman is being assaulted. Though his heart and his instinct as a man of honor tell him to go rescue the damsel in distress, Eli tells himself, "Stick to the path; stick to the path. This is not your fight." He walks away from the battle below and continues on his mission, leaving the poor damsel at the mercy of her attackers.

As I watched Eli walk away, I was somewhat disappointed in him because he was such a good warrior that I knew if he had only come to her aid, he could have saved her from her attackers. At the same time, I also understood the urgency and importance of his mission. Time and purpose would not allow him to stop and rescue every damsel in distress that crossed his path. Some battles he would simply have to entrust to God and just keep focused on his mission, focused on the path that lay before him. Every battle was not his to fight. So it is with us: every battle is not ours to fight. Sometimes the Lord will just have us face our Adversary, show up for the fight to send an emphatic message to the Enemy that we are prepared to duke it out if we have to.

I can recall an incident from back when I was in junior high school where I had to face an enemy. It happened during lunch period. Like most students, I had my few close friends I would sit with while we ate our food in the cafeteria. One day, Linda came and sat down uninvited, to eat at "our table." Linda was not very popular and although I did not dislike her, I really did not want her eating with us simply because she always tried to eat and talk at the same time, with her mouth wide open. This caused her food to fly out of her mouth and spray upon anyone nearby. She could see by my expression that I was not happy to have her at our table. An argument broke out between the two of us over her food flying out of her mouth and into my face. It ended with her calling me on to "meet her at the flagpole" after school, where she vowed to pulverize me. My first internal response was that of paralyzing fear. She was very tall (at least six feet) and she was very big. I was 5'4" and ¾ of an inch tall and weighed only 98 pounds – soaking wet.

That day at school, the classes all seemed to end much faster than usual and before I knew it, it was time to head for the flagpole. "I'm going to get flattened!" I thought. However, I had made up in my mind that I would not run from this battle. I was going to show up and face my enemy. I made my way over to the flagpole, shaking as I went. To my surprise, not only was Linda not there, but no one else was there either! I waited a few minutes, just to appear as though I was braver than I actually felt, and seeing no Linda, I ended my vigil and calmly walked home – the victor! I won by default just because I showed up and she didn't. I never had to lift a finger to fight and Linda never sat at our table anymore after that day.

Some of us run from everything and everybody that intimidates or threatens us. When adversity hits our lives, we pull the covers over our heads and hide, instead of standing in faith on the Word and the promises of God. 1 John 4:4 encourages us by reminding us that the one who is in us is far greater than the one who is in the world. God will not allow His children to be bullied. This is why at times He may tell us, "Show up for the battle, but let Me do the fighting!" That day after school, standing under the flagpole, I only had to show up and somehow God caused my enemy to flee in another direction. If we are convinced that we must fight every battle, then we should consider that perhaps we are in bondage to an argumentative spirit. The spirit of contention likes to fuss; maintaining an atmosphere where contention and drama are always present is exciting to this unholy spirit. This is not of God and we should ask the Lord to deliver us from that spirit. Somewhere there is a gate in serious disrepair and because it is still damaged and not yet rebuilt, we will feel that unless the spirits of strife and conten-tion are present, life is abnormal.

In my years of ministry I have encountered a few women like this. They are constant grumblers and complainers, always looking for a fight. I have tried my best to steer clear of them. They are well aware that their grumbling and complaining has all but sealed their fate in ministry. With missed opportunities and constantly being passed over because of their dreadful attitudes, these bitter, disgruntled women look to soil others by picking fights. Paul warned Timothy, "From such people turn away… they will grow worse and worse, but you must continue in the things which you have learned and been assured of, knowing from whom you have learned them" (2 Tim. 3:5, 13-14, NKJV). "All who desire to live godly in Christ Jesus will suffer persecution" (v. 12, NKJV).

When we are careful and wise to "stick to the path," we have a promise from God that He will fight for us. While we concentrate on rebuilding our gates by continuing to do what God instructs us to do, God deals with our contenders. As we fix our eyes on Jesus and on the path that He has charted for us to walk upon, we discover another sturdy material for reconstructing our gates and that is our faithfulness to our mission. In Isaiah 49:25-26, God promises us, "I will contend with those who contend with you, and your children I will save. I will make your oppressors eat their own flesh; and they will be drunk with their own blood, as with wine. Then all mankind will know that I, the LORD, am your Savior, your Redeemer, the Mighty One of Jacob."

Chapter 15

Abiding in Jesus –
The Discipline of Waiting

"Those who wait on the LORD shall renew their strength"

Isa. 40:31 (NKJV).

"Silence is the home of the word. Silence gives strength and fruitfulness
to the word. Thirdly, silence teaches us to speak."

-Henri Nouwen, *The Way of the Heart*

*M*y Dad was a true animal lover. He loved both cats and dogs, so we always had both in our home when I was growing up. We usually had two cats and at one point, I recall, we also had two beautiful German Shepherds. I loved our pets too, but I was always fascinated by our cats.

Blackie, our female cat, was smart, circumspect, quiet, independent and quick on her feet. However, there was another trait in her that really fascinated me – her ability to sit still, watching and waiting for her prey for long stretches at a time. If she sat quiet and still long enough, eventually a mouse, a squirrel, or bird would unwittingly cross her path. Blackie would stealthily stalk the poor, unsuspecting creature and with a well-timed leap, she would pounce upon it and reap the rewards of her patient vigil – dinner! I can honestly say that I learned a lot about waiting simply by studying my cats. Blackie would not have starved if she never went hunting because we always fed her cat food, but if she wanted a tastier delicacy, she had to exercise the discipline of waiting. If she wanted a freshly slain bird or raw rat meat for dinner, then she had to wait for it.

When Jesus said in John 15:7, "If you abide in Me and My words abide in you, you will ask what you desire and it will be done for you," He was giving us a conditional promise. Both the asking and the receiving are conditional. "*If* you abide in Me, and My words abide in you, *then*, you can ask whatever you will and it shall be given to you." If we will only wait in the presence of God and allow His words to seep in through every one of our gates and saturate our souls, then we can enjoy the delicacies of kingdom living and all that the kingdom lifestyle entails.

What does it mean to *abide* in Jesus? The Greek word for "abide" is *meno* (men'-o)[30] "to stay (in a given place, state relation or expectancy), continue, dwell, endure, be present, remain, stand." This kind of abiding requires discipline. For the 21st century saint, this presents a unique challenge because we live in a society where we must have everything at our fingertips – right now! Our rapidly advancing technology works against our efforts to cultivate the discipline of waiting. There is no time to wait! Why would we choose to wait when we can have whatever we need in a technological nanosecond? Unfortunately, we don't get to ask for the "whatever" with the expectation of receiving it, without exercising the discipline of "waiting" or "abiding."

Consider this: microwave meals and fast food restaurants, which advertise that if you have to wait more than three minutes, your meal is free; IM's, cell phones, blackberries, Bluetooths, iPods, iPads, Facebook and Twitter – all of this technology is designed to make it possible for us to have access to whatever we need in an instant. No more waiting required! In a recent conversation with my sister-in-law, I asked her if she could agree with me that the great technological advances that we enjoy today have served to keep our children alienated from God. She quickly agreed and added that she has never seen a generation so connected technologically, yet so disconnected spiritually. Never were truer words spoken.

The virtue of patience, developed from having to wait, has become such an underdeveloped fruit of the Spirit. The dangerous, subtle, but not-so-subtle message we are being fed is that waiting is not a good thing. However, the admonition from Jesus remains to "watch and pray" (Matt. 26:41). "Watch and pray?" you ask. "Are you kidding?" Today we shrink back at both of these words.

Watching (which also means waiting) and praying are two things that we just do not like to do. It is just too hard to wait and much too hard to pray. We'd rather fly by the seat of our pants, falling short and failing time and time again, than to wait an hour in the presence of God for His counsel and direction. The mere thought of waiting for something or someone gives us anxiety attacks. This is a setup from the Enemy of our souls, because our God will not be accessed by a flip of a switch, or a cryptic text message, but by the one who waits for Him, who watches for Him daily at the door, who communes often with Him in prayer and who expects to find Him. "He is a rewarder of those who diligently seek Him" (Heb. 11:6, NKJV).

God will make Himself known intimately to the one who continues to be present with Him, who does not take long seasons of absence from Him. God speaks intimately to the one who continues to dwell with Him, to the one who recognizes that He is a God who has personhood and He wants, waits and longs to be sought out, known and loved by us. Some of the most profound and life-changing moments that I have experienced in my walk with God have been those times when I laid out on the floor, or sat in my prayer closet, or knelt at the altar with my Lord for hours on end, gazing into His loveliness and meditating on His Word. In waiting upon God in such a manner, at times I discovered that the things I would have asked Him for, I no longer felt the need to ask of Him. What He deposited into my spirit was so much more weighty and precious that I was able to leave that place more than satisfied, feeling no lack.

When David said in Psalm 62:5, "My soul, wait silently for God alone," he was telling his troubled, anxious soul in Hebrew, to *damam* (daw-mam'): to calm down, to stop working in overdrive, to quiet itself, to hold its peace and to be astonished at its God. This is what the Holy Spirit is trying to get to us – a visitation from God that will render us speechless, so that when we encounter the thirsty and the hungry, we will have something of value to say to them that will quench their thirst and satisfy their hunger. He wants to overwhelm us and take our breath away as we wait in His presence. He wants to leave us astounded and in a daze when He walks in the room and His Spirit ministers to us and His hand moves over our lives. Oh bless His magnificent name!

When was the last time we were flabbergasted by Him like this and rendered speechless in His presence? When the Holy Spirit manifests His presence in our lives in this way, every anxious, troubled thought has no choice but to back off! When we wait on the Lord until we receive such a visitation, our problems begin to look manageable. Waiting on the Lord, every negative, doubting word we may want to speak concerning our situations or someone else's becomes trapped behind the gate to our mouths. Finding no exit, they must return back by the way they came. The only words that will exit our mouth gates will be words of victory, strength and faith. Hallelujah!

It's a sad testimony, but the last time some of us were rendered speechless was when we got hold of the latest, hottest technological gadget. The last thing that dazed some of us was a handsome man or a voluptuous woman. The last thing that overwhelmed some of us was not Jesus in all of His glory and majesty, but a new house or a shiny new car. Where a man's treasure is, there also is his heart (Luke 12:34). What excites and delights a man's passion is the thing that he values the most and this is also that on which a man will waste his time. Indeed, it is a waste if the time is spent on things that will decay and rust away, but if it is spent on building intimacy with Jesus, it is an investment into eternity that will never fade and never decay.

God wants us to have an unquenchable desire to know Him in every way that He will allow Himself to be known by us. Satan's strategy is to push God so far out of the frame of our lives until we become completely estranged from Him. This is why we should pray daily that the Holy Spirit would stir up within us the gift of "hunger for Jesus." This cannot be stressed enough. Satan is working hard to pull us away from intimacy with our God. He knows that the day will come for each of us when knowing our God can mean the difference between hope and despair, between possessing God-given, supernatural power to overcome in the face of seemingly insurmountable obstacles and utter powerlessness that will leave us at the mercy of our evil Adversary.

In Daniel 11:32 we find these encouraging words, "But the people who know their God shall prove themselves strong, and shall stand firm, and do great exploits [for God]" (AMP). Webster's dictionary defines *exploit* this way: "to develop, make use of, take advantage of, to make the most of." It defines "exploit" as: an "interesting or daring achievement." This means that when we face difficult times, difficult circumstances, or difficult people, what we would have gleaned from the Lord about Himself and about ourselves by waiting in His presence will be that which we will make use of to stand. In the intimacy of His presence, our Lord reveals Himself to us on levels that He does not to the one who has no time to be a student. He shows us His strength and our weakness. He shows us how He places His strength in us and upon us so that we can accomplish daring achievements directly in the face of what appeared to have been undefeatable obstacles.

When the Word of God abides in us, our asking will line up with the will of God because we know that the will of God is found in the Word of God. When the Word of God is brought to bear on the matters for prayer, the answers will be answers that glorify God. We will have the assurance of having the will of God enforced because He promises us in Isaiah 55:11 that His Word will not return void, but "will prosper in the thing to which it is sent." We will have the confidence spoken of in 1 John 5:14-15 "…that if we ask anything according to his will, he hears us. And if we know that he hears us – whatever we ask – we know that we have what we asked of him."

Active, Not Idle, While Waiting

"Who then is the faithful servant, whom the master has put
in charge of the servants in his household to give them their
food at the proper time? It will be good for that servant whose
master finds him doing so when he returns. I tell you the truth,
he will put him in charge of all his possessions."

Matt. 24:45-46

I am particularly concerned that the children of God be in a constant state of readiness to take up arms in defense of God's truth. At different points in the Word of God, we are made aware of Satan's desire and attempts to "be like God." In the beginning of time, God walked and talked with man in the beautiful garden of Eden. He desired to be in relationship with mankind. Of all the creatures that God had made, the only one that tried to commune with mankind as God had was the Serpent (Gen. 3:1-5). In Exodus 7 and 8, we read of the attempts of Satan to emulate the miracles that God performed through Moses in His many appeals to Pharaoh to let His people go. In Isaiah 14:13-14, we read the very words of Satan when he proclaims, "I will ascend to heaven; I will raise my throne above the stars of God... I will make myself like the Most High." In Matthew 4, Satan has the audacity to try to get Jesus to worship him! "Again, the devil took him to a very high mountain and showed him all the kingdoms of the world and their splendor, 'All this I will give you,' he said, 'if you will bow down and worship me'" (vv 8-9).

As believers, we must commit ourselves to devote much time to reading, studying, meditating on and saturating our souls with God's Word. We must worship, praise and pray as we wait before Him. Our inactivity will set us up to become worshipers of Satan. This is not a far stretch. Jesus said, "Whoever is not with me is against me, and whoever does not gather with me, scatters" (Luke 11:23). Allow me to paraphrase: if we are not on the Lord's side, we are on Satan's side. If we are not working for Jesus, then we are working for Satan. It is just that simple. As the trustworthy servant in Matthew 24 busied himself with the tasks left to his care in his master's absence, so too, the children of God have been entrusted to be guardians of truth. We must keep salting and shaping the world with God's truth while we await His return. We must stay on our posts. Even though His appearance is inevitable, still the children of God must continue to cry out and stand against every deception that Satan tries to weave into the fabric of our world. The gates of our mouths must be as ports harboring truth and our mouths must be the harbingers of truth.

In Mark 13:5, Jesus says, "Take heed that no one deceives you!" In verse 22, He gives us another warning, "For false Christs and false prophets will appear and perform signs and miracles to deceive the elect – if that were possible. So be on your guard!" We are living in a day where the spirit of deception is saturating the land like wildfire. Satan and his demonic troops are actively doing their work of setting the stage for the final deception, which will usher in the Antichrist. For the Antichrist to be able to walk onto the stage of the world without great resistance or astonishment, the minds of the people must have been undergoing conditioning for the deception. Already, we are being fed deceptions in palatable and seemingly harmless doses to help facilitate his appearing so that when he is introduced to the world, he will be all but welcomed. We would have been looking for him, expecting him, just as if he were a guest invited to dinner, with a chair pulled up to the table and a plate set out for him. Amongst the many tools that Satan has been using to soften the blow of his coming deceptions is reality television. This tool of deception has the world captivated! We waste hours, weeks, months and years of our lives engrossed in the many endless series of reality TV shows. The irony of reality TV is that much if it is not even real. It is mostly staged drama and creative editing to make something appear to be what it is not.

I can recall when reality television was first introduced to viewing audiences, most of us were offended as we watched the characters suffer, cry and face humiliation on a national scale. Millions of viewers watched the fate of the poor characters in awe, week after week. However, as time went on we became less offended by the characters' nationally televised humiliation, because something of the presence of that old sinful nature in us took delight in viewing the sufferings of others. That these shows also presented some good feeling to us in the way of giving us a hero, or a winner of some sort, made it easier for us to rationalize the fact that we had so enjoyed feasting on the pain of the losers.

It is often hard to tell while watching reality TV which scenes are real and which scenes are contrived. Is the pain real or contrived? Are those real tears and are the characters really angry with each other? Was that a real fight, or was it all staged? Did he really, actually marry a woman he just met on a television reality show, or is all of this just acting, some good acting, some very bad acting? The point is that around the world, literally millions of viewers are addicted to various reality TV shows and many Christians constitute a large part of the viewing audience. It is important for the saints to discern this type of entertainment for what it really is, a part of the grand strategy to dull our senses to the fact that any and all deception is from the Devil, that it is evil and that it is meant to rob the targets of the deception – that would be you and me – of our ability to recognize the spirit of error and to rightly discern truth. In 2 Thessalonians 2:7, 9-10, we read the Apostle Paul's description of the Antichrist: "The mystery of lawlessness is already at work... The coming of the lawless one is according to the working of Satan, with all power, signs and lying wonders, and with all unrighteous deception among those who perish, because they did not receive the love of the truth, that they might be saved" (NKJV). It is only God's Truth that will preserve the righteous in the face of such massive deception. Jesus said to His children; "Then you will know the truth, and the truth will set you free" (John 8:32). "But when he, the Spirit of truth comes, he will guide you into all truth" (John 16:13). Again He tells us that we will know the Spirit of truth because He dwells with us and in us (John 14:17).

I was one of those who had been addicted to certain reality TV shows until the Spirit of the Lord directed me to pull away from the television completely. At first it was not easy. As with any addiction, I had very strong withdrawal symptoms and was tempted many times to see what my television acquaintances were up to. By God's grace, I was able to hold fast to my commitment to spend more time with God and to leave the TV off! I soon came to realize how much time I had been wasting, spending hours on end completely engrossed in the lives of so many people I did not even know and they didn't have a clue that I existed. I was being a very poor steward over the time that God had given to me.

The Bible speaks of a clan of warriors, mighty fighting men of valor who enlisted to go to battle with King David in 1 Chronicles 12:32. These were the men of Issachar. The scripture records that they "understood their times, and knew exactly what to do." We, too, need an understanding of our times so that we will wage war intelligently as the Spirit of the Lord leads us. Again, I say, it is essential that we know who and what to let in our gates and who and what to keep out. If we are careful to abide in Christ, to sit in His presence, at His feet, watching and waiting for Him, gazing upon His face, reading and studying His Word, He will instruct us and give us great wisdom to know what to do. For some of us, He will instruct us to turn off the television. For some, He may instruct us to turn off the radio or change the station. Still for others of us who may be avid readers of various materials, He may direct us to read nothing other than His pure Word for a season. If we stay in the abiding position, God will reveal to us that this is the hour for the church to rise up and pray. Let me say it again: God is calling for the church, not just the intercessors, but every believer in the Lord Jesus Christ, to be stirred from our stupor and complacency and to lift up our voices in prayer against all such deception and unrighteousness. To that end, God is also requiring that His children uphold the standard for truth, as we ourselves get acquainted with the truth, live the truth, embrace the truth and speak the truth one to another.

Listen to these words from Solomon, speaking of wisdom: "Blessed is the man who listens to me, watching daily at my doors, waiting at my doorway. For whoever finds me finds life, and receives favor from the LORD" (Prov. 8:34-35). We cannot sit at the feet of Jesus and at the feet of any other god at the same time and expect to walk securely and obediently with our Lord. "A double-minded man is unstable in all of his ways" (James 1:8). "Can two walk together unless they are agreed" (Amos 3:3, NKJV)? "No one can serve two masters; either he will hate the one and love the other, or he will be devoted to one and despise the other" (Matt. 6:24). We cannot simultaneously sit at the feet of Jesus and any other god and expect to be able to rightly discern truth. We must make a choice if we desire to walk in the power of Almighty God and if we expect to be kept from the spirit of deception.

There is such an absence of the true presence and power of God in our lives, in our churches, in our families, in our ministries and in our praying. It is because we are not often found watching and waiting in the presence of the One who bestows His glory and who possesses all power. He wants to impart that power into us, but we have to show up for impartation to take place. To "abide in Christ" *we must be present.* In his book *The Pursuit of God*, A.W. Tozer says:

> The world of sense intrudes upon our attention day and night for the whole of our lifetime. It is clamorous, insistent, and self-demonstrating. It does not appeal to our faith; it is here, assaulting our five senses, demanding to be accepted as real and final. But sin has so clouded the lenses of our heart that we cannot see that other reality, the City of God shining around us. The world of sense triumphs. The visible becomes the enemy of the invisible, the temporal of the eternal. We must shift our interest from the seen to the unseen. "Anyone who comes to Him (God) must believe that He exists and that he rewards those who earnestly seek Him" (Heb. 11:6). So be it, every man must choose his world.[31]

If we really want Him, we must really seek Him. Is He not always looking for us?

In Ezekiel 22:30 the LORD says, "So I looked for a man among them who would build up the wall, and stand in the gap before Me on behalf of the land, that I should not destroy it; but I found none."

Why was it that God could find no man, no woman, no boy or girl to stand in the gap, in that hole, that breach, that sever, that place that represents the way things are and the way that they are supposed to be? Why was there no one? Not one person could be found. What were the children of God doing? What were the intercessors doing? Where were they? Were they watching reality TV? Were they gossiping over the backyard fence? Were they wasting time looking at foolishness on the Internet, catching up on their blogs, posting foolishness on Facebook, tweeting irrelevancies?

Is it possible that the children of God and the intercessors were involved in the same sins as the rest of the unsaved world – fornicating, committing adultery, gossiping, lying? Perhaps they had simply fallen asleep because "their eyes were heavy" (Matt. 26:43). Whatever they were doing, they were inaccessible to God because God said, "I looked for a worthy intercessor who could stand in the gap, but I found none!" No one was available to come before God and wait in His presence for a divine war strategy to come against the Enemy's gates.

David said in Psalm 27:8, "When You said, 'Seek My face,' My heart said to You, 'Your face, LORD, will I seek'" (NKJV). Isaiah made sure the LORD knew he was present and ready to be used when he said, "Here am I LORD. Send me." Oh, how many of us, when the Lord says, "Seek My face," our hearts respond with, "Thy face, Lord, will I seek, after I catch a few more winks, after I make this phone call, after I send this email, after I update my Facebook status, or right after I watch this program?" We all know that these kinds of responses end up as "no seeks." We have to show up for truth. We have to show up for godly integrity. We have to show up in defense of honor of the Word of God. If we don't, how else will the world be salted? How often have we been absent and unaccounted for when we say that God has called us to the work of the kingdom, to ser-vice, to prayer and to the ministry of intercession? I keep coming back to prayer, I suppose because at my core, that is what I am, an intercessor. The kingdom of God stands in dire need of more mighty intercessors that will actually do battle in prayer.

I have attended prayer sessions where the same intercessors who say they have been called to intercede never, ever open their mouths to pray. They seem content to let someone else do the fighting for them while they stand or sit on the sidelines, just watching all the other warriors wear themselves out. That's not showing up! That's merely making a weak appearance. They would do better to stay at home. In Judges 8:1, the Ephraimites were incensed with Gideon who went to fight the Midianites, but did not ask them to join the battle. They basically said to him, "How dare you go to battle against an enemy and not invite us to go with you?"

I must say, when I see an intercessor that consistently comes to the prayer sessions, but does not pray, I am convinced that they have not done their homework; they are in sin and feel unworthy to pray, or they are simply intimidated by the complexity of the warfare. Those who constantly come to prayer sessions unprepared are like the slothful child who comes home from school, eats dinner, watches a little television and goes to bed without cracking one book. This child sits in the very back of the classroom with his head down so that the teacher will not call on him because he knows he has not prepared himself to give an answer. God said that He "looked for an intercessor who would build up the wall." That means you've got to *do something!* You've got to open your mouth and say something! All of hell is trying to shut you up, but all of heaven is waiting to back you up, so open up your mouth pray!

You want to know how to walk in the manifested power of a Holy God? It is by actively waiting in His presence. While we wait, we actively prepare for the warfare that is all around us. While we wait, we actively prepare by storing up His Word in our hearts. Daily meditation in the Word of God is a safeguard to our gates against the deceptions of the Enemy. The psalmist said, "Your Word is a lamp unto my feet, and a light for my path" (Ps. 119:105). Proverbs 3:6 tells us that if we acknowledge God in all of our ways, He will "make our paths straight."

While we wait, we actively prepare for His visitation by getting acquainted with His heart. Such preparation readies us so that when He calls, we can voluntarily answer as did Isaiah, "Here am I, Lord send me!" We should be just like the enthusiastic child in the class-room who wants the teacher to call on him because he's done the disciplinary task of sitting still and studying his lessons to be ready with a right response. This is how we should be when God calls on us. We need to have done the homework of abiding in His presence and studying His Word to make room for His Word to abide in us and to flow out of us like streams of living water. If we have failed to learn how to actively wait, then we have failed to build strong gates. If we have mastered the discipline of actively abiding in Jesus, we have managed to incorporate a powerful building material into our gates.

Chapter 16

Are You Ready to Rumble?

"Blessed be the LORD, my Rock, Who trains my hands for war,
and my fingers for battle."

Ps. 144:1 (NKJV)

"People sleep peaceably in their beds at night only because rough men
stand ready to do violence on their behalf."

-George Orwell

$\mathcal{A}$nytime we as God's children open our mouths to beseech our God, our petitions, entreaties, supplications and inter-cessory prayers are supposed to have the Devil sweating and high-tailing it back to his camp of demonic cohorts to strategize on a Plan G, H, I, J, K, LMNOP! When skilled intercessors band together in the spirit of love and unity, in corporate prayer, the Spirit of the Lord will empower us to literally run those demons out the city gates!

"Five of you shall chase a hundred, and a hundred of you shall put ten thousand to flight," states Leviticus 26:8 (NKJV). God will give us insight into Satan's strategies against our families, our schools, our businesses, our finances, our churches and our communities. He will then give us counter strategies that will cancel Satan's assignments and overthrow the powers of darkness. After the intercessors pray, I am telling you, Satan ought to be forced to go on a sabbatical just to recover from the whipping he and his team have received! Glory to God! Hallelujah!

Unfortunately, many of us who have been called as watchmen have fallen asleep on the walls. In Matthew 26:40-41 Jesus rebukes His disciples because they could not keep watch with Him in prayer for one hour during the most significant hour of His earthly ministry. While Jesus pressed through to purpose in prayer, He needed His disciples to help pray Him through, but they were fast asleep, unable to intercede, unable to stand in the gap. As I speak to so many in the body of Christ today, I hear them saying that far too often as they kneel down to pray, they end up falling asleep. This is a strategy of Satan. He has placed a spirit of slumber over the body of Christ that is mostly birthed out of sheer exhaustion. I said it before: we are far too busy doing things that God never commissioned us to do and far too distanced from His presence. I will say this again too, for it bears repeating: Jesus said, "Without me you can do nothing" (John 15:5)!

America really ought to be thanking God for the current woes of our economy because they are what have forced many of us to turn back to Him and back to the place of prayer. As a nation, we have been busy working ourselves to death to accumulate more and more money, more and more material possessions. This has resulted in us having little or no time for God. We have even been working ourselves to death trying to build our churches. This can be a catch 22 because, while we want to encourage excellence in ministry and build the kind of churches that are culturally relevant, we must also find the balance between building great churches and maintaining our personal relationship with the Lord. We have been so busy working that when it comes time to pray, our bodies are spent, completely exhausted, wiped out! The only thing that an exhausted body *can* do is fall asleep.

Wives are sleeping while their husbands are out carousing. When a wife is not attentive to the needs of her husband, when she neglects to build him up and encourage him when life belittles him, when she fails to stand in the gap for him in prayer with all the knowledge that she possesses concerning his personal struggles, she leaves the door wide open for Satan to come in and wreck her home. When a husband neglects to show his wife that he loves and cherishes her through all the seasons of her life, he too leaves the gate to his marriage wide open for demonic infiltration.

Fathers who have abandoned their children are sleeping while their sons and daughters roam the face of the earth like loveless vagabonds, trying to patch the holes in their souls that daddy left with drugs, sex and violence. Mothers and fathers who should be praying with and for their children, building and guarding their children's gates, are instead sleeping while their children are on the Internet involving themselves in dangerous activities with complete strangers. Were I to begin to discuss the dangers presented to our children via the information highway, or the Internet, with its gates to destruction flung wide open, I would have to devote an entire book to that topic alone.

Our children unwittingly expose themselves to depraved and immoral men and women by posting their deepest feelings and desires, their needs, hurts, and pains on the walls of a Facebook page. They naively open their gates wide to invite the Enemy in. The hope is that someone, anyone, will speak into that void place vacated by an absent father or an emotionally absent mother, and bring some type of definition or meaning to their lives. If you listen closely, you can hear the cry of their hearts: "If anyone is out there, please speak to my pain!" Our neglected children are thirsty and they're looking for water on the streets of the information highway. Prayer warriors, called to cover their pastors and churches in prayer, are not even able to pray for one solid hour without becoming bored and falling asleep.

Because we have slept through an Enemy takeover, our churches, rather than looking, smelling and feeling like Jesus Christ, are looking, smelling and feeling more like corporate America. Jesus said, "My house will be called a house of prayer for all nations." Many of our modern day churches could rightly be called "corporations" and that would be a more accurate description than for them to be called "houses of prayer." There is a lot of working, but very little praying. We are merely busy when we should be busy praying. We are sleeping when we should be praying and watching! If we are deliberate in our praying, then we will be deliberate in our watching because we will be anticipating and expecting the strong hand of God to move as we bring His kingdom to bear on the matters for prayer.

In every one of the aforementioned scenarios, it's not just a matter of a single gate being unguarded – it is, in fact, all of the main gates – all of the places of authority that have been left unguarded. The minute the Devil sees that there is no daddy seated at his place of authority at the main gate to the family unit, he violently kicks the door down to try to usurp the authority in that home. When he approaches a church and smells no incense (representative of the prayers of the saints) flowing out of the front door, the Devil knows this is a church that he can wreck in no time at all. No prayer in the church means that poor pastor is working himself to death without a prayer covering over him, his wife, his children, or the church vision. This should not be. I can just envision Satan and his demons catching sight of our fallen, unguarded gates and all of them together shouting "All-ie, All-ie in free!" as they storm every one of our main gates.

I think the body of Christ has forgotten that we are in a war that will not end until Jesus returns. I highly doubt that you would see one of our soldiers in Iraq sleeping on the battlefield. You had better believe that they are suited up for battle and aggressively watching for the enemy. To fall asleep on the battlefield would mean certain death and because the saints are sleeping, the stench of death is in our homes. The institution of marriage, as God ordained it, is dying. Death has boldly stormed the gates of our schools – literally! Our children are murdering each other in the classrooms and the hallways of higher learning. The stench of death is in our streets. Violence on our streets has reached astounding proportions. We are horrified as we watch the cold brazenness of children stomping and beating each other to death in broad daylight, then cold-heartedly blasting a video of the beating on YouTube! This is unparalleled cruelty and a sure sign of the end times fast approaching. In 2 Timothy 3, Paul speaks of the terrible times that we will witness in the last days and of how people will be "…without love, disobedient to their parents, ungrateful, unholy, unforgiving… without self-control and brutal" (vv. 1-5).

The stench of death is in our churches. Pastors, clergy and licensed ministers attempt to minister to the broken, the bruised, the demonically oppressed and the afflicted, but they are unable to meet their needs because they are operating in the flesh, full of flesh and lacking anointing. They have Bachelor's degrees, Master's degrees and PhD's, but I have yet to see a demon expelled by the power of a PhD. We need Jesus! We need the power of the Holy Spirit! Jesus said, "The Spirit gives life; the flesh profits nothing" (John 6:63,

NKJV). Hungry congregants sit in padded pews desperately waiting for words of life to rain down from the pulpits to resurrect their dead situations. Instead, they go home dragging their shameful, putrid, burdensome coffins behind them, only to shove them right back in some moldy, dank, cobwebbed corner of the house with the dull optimism that next Sunday will bring hope to their dead situations.

Those who have been entrusted with proclaiming the Gospel of Jesus Christ have nothing worth saying if they have not spent time waiting on the Lord. It is only when the Spirit of God is poured out upon flesh that we can speak the oracles of God (Joel 2:28; Luke 24:49). Jesus spoke these words to his disciples: "...you will receive power when the Holy Spirit comes on you; and you will be my witnesses in Jerusalem, and in all Judea and Samaria, and to all the ends of the earth" (Acts 1:8). There is no profit, no glory, no help for the afflicted and the oppressed, in the flesh. Paul said, "For I know that in me (that is, in my flesh) nothing good dwells" (Rom. 7:18, NKJV).

The Greek word for "watch" – *gregoreuo* (gray-gor-yoo'-o)[32] in Matthew 26:38 literally means "to keep awake, be vigilant." It is a derivative of *egeiro* (eg-i-ro),[33] which means to rouse (literally from sleep, from sitting or lying; or figuratively from inactivity), to stand." In Mark 13:33 (NKJV) Jesus says, "Take heed therefore, watch and pray." This "watch" is derived from two Greek words – *agrupneo* (og-roop-nee'-ah),[34] which is defined as "to be sleepless, i.e. keep awake" and *hupnos* (hoop'-nos), which means to be "in a state of spiritual torpor, laziness, or lethargy." If we are in a state of spiritual torpor, then we are more or less comatose, in a trancelike state, dull, paralyzed and apathetic. When the saints ask me what they should do to avoid falling asleep when they kneel down to pray, I tell them to get up! Change your strategy! Switch up on your positions. Fight the Devil back! Sing your prayer. Walk and pray. Jog and pray. Swim and pray. Ride your bike and pray. Do whatever you must do to shake that spirit of slumber off of you! We've got to learn how to keep that Devil guessing, "What's she gonna do next?" "I just saw him dozing off on his knees by the bed a second ago! Which way did he go now?" he'll exclaim. That's right! We cannot make it easy for him. If he wants to take us into captivity behind his gates, he is sure enough going to have to work for it!

The saints of God must stay battle ready, always ready to rumble. The Devil is always on the prowl, looking for someone who is weak and unprepared to fight, going about as a roaring lion, seeking someone to devour, to rip in pieces (1 Pet. 5:8-9). Let me tell you, your pastor will sleep better on Sunday night when somebody is praying for him. Your pastor's wife will sleep better when you band with other believers to cover her mind and heart under the blood of Jesus in Spirit-led prayer. A mother will sleep better at night when she knows that the saints are united with her in prayer concerning her child. Your community will sleep better when the community is a praying community.

The Spirit of God strongly impressed upon me to warn the church to stop praying other people's prayers. Lately, the new fad in the church is to distribute CDs, pamphlets and books around that have prayers that someone else prayed, wrote or received from God. There is nothing wrong with those prayers and it's not a sin if you pray them, but they are *other* people's prayers. They are not *your* prayers to God. Those are the prayers of someone else's labor, someone else's abiding. They cost you nothing. David said, "I will not offer up to the LORD that which costs me nothing" (2 Sam. 24:24, NKJV). If we can plop in a CD and just listen to someone else praying while all we do is close our eyes and say, "Amen," this does nothing but make us more comatose and lazy. David said, "In the morning, O' LORD, you hear *my* voice" (Ps. 5:3, emphasis added) and, "In the morning *my prayer* comes before you" (Ps. 88:13, emphasis added). "Let the words of *my mouth*, and the meditation of *my heart* be acceptable in your sight..." (Ps.19:14, emphasis added). Sure, it takes more effort to pray your own prayers, but it's more than worth it.

We read the prayers from pamphlets and books that others have prayed, but we never bother to look up the scriptures that are noted at the end of these prayers. This is like getting in the boxing ring without your boxing gloves. In the boxing ring, the power is in the punch, a strategically landed punch. In spiritual warfare, the punch is in the Word of God! God has exalted His Word above His name (Ps. 138:2). Praying other people's prayers by rote results in powerless praying and Jesus said, "The kingdom of God is not in word, but in power" (1 Cor. 4:20, NKJV). Prayers that are birthed as a result of abiding in Christ, lying in His presence and meditating on His Word, are prayers that have the anointing of the Holy Spirit upon them. They will be filled with power to deliver that strategic knock-out punch!

Prayers that are bathed in the Holy Spirit's presence wield ammunition that the Devil never saw coming! He's already heard you pray that same prayer from that tattered pamphlet for the last two months. He knows that *you* don't even believe what you are praying anymore. However, a fresh prayer, bringing fresh revelation into a present, relevant situation, is more than he can handle! Put that pamphlet down and pray your own freshly anointed, spirit-led prayer that will clock the Devil on his blind side! That pamphlet is disqualifying you from being a serious contender in the ring with your Adversary. It's stopping you from hearing from God on how to wage spiritual warfare against the present needs of your family, your coworkers, your pastor and your ministry.

When Jesus told us to watch and pray, He intended for us to pray with expectancy. He intended for us to pray with fervency. "The effectual fervent prayer of the righteous availeth much!" (James 5:16, KJV). Yes, that's right, we must be living right to get the attention of a Holy God, and to get answers to our prayers. We despise the conditions that must be met to pray prayers that avail much, but again, either we want to live for Jesus, or we don't. It is really just that simple. We must resolve to make Jesus Christ the Lord of our mouths. When we commit our mouths to the Lord, as David did in Psalm 19:14, we will get God's attention and the Holy Spirit's help.

Praying with expectancy adds excitement to the business of praying. The sad truth is that for many of the saints, long periods of unanswered prayer have caused them to enter into prayer in a dull, lifeless state and to exit prayer apathetically. They approach God with that "ho-hum" mentality, which simply indicates that they are no longer even expecting God to answer their prayers and quite frankly, they wonder if He is even listening. Again, this is like a boxer who goes into the ring to fight, jumping up and down, shadow boxing, touching his thumb to his nose like it's *his* fight, but then sheepishly whispering to his coach that he expects to go down in the first round. The fact that he even steps into the ring indicates that he is considered a serious contender. However, he lacks confidence in what he possesses inside of himself and what he has done in preparation for the fight; instead he is more convinced of his opponent's ability than of his own. Amongst my arsenal of favorite scripture is 1 John 5:14-15. It lets us know that we can have confidence in prayer, when praying the will of God, that He will hear us and answer us. We can step into the ring expecting to conquer!

Let me tell you, if the mouth of the wicked can overthrow a city (Prov. 11:11), how much more powerful and how much more good then, can the mouth of the righteous do?" Remember, "the one who is in you is greater than the one who is in the world" (1 John 4:4).

We were all birthed onto a battlefield, and whether or not we accept that fact, still, we must prepare to rumble with our Adversary, or prepare to be knocked out in the first round. If we will step into the ring in faith, Jesus will surround us and will "shield our heads in the day of battle" (Ps. 140:7) and we will have the victory.

In conclusion, I do not suggest that it is an easy thing to sanctify the tongue. Just read James 3 and you will see that possibly the most difficult things for us to control are the words that come out of our mouths. James tells us "If anyone is never at fault in what he says, he is a perfect man" (vs. 2). Since we know that as Christians we are constantly in a state of evolving, of being perfected by God, we know that we must rely on huge doses of God's grace as we undertake the work of rebuilding the gates to our mouths. We need the aid that only His Spirit can give. God is well aware that we are being transformed by the power of His Spirit. We are in process and that's the whole point – the journey. We must be actively participating in our own transformation. We must recognize that we are a work in progress and must do whatever the Holy Spirit instructs us to do to experience deeper levels of authentic spiritual growth in our lives. Abiding in Jesus, the True Vine is so important to this growth and to the reconstruction of our gates. The very act of abiding in Christ postures us to be exposed to transformation. As we remain in such close proximity to Him, His cleansing, consuming fire will wash us, prune us and mold us into His image.

The tongue, James says, is the very best part of us and at the same time it is the very worst part of us. It is the truest barometer of our spiritual condition. "With the tongue we bless our Lord and Father, and with it we curse men, who have been made in God's likeness" (v. 9). It is little, but it is fierce. It can destroy the whole body. "The tongue also is a fire, a world of evil among the parts of the body… and is itself set on fire by hell." (v. 6). No man can tame it, says James, so do we stop praying? Do we stop encouraging? Do we stop ministering to one another? The answer is a resounding *no!* Then what do we do? We humble ourselves before God. We take hold of His grace. We draw near to Him and trust in His great power to cleanse us as we do the work of the kingdom. This is what sanctification is all about. That's what a boxer does when he prepares for a fight. Every time that boxer runs a mile around the track, he is sanctifying himself. Every time he spars in the gym, he is sanctifying himself. Every time he turns down an alcoholic beverage and drinks a gallon of water instead, he is sanctifying himself. Every time he goes to bed early, rather than carousing at clubs for half the night, he is setting himself apart to be battle ready, to take the belt at the end of the fight. We must be willing to do the same as we prepare to war in the spirit. Our tongues must be sanctified – "set apart" for God's use.

As we turn from our sins and cling to God's amazing grace, He purifies us, taking us from strength to strength, and from glory to glory. It never becomes clearer to us how dependent we are upon our Savior than when we see the inadequacy of all our efforts to "get better" on our own. James 4:6-10 says: "But He gives more grace. Therefore, He says: "God resists the proud, but gives grace to the humble. Therefore, submit to God. Resist the Devil, and he will flee from you. Draw near to God, and He will draw near to you. Cleanse your hands, you sinners; and purify your hearts, you double-minded. Lament, mourn and weep! Let your laughter be turned to mourning, and your joy to gloom. Humble yourselves under the mighty hand of God, and He will lift you up in due time" (NKJV).

Remember, Paul says in 1 Corinthians 4:20, "The kingdom of God is not in word, but in power." To be effective, useful and beneficial to God and to others whenever we open our mouths to speak, to minister to others, to encourage others, or to pray on behalf of others, we must have the mouth redeemed from whence come the words of encouragement, healing, or prayers. God said to Moses, "I will be with your mouth" (Ex. 4:15). This is what we need to ask of the Lord, that He be with our mouths and thus sanctify our words. If we know that He is with our mouths, then we can be certain that the gates to our mouths are very secure. We can then speak without fear of our words harming another, speak without regret, and speak words of life and words of power, wielding the authority of God. Oh, that His words might be our words.

Dr. Linda Mintle, one of the keynote speakers at a recent Moody Women's Conference, said, "We [America] used to be a culture primarily influenced and shaped by words, but now we have become a culture that is predominantly influenced by images." Those images are images that promote promiscuity, deceit and violence. They have all but crowded out the life-transforming image of the Savior. We must labor to reshape our culture with redemptive words that have been bathed in the presence of the Holy Spirit, and sanctioned by the Holy Spirit.

> Thus says the LORD; "As the new wine is found in the cluster, and *one* says, 'Do not destroy it, For a blessing is in it,' So I will do for My servants' sake. That I may not destroy them all... the Valley of Achor [shall be] a place for herds to lie down, For My people who have sought Me. But you are those who forsake the LORD... Because, when I called, you did not answer. When I spoke, you did not hear, but did evil before My eyes, and chose *that* in which I do not delight (Isa. 65:8-12, NKJV).

Blessed Savior, may it not be said of this generation that they did not seek Him, that they did not seek Him for His holy words.

We know what to speak, what to do and how to respond because we have been with Him. We have sat and we have waited and we have drunk of His presence. We have feasted on His Word and have allowed it to simmer deep in our spirits before rising to leave the abiding position. Thus has our Lord deposited in us and when we open our mouths to speak, it shall be as living waters springing up into eternal life to those who hear us – to those who hear our words. A sanctified, battle-ready tongue is a powerful tool in the hand of God. Sanctification is another vital building material for the reconstruction of the gates to our mouths.

Part Six

The Mind Gate

"We must see that God's way is the way of the spirit touching spirit. Instead of having our mentality developed or acquiring a storehouse of knowledge, it is by this other means of contact that our spiritual life is built up. Let no one be deceived; until we have found this way we have not found true Christianity. This alone is the way of having our spirit edified or built up."

-Watchman Nee, *The Release of the Spirit*

Chapter 17

Which Way Did I Go?

"If the LORD had not been on our side–

Let Israel say–

If the LORD had not been on our side when men attacked us,

when their anger flared against us,

they would have swallowed us alive;

the flood would have engulfed us,

the torrent would have swept over us,

the raging waters would have swept us away.

Praise be to the LORD,

who has not let us be torn by their teeth.

We have escaped like a bird out of the fowlers' snare;

the snare has been broken, and we have escaped." Ps. 124 (NIV)

"What world is this? What kingdom? What shores of what
worlds? How much longer will you indulge your flaws?"

-Girl, Interrupted

*T*he quote above, taken from *Girl, Interrupted* (1999), recounts the true story of a young woman's stay at a psychiatric hospital during the troubled 60s. Questioning her diagnosis of having Borderline Personality Disorder, she rebels against the two authority figures that can help her the most, the nurse and the chief psychiatrist. She chooses instead to become friends with the resident "lunatics." She learns soon enough that if she ever wants to recover and regain her freedom, she will have to confront the one person who frightens her most of all. That person is herself.[35]

Satan has declared war on the mind of the believer. Since the day that we entered this sin-filled world and until the day that we exit it, our minds will be caught in the crossfire between truth, the immutable Word of God and the perversion of truth, or the lies from Satan. When we say that we believe a thing to be true and yet our living bespeaks quite a different truth, we are operating as double-minded individuals. Our worlds are molded by the truths or the lies that we believe and speak. The kingdom that we labor for, that we build upon and become citizens of, is one that has been fashioned either by truth or by lies. The shores we land upon in the dark nights of the soul will be determined by the truths or the lies that we have chosen either to embrace or to reject in the light.

If you are reading this book, chances are that you are one of the ones who have had something valuable stolen from you from behind your gates, or maybe it escaped through an unguarded gate, or through carelessness you simply lost it. Perhaps you gave it away in ignorance or in a moment of compromise or weakness. The holes that are left in our souls through such deep losses cause a part of us to get stuck or left in the place where we experienced the loss, while the other part of us that must move on does so without the permission of our fragmented self, thus we become like one who stands on a seesaw, unstable and unbalanced. We make decisions for today based on yesterday's hurt and frustration. We choose or don't choose certain individuals to enter the circle of our lives based upon yesterday's hurts, disappointments and betrayals. If the gates to our minds have not been repaired, most of those choices, if not all of them, will be bad choices. In James 1:8 we read "...a double-minded man is unstable in all he does." The phrase "double-minded" is translated in the Greek as *dipsuchos* (dip'-soo-khos).[36] By definition, it means to be "two-spirited." The word "unstable" is defined as "inconsistent, unhinged, restless and disorderly."

It is true that the greatest giant any of us will ever have to confront on the battlefield is ourselves. In the course of our lives, we will all take a beating. We will endure so many emotionally damaging blows, suffer so many losses and experience so much disappointment that we will be left with gaping holes in our souls, bruised to our very core. If the gates to our souls are not being carefully reconstructed along the way, we will end up one big confused mess of a person.

Jesus said in Luke 4 that he was sent by God to "heal the brokenhearted, to proclaim liberty to the captives and recovery of sight to the blind, to set at liberty those who are bruised" (Luke 4:18, KJV). This "bruising" in the Greek is *thrauo* (throw'-o), which means: "to crush"[37] and *agnumi*, which is to "break, wreck or crack," to sunder (by separation of the parts; a shattering to minute fragments); "to disrupt."[38] This "shattering" comes to interrupt and to disrupt our lives so that we are never the same, so that we will be doomed to roam the face of the earth as lost, partial souls, never finding our way back to the path that leads us to our destiny, the path that leads us back to Abba. This is Satan's goal in the bruising, that we be completely shattered, cracked asunder. He banks on the fact that our broken hearts will result in a mental disconnect wherein our capacity to think clearly is truncated. When the head and the heart are not in sync, every other part of the body is pretty much doing its own thing as well, on a fast track to destruction. However, the goal of God is that our brokenness will lead us back to Him and make us more useful to Him.

You remember the story of Hansel and Gretel. They were the children of an old woodcutter and had a wicked stepmother. The family had fallen on hard times because there was a famine throughout the land. The evil stepmother, seeing the children as only two extra mouths to feed, devised a plan to get rid of them by leading them far off into the woods and abandoning them there for the wild beasts to devour. She gave them each only one small piece of bread to sustain them. Although the father's heart was very grieved over the plan, he agreed to the evil woman's scheme. However, as they were led into the forest, Hansel dropped bread crumbs all along the way with the hopes that he and Gretel could follow the path of the broken bread crumbs back to their father's house. This is our heavenly Father's goal for us too, that as we turn to recover, retracing the path where the brokenness in our lives occurred, we will also discover Jesus to be the "broken bread" which, if we will only pick it up, will lead us straight into the Father's loving arms. When we place our broken pieces into the hands of the One who was broken to pieces for our restoration, He gives us back a whole loaf. His love makes us completely whole. Glory to God!

Unlike the old woodcutter, our heavenly Father promises us that not only will He not allow anything to separate us from His love, but that He will also make all things work together for our good. Even the things that shatter our lives He will cause to benefit us as we cultivate our love for Him and as we answer His divine call concerning our life's purpose (Rom. 8:28).

I can liken the state of one who has experienced such shattering in their lives to that of a 1,000-piece puzzle. The puzzle starts off as one whole image that someone decides to break down into a thousand tiny fragmented pieces. With all its thousand pieces in the box, it is yet one whole puzzle, just sectioned off. Now, if you take the thousand pieces and toss them straight up in the air, what you will catch in the box as they fall back down will only be a portion of the whole puzzle. Try putting the puzzle together using only those sections that remain in the box and you will see only a mere fragment of the whole. You will not be looking at the entire picture as it was originally created and it will be difficult to understand the image. This is because it was not intended to be understood in part, but in whole.

Many of God's children are just like that fragmented puzzle. We started off as one whole individual, but then life came at us, hit us from all different directions and shattered us into tiny pieces. The fragmented pieces of our lives can be found in our childhood homes, where perhaps we were abused or traumatized in some way. We may discover some fragments left in our old junior high school where some football jock bullied us, or a popular "mean girl" cheerleader made us feel as if we were ugly outsiders. It is for sure we will locate fragments in the home that we once shared with an ex-spouse, or at the gravesite where we buried a dear loved one. Many saints have left fragments of themselves on the pews of former churches where they were wounded by church leadership that they had come to love and trust.

We must bear this in mind as we interface with unbelievers and as we co-exist and co-labor with our brothers and sisters in Christ. That is, that we are not seeing the whole picture, only a fragment of the person God created them to be. With this understanding, we should be more willing to extend compassion, mercy and love towards each other. Additionally, because most of us have sorely neglected our own mental and emotional health, we are often functioning out of our fragmentation as well. Sometimes we love like Jesus, but sometimes we hate like the Devil. Sometimes we embrace our brothers and sisters in Christ, other times we almost "Dare anybody to try and touch [me] today! Don't hug me, speak to me, or even look at me!" Sometimes we are full of encouraging words, other times we won't even open our mouths to say, "Good morning." When the sun is shining and our paychecks are steady, we believe all the promises of God in Christ Jesus are yea and amen (2 Cor. 1:20), but let the clouds darken the skies, a little rain fall and we get a flat tire all in one day and we're no longer even sure if there is really a God "up there." We are essentially two-souled, double-minded and unstable.

The very act and process of the fragmentation of our lives results in a breakdown of our emotional and mental stability. Fragmentation can make us come unhinged. It can make us inconsistent, restless and disorderly. When people look at us and watch our lives, consider our responses, actions and reactions, our fragmentation makes the picture of our lives difficult to comprehend. We are all straining, as it were, to try to understand a mere part of each other. It is for this reason that I believe Jesus urges us to "love one another" and He adds to this commandment: "just as I have loved you" (John 15:12). This means that we are to love each other, flaws and all, to the death. "Greater love has no one than this: that he lay down his life for his friends" (v. 13). Lest we think that Jesus's commandment to us to love each other was only to be practiced amongst friends, we must remember His words from His sermon on the mount, "Love your enemies, and pray for those who persecute you."

I believe that God had our fragmentation in mind when His Spirit breathed these words through Peter, "Above all, love each other deeply, because love covers over a multitude of sins" |or "faults" in some translations| (1 Pet. 4:8). In 1 Corinthians 13, as Paul discusses the topic of spiritual gifts, he exalts love as the most excellent of all of the gifts. Without the gift of love in operation with all the other gifts, we are nothing more than "a resounding gong or a tinkling cymbal;" translation – a noisy irritation. Paul says that we know only a part of all that there is to know. What we see is imperfect and we view the imperfect through a cloudy mirror (vv. 9-12).

Our fragmentation deeply grieves the heart of our loving Savior, Jesus Christ. We know this because we see repeatedly how Jesus labored tirelessly to heal the sick and afflicted. He labored to undo and to destroy the works of the Devil (1 John 3:8). Matthew 8 tells of healing after healing that Jesus performed, first on the leper, then the centurion's sick servant, then Peter's mother-in-law and finally, He healed two demon-possessed men who were out of their minds, living amongst the tombs, scaring anyone who dared try to pass their way. In chapter 9 the healing continues and in verse 36 we read that Jesus looked out over the multitude of those who were coming to Him for healing and was "moved with compassion for them, because they were weary and scattered, like sheep having no shepherd" (NKJV).

We know that the heart of Jesus is deeply grieved over our fragmentation because Isaiah 53:5 tells us that He allowed Himself to be pierced through, so that by His wounds we could be put back together again. He wants us to operate with a sound and stable mind. We do not have to remain fragmented. 1 Corinthians 6:17 reads, "…he who unites himself with the Lord is one with him in spirit." The psalmist David said, "He restores my soul" (Ps. 23:3). The Lord wants to rebuild the gates to our minds by working stability into the structure of our gates, thus making us mentally whole.

I Will Survive

"The people who survived the sword found grace in the wilderness… Again I will build you and you shall be rebuilt"

Jer. 31:2, 4 (NKJV).

Statistics noted in medical doctors Dianne and Robert E. Hales' book, *Caring for the Mind*, show that one out of every four individuals suffers from a mental disorder. According to their surveys, problems of the mind touch the lives of more persons than illnesses such as heart disease and cancer. Although mental illnesses can be horrendously disabling, even fatal, most people never seek treatment.[39] Millions suffer unnecessarily, not knowing what is wrong, not knowing that there is hope. There is hope – in Jesus Christ! In Exodus 15:26 God declares, "…for I am the LORD who heals you." The gate to our minds arguably undergoes the most severe and the most repeated attacks of all the gates. It is the Devil's primary battlefield, so it is only fitting that there be so many ways for us to *lose our minds*.

The contributing factors to mental disorders are plentiful. Some are brought on biologically through genetics caused by brain infections, brain defects, brain injury, prenatal damage, toxins and poor nutrition. Other contributing factors are psychological, such as when a child suffers severe psychological trauma emotionally, physically or sexually, or through the early, significant loss of a parent, which can also result in the child being neglected. These are all common psychological causes for the development of mental disorders. Still others have their root in environmental and sociological factors such as the dysfunctional family, living in abject poverty, any type of substance abuse, a change in lifestyle either with a new job or a new school, death, divorce, feelings of not measuring up to one's own standards or the standards of others, low self-esteem, anxiety, anger, depression, loneliness and rejection. All of these come as battering rams against the gates of our minds.

In cases of severe mental disorders, medical intervention is most often necessary and I do not want to minimize its importance in the treatment of some mental disorders. In my studies to become certified as a licensed Christian Counselor through the American Association of Christian Counselors, I came to understand the importance of such intervention. God does use the knowledge and skill of psychologists and psychotherapists to treat and cure mental illnesses. After all, it was Jesus who stated that sick people need doctors (Matt.

9:12). This means that, very often, doctor-prescribed medications will be used to assist in treating the disorder(s). However, along with the medicinal cures, there is also the need for the spiritual cure. If we fail to acknowledge the need for the soul to be healed, all the medicine in the world will simply fail to make one completely whole.

Scripture tells us that it is the Lord Jesus who makes us completely whole. We see evidence of this in Luke 17:11-19. Here we read of ten leprous men who cried out to Jesus to be healed. Jesus directed them to go and show themselves to the priest. The scripture records that all ten were cleansed of their leprosy on their way to see the priest, however, only one of the ten lepers returned to tell Jesus, "Thank you" and for this simple act of gratitude, the Bible records that this was the only leper who Jesus made "completely whole." This word *whole*, in the Greek (*sozo*) means, "to save... deliver or protect."[40] Along with being cured of his physical disease, Jesus also cured him of his soul's disease, that which had impaired his mind, will and emotions. The Devil does his best work erecting strongholds in our minds when he discovers an opportunity to begin the work while we are still mere, defenseless, innocent little children.

Casey is a thirteen-year-old girl who comes from a home where abuse of all forms has been present for as long as she can remember. Before she leaves home a full-grown woman, every one of her gates will have been violated, broken down and trashed. In a child's way, she will have utilized every conceivable coping mechanism that is available to her just to maintain some measure of normalcy and sanity in her severely distorted world. The task of reconstructing her gates will be arduous and overwhelming as she matures into adulthood and discovers that she is *broken*. She will spend the rest of her life trying to undo the damage done to her mind, body and soul.

Many innocent children are born into antagonistic environments in homes filled with drugs and all manner of substance abuse. Like Casey, they have either witnessed or been the victims of prostitution, child abuse, molestation, rape, pornography, substance abuse and violence. For these children, the matters of justice, of right and wrong, are issues that are cloudy and constantly challenged. What is their truth when the primary authority figures in their lives, mother and father, who should also be the primary dispensers of justice, love and compassion, are instead the sources of injustice, mass confusion and unspeakable pain? They, too, may very well spend the rest of their lives in a state of recovery.

With no sense of security and with the constant threat of personal injury looming in the atmosphere, the child living in traumatizing surroundings must devise a mechanism of survival. Most often, this mechanism is formed in the mind. It is here where the child begins to make resolutions that are greater than his/her ability to live up to, such as, "No one is ever going to hurt me again!" "I'm never going to let anyone boss me around. I am my own boss!" "I will never allow anyone to get close to me!" These are impossible resolutions to uphold, impossible because the times and the seasons of life will eventually change. The people who will enter and exit their lives will change. The situations and the surroundings in which they will find themselves will change. All such change will require a flexibility that these adults will be unable to summon. Oh, how the Word of God becomes a fortress and a stronghold for us when we undergo such trials! The LORD encourages us in Isaiah 43 with words that strengthen and bring so much hope. He says, 'You don't have to be afraid, little one. I formed you. I have seen everything that the Devil has thrown at you to destroy you, and I am fully aware of everything that I, Myself, have allowed to come your way, in order to mold you. I know your past, your present, and your future. I know what you are made of. It is I who formed you in your mother's womb' (Ps. 139). 'No matter what you go through, be it fire, or overwhelming floods, I will be with you' (Isa. 43)! 'I Am your Redeemer. I will make you over, and you shall give Me praise' (Isa. 41)! Hallelujah!

The words of the prophet Nehemiah in chapter 1, verse 3, give us a pretty good description of the kind of devastation that survivors of various traumatic events in life must press through: "Those who survived the exile, and are back in the province, are in great trouble and disgrace. The wall of Jerusalem is broken down, and its gates have been burned down with fire." Do you remember the lyrics to the Gloria Gaynor song "I Will Survive"? Here's a sampling from that song that brings to mind what happens when we bypass the work of reconstructing the gates to our minds:

...and so you're back
from outer space
I just walked in to find you here
with that sad look upon your face
I should have changed that stupid lock
I should have made you leave your key
If I had known for just one second
you'd be back to bother me.

That's right – the Devil comes back to bother us again! Take a look at the end-time prophecy found in Ezekiel 38. Here we see an enemy scheming to invade a people who have just recovered from an assault and have begun to settle down in peace. While they are trying to put their lives back together again, the enemy plots to catch them off guard, "a peaceful and an unsuspecting people, all of them living without walls and without gates and bars. I will plunder and loot and turn my hand against the reset-goods, living at the center of the land" (vv. 10-12). To be sure, our evil Adversary circles back to upset all that we have painstakingly reset. However, the battle will not go according to his plan, because if you keep reading to the end of Ezekiel 38, you will see that God will foil the plan of the enemy. This is exactly why we must be certain that we have gone to God to assist us in the reconstruction of strong walls and gates: the Devil looks to return to finish us off.

Adult survivors of childhood trauma may very well have survived their unique, awful childhood experiences, but they are now as adults, mentally, spiritually, emotionally and even physically in great trouble and much disgrace. Finding themselves "back in the province" so to speak, in situations where they have to submit to a cruel supervisor, or in a marriage with an abusive spouse, or trying to raise a troubled teen who is strung out on drugs, they soon discover themselves to be emotional handicaps. They are disgraced by having to repeat history because they have not sought a cure for their souls' *dis-eases*. They are disgraced by the sheer haunting memories and ill-timed, triggered flashbacks of yesterday's shameful abuses. They are in trouble and disgraced because their own traumatic childhood experiences, having gone unattended, have rendered them incapable of possessing the tools necessary to successfully resolve their all too strangely familiar present difficult life issues. Their walls and their gates have been burned down by the fires of extreme trauma to mind, body and soul. When they run into anything along the road of life that even slightly resembles their past trauma, they resort to their trusty childhood coping mechanisms. Psychologists refer to this behavior as the "shutters coming down," which simply means that they choose not to deal with the unpleasant situation by creatively shutting it out. Let me explain.

Usually, when we close the shutters on the windows to our homes, it is because daylight has gone and nighttime has arrived, which means that outside it is now dark. We may not be ready to deal with the darkness, so we close the shutters and turn on the lights inside our homes. Inside, it is as if it is still daylight and the darkness outside has been erased by simply not dealing with it, by focusing on the light that we have created. Likewise, when a survivor of childhood trauma runs into a dark night of the soul that threatens to take them back to some horrible memory, they simply close the shutters on the dark memory by using one of the following three coping mechanisms: *repression, denial, or dissociation.* These three mechanisms have the ability to take them out of the dark moment and transfer them into an artificial light in a place they have created somewhere in their minds. I refer to it as an artificial light because such light is formed out of deception and illusion. It does not have its foundation in truth.

In her book *Counseling Survivors of Sexual Abuse,* Diane Langberg states that because abuse is so overwhelmingly damaging to a child's thoughts and feelings, that child will sacrifice a sense of coherence for the sake of survival. "In essence, the child says, 'I cannot live with these feelings and survive, so I will make them not mine.' Survival is gained, but there is great loss to the developing self. A sense of wholeness is lost, of being real, spontaneous and aware of one's own inner workings. In essence, what is lost is the integrity of the self." In *repression,* the coping mechanism is simply to "forget that the abuse ever happened," to store it away neatly in a little suitcase, place it somewhere in a dark corner up in an unused portion of the attic of one's mind, turn and walk away.[41] Out of sight, out of mind! *You don't bother me, I won't bother you!*

Those using the coping mechanism of *denial* will literally just deny that the abuse is occurring. "This is not happening." This mechanism must incorporate delusion and a perceptual distortion of reality. Langberg points out that this form of accommodation only puts the individual in danger of "retraumatization, in that she has trained herself to fail to recognize the signs that would remind her of the original trauma." Consequently, "the child loses continuity in her experience and learns to ignore aspects of herself that are, in fact, vital to her wellbeing."[42]

Dissociation, which is the most damaging coping mechanism, has the child saying either, "This is not happening to me," or "This is happening to someone else." Langberg points out the following steps that must occur for a child to dissociate: she must alter her thinking, disrupt her sense of time, alter her body image, distort her perceptions, experience a loss of control, alter her emotional responses, change the meaning of things and become hyper-suggestible. This type of coping mechanism results in fragmentation of the self and the fragmented parts become inaccessible to her. She is no longer her "self" in any sense of the word.[43] Perhaps now we see why it is imperative that we make it our responsibility to be engaged in the process of becoming whole.

Take a moment to go back and read through the steps that a child must follow, according to Langberg, to dissociate from an abusive situation. For God's children, every one of those steps can and will spell disaster as we attempt to hear from God on the matters for prayer for ourselves and for others. If we are involved in a prayer ministry within a local church, or worse yet, if we have somehow gained the position as leader of the intercessory prayer ministry within our local church, that poor pastor had better look out, trouble may be on the way!

In Ezekiel 22:30, God said that He was looking for someone to stand in the gap. What is the *gap*? Remember, we said the gap is "a breach, a hole or a severed place." It represents the difference between the way things are and the way they are supposed to be. To stand in the gap you must be a whole individual, or at the very least, you need to have dealt with the major areas of fragmentation and incongruity in your life. We cannot effectively intercede, pray, or stand in the gap for anything if our perceptions on critical matters are distorted, if we are subconsciously trying to regain the control that was stolen from us through abuse while we were still a child, if our manner of processing things mentally has been severely altered from normal, or if our past coping skills have taught us that it is necessary to "change the meaning of a thing" to make its existence more palatable. If we are fragmented souls, having no sense of who we are, to position ourselves in such a highly charged spiritual atmosphere (standing in the gap), waging war against demonic principalities and powers of darkness, is a dangerous thing. Indeed, until we have undergone healing, we really need someone to stand in the gap on *our* behalf until our mental gates have been reconstructed and we have become strong enough mentally and spiritually to go to greater depths of warfare in prayer.

Repression, denial and dissociation are the three main defense systems, or coping mechanisms, that a child living in trauma will use in abusive situations to manage the horrific experience of trauma. However, when as an adult one still employs one of these three coping mechanisms to face life's challenges, it is clear evidence of a fragmented soul, an individual who has not matured properly and who has not been made whole. Paul said in 1 Corinthians 13:11, "When I was a child, I did childish things, but as an adult, I now do things the way that an adult should do them." I believe that God has given children these coping mechanisms as a means to survive the trauma. Looking back over my own life experience, this was certainly true for me. However, as adults we must put away childish things and begin the hard process of working out our souls' salvation with much "fear and trembling" to face the challenges of adult life as healthy and whole beings (Phil. 2:12).

When we bypass the healing process on life's journey, we will remain emotionally, spiritually and mentally handicapped, never reaching our full potential in life or in God. Such healing requires that at some point, whether we want to or not, we will have to return to the place where truth was lost. This will be quite a challenge because repression, denial and dissociation are launched from the springboard that demands that one never looks back. However, to know where we are going, we must know from whence we came.

In the mental stronghold that Satan builds in the mind of the traumatized individual, he strategically piles one lie upon another.

He knows that fear is an almost impenetrable stronghold. Fear is a demonic prison gate that can hold us captive for the span of our lives. You see, the Devil does not so much concern himself with *what* you are afraid of as much as he does with just making sure that you stay afraid. Afraid of what? Of whatever! It is his job to simply plant the seed of fear. That small seed, firmly planted, can grow into a monstrosity of a tree that has the capacity to house many animals. In Luke 13:18-19, we read: "Then Jesus asked, 'What is the kingdom of God like? What shall I compare it to? It is like a mustard seed, which a man took and planted in his garden. It grew and became a tree, and the birds of the air perched in its branches.'" The same principle is true of the kingdom of Satan. Once that seed of fear has been planted in the soil of our minds, it will continue to grow until it monopolizes every facet of our thoughts. That spirit of fear can and will take on many forms until everything that we are afraid of is sitting, perched in the tree in our minds, just daring us to try to make a move in spite of them. I tell you the truth, as Jesus would say, you will not be able to make a move in life without first considering your fears.

From behind the gate of fear, the traumatized child unwittingly joins his adversary in further imprisoning himself as he begins laying the foundation for the lies that he will tell himself out of sheer fear of his victimizer. Satan then comes and builds on the foundation of lies that have already been laid through repression, denial and dissociation by adding his own lies, such as, "Looking back can be deadly," or, "You are safe in this fortress of lies. Why open a can of worms now and spoil everything?" "Digging for the truth after all these years is only going to result in unnecessary pain for everyone. Let sleeping dogs lie and just keep moving forward." Satan will do whatever is within his power to keep you imprisoned behind his gates. Remember the words of Jesus Christ, the True Gate for the sheep. His words of life bear repeating. He is the One who gave up His own life so that you and I can be free. He says in John 10:10, "The thief does not come except to steal, kill and destroy. I have come that they might have life, and that they might have it more abundantly" (NKJV). When we fully understand the Devil's mission, we will better equip ourselves to come against his works in our lives.

How many times Jesus, our Big Brother in the faith, comes to set us free as He breaks down those gates of fear, destroying Satan's strongholds with His command to us over and over again, "Fear not, for I Am with you" (Isa. 43:5). He lets us know that we do not have to fear anything, not even the truth. Quite the contrary, He tells us that our deliverance, our liberation will come as we ourselves come to know the whole truth (John 8:32, 36). That truth will set us free! Having the courage to confront ourselves, our inner giants and our fears is great building material for strong gates.

Chapter 18

A Candidate for Change

"Do not be conformed to this world (this age), [fashioned after and adapted to its external, superficial customs], but be transformed (changed) by the [entire] renewal of your mind [by its new ideals and its new attitude], so that you may prove [for yourselves] what is the good and acceptable and perfect will of God, even the thing which is good and acceptable and perfect [in His sight for you]." Rom. 12:2 (AMP)

"Progress is impossible without change, and those who cannot change their minds cannot change anything."

-George Bernard Shaw

Studies in behavioral psychology have shown that the human personality is developed in community with other people. In her book *The Healing Presence*, Leanne Payne states, "Because heaven and earth are crammed with living creatures and concrete things, awesome to know in their reality, man is only becoming whole while reaching out to them;—i.e., when he is outer-directed. He can only know himself by knowing others..."[44] Having the freedom to interact with a variety of people types in a variety of social settings, is therefore vitally important in the development of healthy social skills – skills necessary to the reconstruction of the gate to a severely damaged human mind. We must be candidates for change and willing to let God work transformation into our lives.

However, survivors of childhood trauma are very often loners. Indeed, one of the contributing factors to their being a social misfit is that their abusers will perform their horrific deeds against these innocent children in highly controlled environments, under cover of darkness. There, in the dark, the child is made to feel isolated through fear tactics used against them by their abusers. The fear itself becomes a stronghold powerful enough to box them into a small, small world for the rest of their lives. With Fear come its traveling companions – Shame, Anger and Rage. This confining spirit of fear can be likened to the oft-told story of the dog that had been chained to a pole all its life. The chained dog could only roam as far as the length of the chain would allow. One day after the dog had become old, its owner, no longer fearing that the dog would run away, decided to remove the chain. The poor dog continued to roam only within the limitations of that chain, long after it had been removed from around its neck. He never understood that he was free to travel as far as his eyes could see, if he so desired. In his mind, the dog still believed he was chained to a pole.

In much the same way, many survivors of childhood trauma still feel the confines of their chains as adults. The secrecy, the lies, the threats, the belittling, the pain and the shame all served as mental and emotional chains, or strongholds. The strongholds become prison cells and the prisoners behind the gates have become trapped within their own bodies, within their own minds and within their own souls. Until they understand that they, too, can be free to expand their horizons, they will continue to roam only as far as their mental chains will allow.

Psychologists will tell you that the emotion of fear causes the body to produce a rush of adrenaline that is meant to empower the one in danger to either run or fight back. This is what is commonly known as the *flight or fight* syndrome. However, in most cases, a small child is neither able to fight back nor to flee, thus the gates are open for this child to subconsciously and unknowingly house the spirits of anger and rage beginning from that very moment when the gates have been violated. These destructive spirits will continue to dwell in the "house" or the spirit of that child and to wreak havoc until the child discovers the root cause of her rage and actively seeks to uproot the trespassing spirits. Unfortunately, the discovery may not come until many, many years later in her life, after many lives have been damaged by her own misguided anger and rage.

It has been said, "A rose garden cannot grow where a volcano lies." Many relationships that could have survived are doomed to fail because one or both of the partners are dealing with unresolved issues that keep a spirit of rage alive just under the surface of their "good behavior." Let just one thing not go their way and you will see what appeared to be a loving, fun, tenderhearted person transform into a self-centered, rage-filled and abusive person. This is why we see so many husbands and boyfriends are killing their partners. These demons have not been aggressively dealt with. You see, when the Devil trespasses and violates the gate to the mind, he moves in with all of his messy baggage and he moves in with a vengeance. His resolve is to take up permanent residence in the territory of our minds, so there he begins to unpack all of his "stinkin' thinking," (a phrase coined by Charles Tremendous Jones).

For us to regain our mental stability, we must wage war on our own out-of-control thoughts. Jesus said, "Behold, I stand at the door and knock" (Rev. 3:20), but being the gentleman that He is, He will not knock down the door to force His way in. He waits for His invitation. Since He will not have the Devil as a roommate, there must be an eviction and that responsibility rests upon us, the gatekeepers. In her book *Honey, I Shrunk the Devil* Dianne Sloan writes, "Satan is a destroyer, and don't forget it! He will cover the walls with graffiti and destroy the house. He is not an owner, so he will not occupy with an owner's mentality. He will just use the place and destroy it, leaving you with a heap of ashes."[45]

Dianne is correct; there must be an eviction, or else the Devil will end up driving us out of our own minds. By the time he is finished with us, we will be ripe and ready for nothing but the cuckoo's nest! This means that the landlord has got to stand up to the encroacher and tell him to pack his bags and get out! By the way, that eviction notice is not just reserved for spirits. It can be served on so-called friends and family members who keep popping up at your home, unannounced and uninvited, bringing strange spirits with them. They crash in your bed, eat up your food, trash your living quarters and make you uncomfortable in your own home. As encroachers, they occupy space in your mind by causing you to stress out and become filled with anxiety wondering, *"When will they ever leave?"* In fact, I know a woman whose adult children stressed her out so much by returning home every six months to a year that she finally packed her bags and moved out of her own home.

When you make up your mind to regain possession of the gate to your mind, you have set the wheels of prophecy in motion over your life. In essence, you are telling yourself prophetically, "That's it! Enough is enough! The Devil's reign of terror in my life is over. I'm coming out of this bondage, in Jesus's name!" We must regain control of our thoughts to rebuild the gates to our minds and Romans 12:2 confirms this when it says, "...be transformed by the renewing of your minds." Well then, what does it mean to be transformed? The dictionary definition of the word "transformation" is "to shift, to mutate, a conversion (gradual change), revolution, metamorphosis, to turn the corner." A few years ago, I saw the movie *Transformers*. I was quite impressed at how a common old car was transformed into a powerful superhero. In its transformed state, the old-car-turned-superhero could go places it could never go before and do things it could never do before.

The Transformers had incredible power, strength and courage. Of course, this was just a movie about some very cool toys, but the basic concept is the same for us when we allow the Word of God and the Holy Spirit to transform our lives from the inside out. Things we could never accomplish in our old, sinful, bound state, we can now accomplish in our transformed state, that is, in the Spirit's power. Places we could never go physically, spiritually, emotionally and mentally, having been bound by the traumatic experiences of our childhood and controlled by our own irrational resolutions, we are now gradually freed to go as we walk in step with the Holy Spirit through a renewed mind; a mind that has undergone a radical conversion. I am reminded of the directive given by the stewardess on the plane once the airplane has lifted and has stabilized in the blue skies. She says, "Ladies and gentlemen, the Captain has turned off the seatbelt sign. You are now free to move about the aircraft."

You may not have even realized why you kept running from the will of the Lord, saying "No" to His will and to His plan for your life. With a transformed mind you are now *free* to say, "Yes, Lord. I'll go where You want me to go. I'll do what You want me to do. I will say what You want me to say!" "I am *free*. No more chains holding me!"

With a transformed mind, you are now *free* to invite other people into your world and to step into the lives of others without paralyzing fear. With a transformed mind, you are now *free* to extend Christ's love to others and to accept and embrace that same love extended to you. You are *free* to enjoy pure and healthy loving relationships and are no longer doomed to keep partnering up with toxic people. The Captain, Jesus, our Savior, Redeemer and Liberator, has turned off the seatbelt sign and we are no longer confined, nor sentenced to do time in a small, small world. Isn't that liberating? We can achieve a renewed mind as we are deliberate to make daily applications of the truths found in the Word of God directly to the particular areas of struggle in our lives. The work is hard, the journey is long, but little by little change is realized. Eventually we get to round the corner to a whole new world of possibilities we never would have imagined. As has been aptly stated: no pain, no gain!

In Chris Thurman's book *The Lies We Tell Ourselves,* he points out that many people with mental issues want to get better without having to do the required work to become whole. He suggests you make a list of the things you find most difficult to do along your road to recovery, then pick one of them and *go face your pain!* He recommends an accountability partner who will agree to check in with you daily, if necessary, to encourage you to stick with the work that you committed to do. "Whatever it takes to get it done, do it! *Do the pain; get the gain.*"[46] The character builders are found in the journey to transformation and liberation, not in the act of liberation.

This, too, is what God esteems – the journey. It is in the journey to healing where God allows, controls and creates circumstances and situations that are intended to mold and build our character. He works to correct and reshape a character that has been damaged by perversions, lies, unhealthy secrets, and hypocrisy.

When you have been the victim of perversion, lies, deceit and hypocrisy, the Devil tries to capitalize on your victimization by attempting to set you up to become just like your abuser. Understand that perversion begets perversion. Lies beget lies. Hypocrisy begets hypocrisy. When a child is being abused, doors are being opened up in their spirits that will house these demonic spirits. The Devil prowls about looking to take up residency within that child to ensnare him, well into adulthood, to continue to operate in the only thing that he knows and what he knows are those familiar spirits of perversion, deception, lies and hypocrisy.

As with the oft rebellious and stubborn Israelites, God is in no hurry to repair and restore us if we also choose to rebel and prefer our own stubborn ways when He is trying to bring about deliverance in our lives. If it takes forty years or more for Him to repair our gates and redeem our damaged minds, He will do in His sovereignty what is best for us. We must learn to humble ourselves and say, "Have thine own way, Lord." In 1 Corinthians 5:6-8 we read: "Do you not know that a little leaven leavens the whole lump of dough? Clean out the old leaven, that you may be a new lump, since you are truly unleavened. For Christ, our Passover has also been sacrificed.

Therefore let us celebrate the feast, not with old leaven, nor with the leaven of malice and wickedness, but with the unleavened bread of sincerity and truth" (NASB).

It has often been said that we cannot change what we do not acknowledge. We must realize the necessity of acknowledging our sin before a God who already knows more about us than we do ourselves. In the words of David:

> O LORD, You have searched me and known me.
> You know when I sit down and when I rise up;
> You understand my thought from afar.
> You scrutinize my path and my lying down,
> And are intimately acquainted with all my ways.
> Even before there is a word on my tongue
> Behold, O LORD, You know it all.
> Ps. 139:1-4 (NASB)

Adult survivors of various childhood traumas have been exposed to so many lies and deceptions that they can themselves become wired to lie. When the Holy Spirit reveals a lying spirit in such an individual, they must quickly agree with Him about that sin, humbly repent, and look to the Savior for deliverance and direction. The psalmist David said, "When I kept silent, my bones wasted away through my groaning all day long, for day and night your hand was heavy upon me; my strength was sapped as in the heat of summer.

Then I acknowledged my sin to you and did not cover up my iniquity. I said, 'I will confess my transgressions to the LORD' – and you forgave the guilt of my sin" (Ps. 32:3-5).

In Proverbs 28:13 we read, "He who conceals his sins does not prosper, but whoever confesses and renounces them, finds mercy." "Well," you may say, "it's too late for me," or "My situation is impossible! I've been bound in this way of thinking for too long now." You may think that the damage done to you was so severe that it can never be reversed. Perhaps you are feeling completely hopeless about transformation. You believe it for others, but not for yourself. I want to remind you that God specializes in doing the impossible. Our God is the same God who makes the deaf to hear (Mark 7:32-35), the dumb to talk (Matt. 9:32-33), the blind to see (Mark 8:22) and the lame to walk (Matt. 15:29-31). He is the God who raises the dead (John 11:38-44) and who restored life to a valley of dry bones (Ezek. 37:1-10). What makes you think that He cannot renew your damaged mind and transform your life? What makes you think that He cannot rebuild the gate to your mind?

The power of life and death are in your own mouth! You must begin to speak new life and restoration to your own mind. Believe that God can and will heal your mind. God wants us to have an impossible healing testimony so that we can encourage someone else in their impossible situation and thus assist them in rebuilding their gates.

Chapter 19

My Mind's Made Up

"You knit me together in my mother's womb. I praise you because I am fearfully and wonderfully made" Ps. 139:13-14a.

"The flesh endures the storms of the present alone; the mind, those of the past, present and future."

-Epicurus

The human brain is like the motherboard of the body. If it is not functioning properly, then everything else we do is rooted in error. For this chapter, I have relied on information from researchers who have studied the early development of the brain. I've included this information because I believe that it will not only help us to understand our own mental behavior better, but it will also help us to appreciate the mighty hand of God in preserving our minds and in restoring its gates. Let us now take a closer look at the human brain and how it develops and functions.

More and more, researchers have come to the conclusion that early childhood affects physical changes in the way the brain functions. Clinical studies have shown the damaging effects that childhood trauma has on the development of the human brain. We know that the brain is composed of raw material known as neurons. These neurons are connected by *synapses* that organize the brain by creating pathways that govern everything we do, from breathing and sleeping to thinking and feeling. Research and clinical studies conducted by Jenni Whitehead have shown that brain development and learning involves the strengthening of some synapses and discarding others and this process is highly dependent upon stimulation and environment.

According to Whitehead, synapses develop rapidly in the early stages of a child's life. However, by adolescence, about half of the synapses have been discarded and those remaining will exist for the rest of the person's life. The early overproduction of synapses is believed to be the result of evolution that has led the brain to expect certain experiences. For instance, all babies appear to be pre-wired to respond to the sound of the human voice. Early synapses need reinforcement if they are to be strengthened; if they are not strengthened through repetitive use, the brain may discard them. For example, a baby's genetic predisposition is to form strong attachments to their primary caregiver. If the primary caregiver is unresponsive, threatening, or rejecting, or if the attachment process is disrupted [by abuse or neglect], then the child's ability to form healthy relationships during later life [will] be seriously impaired.[47] While the research does not conclude that the damage done cannot be repaired, relearning later in life is certain to be a much more arduous task.

Remember what we discussed earlier about the power of a resolution. If we look at how the brain cells function and are formed, we see that in unhealthy relationships, where the child is repeatedly neglected, rejected and mistreated by the primary caregiver, the synapses for that type of unhealthy interaction are strengthened. Meanwhile, the synapses for healthy bonding are discarded, making it possible for the child to grow up and be pretty good at keeping those irrational, self-imprisoning resolutions that we discussed in previous chapters.

Even if they wanted to and as much as they admire each other, the little boy and the little girl who share a secret of having been victims of child abuse, as adults, will never marry because they have both made resolutions to never let anyone get close enough to hurt them ever again. Try as she may, the little traumatized girl, now a married woman, will never be able to submit to her husband because she has made a resolution to never come under anyone's domineering control again. As much as he wants to be promoted in the firm and as hard as he works, the little boy, molested at the age of seven by his schoolteacher, will never advance in the firm because his resolution is to never trust or submit to an authority figure again.

We can clearly see now that damage done to brain cells during the early stages of development is difficult, if not impossible, to repair and restore. Therefore, to suggest to such individuals that they need to just "change their minds" about how they act or react in certain situations affected by this type of severe damage to the gate of their minds is simply unrealistic and unreasonable. The issues are much more complicated than that. Their minds appear to have been made up by those who controlled their early life experiences.

For those whose gates have been violated in this way, connecting and staying connected to others is more abnormal than normal. Normalcy is being isolated. Normalcy is being rejected and even though rejection is painful, it is at least familiar. Normalcy is having a strong urge to be loved and touched in a pure way, but resisting it with everything within them, because that's not what they are used to. That's not normal. Daddy didn't hug them. Daddy slapped and beat them. Mommy didn't cuddle them. Mommy abandoned them, if not physically, then emotionally. Normal, for them, is experiencing touch from another human being in ways that always bring pain, or not having the experience of a loving touch at all. Understandably, under their breath, they make foolish vows.

These individuals may long have forgotten the binding resolutions that they made, but such resolutions are powerful and far reaching. Once they are made, they dictate actions, responses, thought patterns, relationships, lifestyles, occupations and on and on their influence travels, impacting every aspect of life. What the mind thinks determines where the body will be allowed to go. If perchance the boy and girl mentioned above do grow up and marry, without taking the necessary steps to be healed both psychologically and spiritually, most likely their marriages will not last. When the marriage begins to hit the rough spots and it will, without a clear understanding of the real source of their strongholds, they will simply be trying to fix their issues by force of will. The same holds true of the little girl, now grown up and married trying to force herself to submit to her husband and of the boy, now a grown man unable to advance on the job because of his early resolution to take a stand against all authority figures. It is also true of the man or woman who is unable to experience intimacy with the Lover of their souls, Jesus Christ. Attempts to build, grow, or advance from a cornerstone built of flesh are all vain attempts. The building will crumble. The attempts will amount to nothing. The growth will be stunted.

The road that leads to deliverance for a mind that is imprisoned by ungodly thought patterns is called brokenness. Authentic brokenness leads to repentance. This is the starting place where God can begin to rebuild and reconstruct our gates. He often waits until we are reduced to nothing as a result of our own stubbornness, pride, self-righteousness and rebellion, before He can produce His best work in us. Our old, hardened flesh only gets in His way and God will not build something new in us while the old remains. In Mark 2:22 we read, "No one pours new wine into old wineskins. If he does, the wine will burst the skins and both the wine and the wineskins will be ruined. No, he pours new wine into new wineskins." This is the way of God. He tears down so that He can build up. He wounds so that He can heal. "See now that I myself am He! There is no God besides me. I put to death and I bring to life. I have wounded and I will heal, and no one can deliver out of my hand" (Deut. 32:39).

Remember the dilemma Paul found himself in, in Romans 7? Paul was struggling with trying to fix himself. He was trying to deliver himself from the power of sin active in his life, but each time he made up his mind to do the right thing, the power of sin got the better of him and he ended up falling back into sin. He said, "For what I am doing now, I do not understand. For what I will to do, that I do not practice; but what I hate, that I do...O, wretched man that I am! Who will deliver me from this body of death?" (vv. 15, 24, NKJV) Paul came to the conclusion that he was powerless to deliver himself and that only through Jesus Christ could true deliverance be achieved (v. 25). From what we read in Zechariah 4:6, we further understand that anything we are going to accomplish in this life that is going to be lasting and beneficial to us, to others and to the kingdom of God must be accomplished by the Holy Spirit, not by force of will, or by our little, bitty, finite strength. "'Not by might, nor by power, but by My Spirit,' says the LORD Almighty." As Paul learned, we too must come to understand that we cannot fix ourselves either. If we desire to be used of God with maximum effectiveness, we must be certain that we have received deliverance from God from all such bondages and hindrances, embracing brokenness wherever we have allowed ourselves to become hardened by the assaults of life. We must daily seek out and welcome personal, spiritual, emotional and mental transformation that only our Redeemer can give.

It may astound you to know the number of saints who are involved in various levels of ministry who have deep emotional, spiritual and mental scars for which they have never sought a cure. Some of them are carrying around twenty, thirty and forty years of baggage. They have never told anyone that they were raped, abused or molested. They have never undergone any type of counseling to work through and work out the issues. This is especially dangerous for those operating in the more spiritual aspects of ministry, such as altar work, intercessory prayer and spiritual counseling. In the infinite sovereignty and grace of God and I speak from personal experience, such an individual can be effectively used of God, provided their hearts are pure, but God will only allow them to go so far before He insists that they seek a cure for their damaged souls.

Have you have ever known an anointed man or woman of God who was advancing in ministry and then all of a sudden he or she seemed to have hit a ceiling and could go no further? It could very well be that God had called a time out for the express purpose of giving them the opportunity to focus on becoming whole. The love of God is so rich and all-consuming, so incomprehensible and yet so magnetically wonderful that He will arrest us in our steps, even as we are doing His will, to minister to our souls' illnesses.

Ministry can become so rewarding to us that were it entirely up to us, we would just keep going, ministering to others while all the while knowing that we are not whole. It's like that annoying tooth that keeps aching, you know the one. I am talking about that tooth that every time you accidentally bite down on it, you experience pain that shoots from the tip of your toes to the ends of every hair on your head. You know that you need to go to the dentist and have that tooth repaired, but you decide to just chew on the other side of your mouth to avoid that visit to the dentist's office. Eventually, if you ignore that tooth long enough, it will rot and completely decay, even causing damage to the surrounding roots of other, healthy teeth. Whereas it could have been easily repaired and saved, your delay in dealing with the early warning signs have now resulted in a total extraction. Isn't this just what Jesus said that His Father would do to us in John 15? "He cuts off every branch in me that bears no fruit..." (v. 2) Extraction, amputation, root canal... call it what you want, but God will radically deal with our disease, either by cure or by eradication. God wants us healthy and whole and He does not want our diseased branches to infect other healthy branches around us.

We have a way, don't we, of avoiding the reality of the severity of our wounds. We seem content to just keep replacing our old, dirty bandages with new ones, avoiding exposed, damaged nerves and covering festering sores that have never been treated or closed over. God can and will allow us to keep going for a little while. He will allow us to taste and experience the awesomeness of having His hand upon us to do rewarding ministry in His kingdom, but then He will permit us to hit a wall and will call a time out to lead us beside the still and quiet waters, away from all the noise and confusion, to restore our souls (Ps. 23:3).

The foretaste of fruitful ministry encourages us that God will use us with even greater results once we have submitted to the process of healing that begins with our brokenness and repentance and once we have allowed Him to make us completely whole. Though we may not fully understand His supervision of our lives at such times, the humble and the pure in heart will not resist the hand of God when He ordains a timeout for us on the sidelines while He works deliverance in our lives. We would do well to submit to the wisdom of our loving and merciful Savior and Redeemer. He is that Balm in Gilead. In His hands we find the cure for our souls. It is He who has the power to renew our minds. Although others have controlled the paths of our thoughts through abuses, God created our minds. The One who made our minds can restore and remake our minds.

Certainly it will take the help of the Holy Spirit to repair such damage to the soul. It will take the help of the Holy Spirit to restore the brain to a healthy state where it can begin to expect good and not bad out of relationships and life experiences. When the finger of God reaches in and touches the damaged cells in our minds by repeatedly showering us with His never-ending love, we will begin to believe that we are worthy of being loved and accepted. When we experience the great faithfulness and the tender mercies of God morning by morning, we will come to believe that there is Someone who will never leave us or forsake us, whose thoughts towards us are compassionate to show us compassion, kind to show us kindness, merciful to shower us with mercy and loving to show us true and incomprehensible love. When the healing hand of a loving Savior touches us, soon all the healthy synapses, once discarded as a result of having never been used, will be restored. Remember what the psalmist David said, "He restores my soul" (Ps. 23). For the believer, there is always hope in a powerful, loving Savior and Redeemer who is able to destroy every work of the Enemy in our lives.

In Psalm 107:10-16 and 20, we read of a people who have been robbed, whose gates have been violated, a people sitting in darkness and in deep, deep gloom, "prisoners suffering in iron chains, for they rebelled against the words of God, and despised the counsel of the Most High." God allowed them to be subjected to "bitter labor" because of their disobedience to Him and because they rejected His counsel. However, when they turned, repented and cried out to Him, to the only One who could deliver them, the Word of God says that God heard them. "He brought them out of darkness and the deepest gloom and broke away their chains." He broke down "the gates of bronze and cut through the bars of iron... and He sent forth His word and healed them." He will do the very same for us when we repent of holding to our own way, repent of ignoring the severity of our wounds and spurning His prompting and counsel to seek a cure. God will gladly heal us when we cry out to Him for healing.

It doesn't matter how long we have been in the condition we're in. When God sees that we have positioned ourselves for deliverance through brokenness and repentance, He only asks us "how long have [we] been in [our] condition," just so that we will understand that no captivity is permanent. You can be blind (John 9:1), bent (Luke 13:11), lame (John 5:5), crazy (Luke 8:27) or dead (John 11:17), but when Jesus says, "Be loosed!" no devil in hell can keep us bound!

How vitally important repentance is to the reconstruction of our gates when we have stubbornly held onto our own ways, knowing that they are contrary to what God seeks to accomplish in our lives. Our brokenness before God will lead us to the place of repentance, healing and restoration. We unleash God's hands to rebuild strong gates for us when we fully embrace brokenness and repentance in our lives.

Chapter 20

Looking Back

"Forgetting those things which are behind and reaching forward to those things which are ahead, I press toward the goal for the prize of the upward call of God in Christ Jesus" Phil. 3:13b-14 (NKJV).

An excerpt from my journal:
5/11/7 – After being out of school for twenty-five years, I returned to college to get my degree. I graduated from Pratt Institute today! Thank you Jesus! God, you are so good to me! Kareama, James and Ariel were there to celebrate with me. Wow! After the ceremonies, I went to a few of the buildings on campus and tried really hard to put myself back in *yesterday*. For the life of me, I couldn't do it, couldn't place myself back in those buildings. Then, I heard His voice in my spirit say, "Daughter, I didn't bring you back here for you to put yourself back in your yesterday. I allowed you to come back here just to get your stuff. Now, get your stuff (my diploma) and let's go! Move on!"

"Life can only be understood backward, but it must be lived forward."
-Soren Kierkegaard

*F*rom personal experience, I can share with you that once I made the decision to look back, I too was overcome with overwhelming fear. You see, I had never denied my past, but had simply tucked it away, stuffing it into a drawer that never seemed to shut completely. I also realized that I had never really extended forgiveness to those who had hurt or traumatized me. It wasn't until I finally stopped running and turned back to face the totality of all that the Devil had tried to do to destroy me that I realized the full depth of the damage that had been done and just how much forgiveness I needed to extend.

Although I earnestly desired to be delivered from my past demons, my thought process up to that point had been simply this, "Keep moving forward. Don't stop. Don't look back." However, as I worked out my soul's salvation with a trusted Christian counselor (Pastor Pam), I was challenged to stop moving. I was challenged to draw my strength from God to turn and look back. I knew that if I had turned to look back on my own and in my own strength, I would have perished in the ocean of pain that awaited me, but with God's help I could look back and gain a clear understanding of my past. This would help me to have a better understanding of my present, which would in turn give me the release that I needed to live in forward motion. I would not have to keep looking over my shoulder in fear anymore.

In all candor, I absolutely panicked at the thought of looking back, because all of my life it seemed I had been running full stride from my past. My mind went into overdrive with harassing thoughts that came to hinder and stop any progress that I was about to make in the repair of my own gates. You see, I knew there were parts of me strewn all over the place, so much that I often felt that all that was left of me was a mere vapor floating in the atmosphere and I couldn't even put my finger on *myself.* In other words, I was completely out of touch with me. I could not find me! I hadn't the slightest idea who I was; even more painful was the fact that I didn't even know that I did not know who I was. How I praise God for His Word that encourages us that when the Enemy comes in like a flood to overwhelm us, His Spirit will lift up a standard against him that will empower us to ride the turbulent tides victoriously! (Isa. 59:19) Our mighty God will demolish the Devil's plans to destroy us and then clear a path for us to cross over triumphantly to victory! Glory to God!

With my merciless past barreling down on me like a gigantic, monstrous eighteen-wheeler just on my heels, I *had* to keep running. When Pastor Pam challenged me to stop running, all I could see was a fast-moving eighteen-wheeler slamming into this poor little vapor on the run, scattering the nothingness that was left of me into an irretrievable oblivion. Deliverance for me would mean that I (such as I was) would surely be lost forever. My challenge was this: Do I hold on to my nothingness and keep moving, to where I didn't know (I always seemed to run into some sort of impasse anyway), or do I stop, look back and risk being blasted into outer space by a giant Mack truck hauling all of my past pain?

After agonizing in much prayer to the Lord, I accepted the challenge to stop running and face my pain. As the Holy Spirit illuminated my understanding, I realized that I could not press on toward that upward call of God in Christ Jesus until I reconciled my painful past. I had an assurance from the Lord that He would be with me and that His love and compassion would enfold me; His grace would enable me. It is one thing to petition the Lord in prayer; it is quite another to position one's self for a response. This means one has to wait in the presence of God, listen in silence to receive the Holy Spirit's direction, then watch for the Lord's hand.

As I sought the Lord regarding the challenge placed before me, I waited still and quiet in His presence. The Holy Spirit reminded me of a promise that He had given to me from Deuteronomy 7, almost twenty years earlier:

When the LORD your God brings you into the land you are entering to possess and drives out before you many nations – the Hittites, Girgashites, Amorites, Canaanaites, Perizzites, Hivites, and Jebusites, seven nations larger and stronger than you, and when the LORD your God has delivered them over to you and you have defeated them, then you must destroy them totally. Make no treaty with them and show them no mercy (vv. 1-2). You may say to yourselves, "These nations are stronger than we are. How can we drive them out?" But do not be afraid of them; remember well what the LORD your God did to Pharoah and to all Egypt (vv. 17-18). The LORD your God will do the same to all the people you now fear. Moreover, the LORD your God will send the hornet among them until even the survivors who hide from you have perished. Do not be terrified by them, for the LORD your God, who is among you is a great and awesome God. The LORD your God will drive out those nations before you, little by little. You will not be allowed to eliminate them all at once, or the wild animals will multiply around you. But the LORD your God will deliver them over to you, throwing them into great confusion until they are destroyed. He will give their kings into your hand and you will wipe out their names from under heaven. No one will be able to stand up against you. You will destroy them (vv. 19b-24).

Praise God! The passage of scripture above gave a liberating answer to every lie that the Enemy was trying to plant in my mind. Jesus said, "I have much more to say to you, more than you can now bear. But when he, the Spirit of truth comes, he will guide you into all truth" (John 16:12-13). It was both reassuring and strengthening to know that God was not going to allow me to be bowled over by this giant, but that deliverance would come at the destruction of one giant at a time, little by little as I could bear it. This also told me that God knew how much I could bear at any given point along the road to deliverance. I trusted in the fact that He would surely bring about deliverance in my life and reveal truth to me in stages, not requiring more of me than I could bear and that in His loving, compassionate way, He would allow rest stops along the journey, should I require them.

Armed with the knowledge that He was wise and discerning enough to know when to call a time out should I become over-whelmed, I was now ready to go back and slay the giants of my past. God and I had a strategy against my enemies! He would go in ahead of me to drive them out and hand them over to me one at a time and I would destroy them. I really liked the part about Him going in ahead of me and trust me, I had no problem following behind Him. I would not have had a problem with Him killing all the giants too, but I realized that in destroying them myself, I was working out my soul's salvation by participating in my own deliverance. I was taking back possession of land that had been stolen from me as a child. I was also taking back land that I had forfeited in the ensuing years through the poor choices that I had made from a mental state that was yet in bondage to its traumatized past.

The path to deliverance that the Lord chose for me straight out of Deuteronomy 7 has convinced me that not only is deliverance a process, but that it is a process in which God wants us to clearly understand that which we are being delivered from. I feel this is necessary to say because for years I have watched individuals standing before pastors, deacons, elders and ministers at their local churches, needing deliverance, but finding none. These leaders would anoint the poor, bound souls with oil, lay hands on them and pray for them. The parishioners would fall out, "slain in the spirit," get up, go home and be right back in the deliverance line the following week, seeking deliverance for the same problem. This would go on week after week and for some, it would continue for years. Sadly, most of them never walked in deliverance, at least not in the years that I knew them. They were always in the deliverance line, back at square one. It is not enough to simply experience the emotional high and the sensationalism of being slain in the spirit. God wants us to understand exactly what we are being delivered out of and into. He wants us to benefit from the profound ministry of the Holy Spirit who works deeper levels of deliverance into our lives, taking us from strength to strength, faith to faith and glory to glory. This is why He drives the giants out one by one, little by little and by name.

Right now, you may be dealing with giants of alcoholism, pornography and infidelity. The Lord is not going to drive all three of these giants out to stand before you at the same time. That would be too much for you to handle. You would be overwhelmed and confused because those three giants are simply the manifestations of a bigger giant, or what the Bible calls "the strong man" (Matt. 12:29).

He is going to first drive out the giant that molested you as a child so that you will be able to deal with the root cause, or the doorway, by which all of the other giants gained their entry into and ultimately took possession of your gates. Jesus said, "But no one can enter the strong man's house and plunder his property unless he first binds the strong man, and then he will plunder his house" (v. 29, NASB).

The scriptures teach us that knowledge is power. God knows that once you can see the reason behind a thing, it won't be long before enough revelation comes to make light begin to shine out of the darkness of your soul. Understanding is coming to you as your blurred vision begins to clear up. This is why the Word of God admonishes us in Proverbs 4:7b, "Though it cost all you have, get understanding." That truth which was once hidden from you is surely being revealed (John 16:13).

See, you really never knew the *why* behind your alcoholism. All you knew was that one day you opened your eyes and looked up to the sky from the vantage point of a cold manhole cover and realized that you had become *him*, an alcoholic. However, now the Holy Spirit is illuminating your mind as you seek Him for understanding and truth. Now you see that you drank to forget the fact that Uncle Smitty, an alcoholic himself, used to pulverize you for no reason at all when you were only four years old. The Spirit of Truth is revealing truth to you. The psalmist said, "In your light we see light" (Ps. 36:9).

It is also here where God administers deeper levels of grace to us so that we can identify with Him as He identified with us in extending forgiveness to our offenders. Jesus knew beforehand, all who would betray Him, torture Him, abuse Him, humiliate Him, crucify Him and reject Him and yet, He forgave us all and loved us all before the foundation of the earth, with an everlasting love (Luke 23:34; Eph.1:1-14). In Luke 23:34, as he hung on the cross, Jesus said, "Father, forgive them, for they do not know what they are doing." We must be able to extend that same measure of forgiveness once we begin to see the full extent of the damage that was done to us by anyone who has caused us pain. In truth, often it is just as Jesus said – they really do not know what they are doing. The Holy Spirit wants us to see clearly and yet forgive entirely. It is for certain that one day we, too, will stand in need of great forgiveness, for who among us can say that we have never hurt or offended anyone? In the rebuilding of our gates, forgiveness is a very strategic building material.

Once your mind's eye begins to clear up, your vision is restored and restored vision brings renewal, restoration, health and righteousness. Light is coming into your situation and your ability to see around and through the darkness is getting stronger. It won't be long before you are walking in the light of God's truth. David said, "You, O LORD, keep my lamp burning; my God turns my darkness into light" (Ps. 18:28). We cannot live fruitful, meaningful lives without vision, "Where there is no revelation, the people cast off restraint"

(Prov. 29:18). Without the ability to see with our mental sight, with understanding, we will keep right on doing what we have been doing – destroying ourselves. Simply put, we die without vision.

In Deuteronomy 7 God names each of these seven giants that must be destroyed before possession of the land can occur. He hands them over to us one at a time, by name, then commands us to completely destroy them: "Make no treaty with them, and show no mercy." He further commands us, "Don't marry them or let your children marry them." In other words, make sure your giants do not become your children's giants. God says, "Here is what I want you to do to them: break down their altars, smash their sacred stones, cut down their Asherah poles, and burn their idols in the fire" (v. 5). "Don't look on them in pity and do not serve their gods... The images of their gods you are to burn in the fire. Do not covet the silver or the gold on them, and do not bring a detestable thing into your home" (vv. 25-26). What is God saying here? Here's what I believe He is saying to us: whatever we thought was sacred, precious or of value to us about this particular giant, God is saying, "I want you to carefully consider all the reasons why you esteemed this giant so, and then have none of it. Have none of its habits, none of its customs, none of its ideals or influences, and none of its belief systems. Completely destroy it!" Let's dig a little deeper into this process of deliverance.

In Deuteronomy 7 God names the seven giants, or the seven "ites:" the Canaanites, the Hitites, Jebusites, Girgashites, Amorites,

Perizzites, and the Hivites, but let's say that the first giant that an adult survivor of trauma must face is named *Fear*. As He hands this giant over to you, God wants you to thoroughly consider everything about this giant. Consider how it entered your life. Think about the gate or gates that may have been unguarded that allowed this giant access. Consider how it traumatized you as a child and how it pervaded every area of your mind, body and soul. Consider how, as an adult, you did nothing to rid your life of Fear's overwhelming presence. Consider how you allowed it to reign in your mind, body and soul, controlling every aspect of your world.

You made Fear your god, consulting it before ever you made a move. You had mercy on Fear as you let it dictate your responses and lead you into compromise and bad choices, even though you knew there was a better way, a better response. Fear gagged your tongue so that you would not say what God wanted you to say. Fear has gagged the mouths of many modern day prophets, hence, the Word of the Lord – intended to tear down, warn, correct, rebuke, build and plant – has been hindered by a spirit of fear operating amongst God's prophets. This big, bad giant stopped you from giving as much as God wanted you to give and from receiving as much as He wanted you to receive. You allowed that giant to stop you from loving yourself and from loving others, therefore, you let it stop you from loving God. You wonder why your relationships never go to the next level of intimacy and transparency – his name is *Fear!* You wonder why you cannot hold down a job for longer than six months, or stay long enough to move up in the ranks. It is because of the giant called Fear.

Just like the ordinary, old, rundown car before it became a dynamic Transformer, you let the giant of Fear stop you from going where God wanted you to go and doing what He wanted you to do. If you are afraid that your old bald tires are going to blow out, or your old engine will burn out, you will avoid highway driving at all costs. God wanted to fast-track you in some areas of your life, but you were afraid to trust Him on the highway. Fear made you worry about the tires, the engine, the washer fluid, the fact that you only had a four-cylinder car, etc. You allowed the details to hold you back. You forgot that if God makes a way for you, He has already gone ahead of you and worked out every detail. God wanted to use you, but instead had to use someone else because you yielded your members to be controlled by a spirit of fear rather than by the Holy Spirit.

You served the god of fear when you allowed your life choices to be limited by the constricting boundaries dictated by this debilitating spirit, thus you failed to enter into the abundant life that God intended for you to enjoy. You became a stumbling block to your children and to your children's children – this is only giant number one. We've got six more to go! Don't be discouraged. You see, God wants you to know exactly what your issues are. He wants you to fully comprehend when, where and how you got to be in the sick mental condition that you are in, because knowledge is power. When you thoroughly know which giant you are going to fight, you know which scripture to use to annihilate it. You know at which gates to stand guard and you know which building materials to use in the reconstruction of those gates.

Does the Word of God not say that we perish for the lack of knowledge? A painter must know his canvas to know which brush or which tool to use on it to achieve a certain effect. A mechanic can know a car so well that all he has to do is hear a noise and without even getting up under the hood, he has already identified the problem and knows which tool to use to rectify it. A good cardiac specialist knows the heart so well that he can simply listen to it and know where there is trouble and thus what actions must be taken to remedy the condition. We, too, must know the giant that we are facing to skillfully use the Word of God against it.

It is in the very process of the battle against the giants, against those strongholds in our minds, that deliverance is achieved. We must be prepared to gird up the loins of our minds and face our giants. God has made available to us a certain grace to give us strength and to empower us to endure the process. "…for he knows how we are formed, he remembers that we are dust" (Ps. 103:14) and His grace is sufficient, for when we are weak, His strength is perfected in us (2 Cor. 12:9).

The coping mechanisms of denial, repression and dissociation, which we spoke about in chapter 17, all work against an individual's attempts to stay committed to the process, because all three of these methods of coping do not allow the individual to work out and work through the issues, but rather to find a way to escape. God is committed to repairing the breaches in our lives and maturing us in the faith, therefore, He insists that as adults we learn how to work things out. He insists that we solve our problems, not try to escape from them. However, working out our issues means a humbling of oneself must take place as the Holy Spirit begins to shine the light on areas in our lives where we have walked in error concerning the manner in which we have processed truth.

Traumatic experiences such as rape, molestation, physical and mental abuse, witnessing a brutal murder or some horrific tragic event are so dark and looming, so frightening, overwhelming and larger than life that the survivor of the trauma will often, but not always, have a tendency to speak in exaggerations when referring back to the event. This tendency to embellish will usually evolve into a serious character flaw. They may tell you that there were 300 people at church today, when in reality there were only 200. They may tell you that they witnessed a ten car pile-up on the interstate on the way to work, when in reality the fender-bender only involved two cars. This is also in part due to the fact that years of living in trauma has made them so accustomed to existing in shock mode that the mundane is not enough to satisfy their heightened senses. This is why many survivors of long-term trauma end up on drugs. They still need a high. This also accounts for the reason why some of the nicest people that you know seem to never be content unless there is some kind of drama going on in their lives. No one in their right mind wants to stay in a toxic relationship, but for these individuals, toxicity in relationships is familiar to them. It's all they know.

These are vital aspects of looking back – getting a clear understanding as to why you do and say certain things and behave in certain uncharacteristic ways. How and when did you start lying? How and when did you develop this need for drugs and alcohol? What made you, as a woman, become attracted to other women? When did it all start? It is important to discover and uncover the root. It is because of the hidden roots that many of us are still locked up behind the Enemy's gates. Moreover, in an atmosphere where abuse is present, lies are also present in abundance. "If they ask you at work what happened to your eye, just say that you bumped into a door." "If the teacher asks you what happened to your arm, tell her that you fell off your bed." "You'd better not tell anyone that I touched you or something bad will happen to you and to your mommy, your daddy, your grandpa and your little dog, too!" I said it earlier – lies beget lies.

Many adults who spent years, or most of their childhoods, in traumatizing or abusive surroundings where everything existed solely on the strength of a lie and their environment evolved from and was held together by a lie, may find it extremely difficult to see any benefit in truth. Since they themselves witnessed firsthand the power of a lie, having been held captive by it, controlled by it, stripped by it, shamed, humiliated and demoralized by it, they may find it easier to default to it as a means of exacting what they want from people and from this world. The Holy Spirit hovers over the darkness in their souls, longing and waiting for the opportunity to show them a better way. He desires to guide them down the path to truth. He wants to reveal to them that a lie is not their friend and that the only thing that has the power to set them free is God's truth. This is why, when we put on the full armor of God, we must never neglect to strap on that belt of truth (Eph. 6:13-14). When worn loosely, the Devil will strip it off of us and whip us with it. When worn securely, it has the power to set us free! All of this comes to us, this understanding, this illumination, this liberation, from a journey backwards.

When we come to know the power of God's truth to free us from every lie that the Enemy of our souls had sown into our minds when the gates were burned down, then we will prefer truth. When we come to know the power of God's truth to strip us of what we thought was a regal robe, but in God's eyes was nothing more than a tattered and raggedy cloak of deception, we will strive for truth. When a survivor of trauma realizes the power of God's truth to silence the stormy waters that rage over their troubled minds concerning every tormenting, unanswered question about their traumatized childhood, then will the covenant with the grave be annulled. Only then will they cease to lean upon a lie and to depend upon a lie as their most trusted power source. Isaiah 28:14-18 (NASB) says,

Because you have said, "We have made a covenant with death, and with Sheol we have made a pact. The overwhelming scourge will not reach us when it passes by. For we have made falsehood our refuge and have concealed ourselves with deception." Therefore thus says the LORD God, "Behold I am laying in Zion a stone, a tested stone, a costly cornerstone for the foundation, firmly placed. He who believes in it will not be disturbed. I will make justice the measuring line, and righteousness the level; then hail will sweep away the refuge of lies, and the waters will overflow the secret place. Your covenant with death will be canceled, and your pact with Sheol will not stand."

God loves us too much to let us dwell in error. He will shake the bed and pull the covers off of us so that we become extremely uncomfortable curling up with a lie. He wants us to prefer truth. Proverbs 16:6 says, "In mercy and truth, atonement is provided for iniquity." David prayed, "Teach me your way, O LORD, and I will walk in your truth" (Ps. 86:11). In His effort to deliver us from the stronghold of lies, God will give us wakeup calls, shaking us up and rattling us, but He will not force Himself upon us.

In Revelation 3:20 Jesus says, "Behold, I stand at the door and knock. If anyone hears my voice and opens the door, I will come in and dine with him, and he with Me" (NKJV). You've got to get the picture in your mind. When someone knocks on your door, it is up to you whether or not they get to come in. It is your house. You can choose to completely ignore the knock as if no one is even there – you know, give them the old *snub-er-roo* – or you can peek out the window to see who it is, then make your decision to let that person come in or stay outside. Whatever you decide, you are making a strong statement, both about yourself and about the one who is knocking. When Jesus is knocking, truth is knocking. You have got to ask yourself, "Am I ready for truth? Does truth get to come in today?"

The first truth that survivors of trauma must learn how to properly process is the truth about God. For them, many questions arose in their minds concerning God as they were being molested and abused. They have wondered, "If God is omnipresent, then where was He while I was being molested for seven years? If He was standing right there, then how could He say that He loved me but not rescue me?" The answers to these questions are not easy, however, the truth remains that God gave His only begotten Son for you and me and for all victims of injustice precisely because of His great love for us. Jesus willingly went to the cross and died for just such victims and He, too, was subjected to humiliation. He was abused mentally, emotionally, spiritually and physically. In all His sufferings He has identified with the sufferings of every victim of such heinous crimes committed against their personhood (John 3:16; Isa. 53; Heb. 4:14-16; Heb. 5:7-10).

The truth is that we live in a fallen world where people are greatly influenced by Satan and his demonic hosts. Injustices will occur on this earth daily and who knows whose turn it will be to suffer next, but Jesus does stand in the midst of our sufferings with us. When we suffer abuses, humiliation, tortures and torment, our Savior's heart is greatly grieved. As He wept at the tomb of Lazarus (John 11:35), so He weeps over us, so great is His love for us. The Holy Spirit comforts us when it seems that no one else cares and we feel that we cannot be comforted, for He has said, "I will not leave you comfortless: I will come to you" (John 14:18, KJV).

As He is there for the one who has suffered abuses, He is there for the heartbroken, comfortless mother sitting helplessly at the bedside of a precious child who is dying from cancer. He is there for that grief-stricken father who has just received word that his sixteen-year-old daughter was killed in a car accident by a drunken driver. He is there for that promising young athlete whose annual routine physical has just revealed that he has leukemia. He is there for the single mother of four children who, even though she has been working two jobs to make ends meet, has just received notice that her house is in foreclosure. The Holy Spirit is there for that fifty-year-old husband and father who was just laid off his job and He is there for the wife whose husband has left her for a younger woman after thirty years of marriage. In instances such as these, the one who is left holding the pain often accuses God of being "missing in action" when He was needed most. It is the love of God that holds us together whenever we undergo unbearable suffering.

Our God gives us the strength to endure and by His blood we overcome and are healed. By His love and grace we recover and our testimony of victory gives life and strength to another who must walk a similar road (Luke 22:31-32). However, the understanding of it all comes only when we, by faith, courageously accept the challenge to journey back to the place where our gates were seized by the Enemy. It is a necessary and worthwhile journey. You will only have to make the journey once and your world will be forever changed. This is all to God's glory.

Chapter 21

Delivered From Shame

"Instead of their shame my people shall receive a double portion, and instead of disgrace they will rejoice in their inheritance."

Isa.61:7a

"Where there is shame, there is also fear."

-John Milton

*T*he giant of Fear always has Shame as its traveling companion. Remembering my childhood, I vividly recall that when our dogs were mere pups, if ever one of them were to relieve itself on the carpet or the kitchen floor, my mother would look down at it contemptuously, shake her finger vigorously at the dog and exclaim, "Shame on you!" to which the cute little pup would lower its big, beautiful brown eyes, curl its tail between its legs and slink away to go and hide somewhere, in great shame.

Let me expose another area where demonic activity may occur for the individual whose mental gates were ransacked after having endured some sort of traumatizing abuse. The violation of these gates causes great shame for the survivors, often manifesting itself in feelings of anger, mean-spiritedness and fits of rage. These individuals will discover that feelings of shame will greatly hinder their ability to receive the grace needed to humble themselves as God points out the erroneous thought patterns in which they have been operating.

God is resourceful and creative. As He undertakes the great and wonderful task of restoring our broken places, in this case restoring the gate to the mind, He will use various scenarios, employing coworkers, family members, supervisors, church leadership and the like as irritants meant to flush out evil. Survivors of abuse may incorrectly discern the healing hand of God in such instances and erroneously interpret such activity as the Devil trying to come against them just to harass them or make them feel bad about themselves. This is a clear example of the battle still raging in the mind of one who has suffered abuses that result in humiliation and shame. In reality, it's simply God working saying, "Hey! You asked me to help you get rid of your evil attitude. Now these are the people and the scenarios that I have chosen to use to do just that!"

In his book *The Release of the Spirit,* Watchman Nee makes this observation, "Has the Lord for years disciplined us, but instead of recognizing His hand we blamed it on other people or on fate?

May we be reminded that *everything is measured by God for us*. He has predetermined its time, its boundary, and its force, in order to break our hard-to-deal-with outstanding feature."[48] Our own failure to recognize the marvelous hand of God will only serve to lengthen and delay the process of deliverance because we will fight tooth and nail, trying to avoid the dishonoring feelings of shame. We will miss God many times over, refusing to humble ourselves under His mighty hand that He might lift us up in due time (1 Pet. 5:6). Why? It is because humility feels too much like shame; but there is a difference.

A person who has been shamed has been dishonored, disgraced and humiliated. Webster defines "shame" as "to be stained or tarnished, and to have one's glory stripped away." A young boy or girl who has been molested carries the shame of that violation. Rape victims carry that shame, as do those who have been physically, verbally and emotionally abused over long periods of time. Shame leaves one feeling embarrassed and belittled, timid and fearful. One who has been shamed has had their self-esteem stripped from them, leaving them to wrestle with the lie that they are valued less than others, both in the eyes of man and God. Like my scolded dog, shame causes us to put our proverbial "tail between our legs" and hide all through life, preferring to stand behind the curtain of life, rather than to face the agony of being seen or heard. This suits the Devil just fine because he can now sit comfortably at the place of authority at our gates and decree whatever he wants over our lives.

He has our chair and he has our voice. He knows that we don't want either of them.

Acts committed against individuals that result in feelings of shame have forcibly humbled them without taking into consideration that they are persons of great value and worth, created in the image of God. Proverbs 18:3 reads, "When wickedness comes, so does contempt, and with shame comes disgrace." Indeed, the intent of Satan in causing any of us to be disgraced, or *dis-graced,* is to undo or dismantle the grace of God over our lives. He wants to snuff out all possibilities of us ever shining for Jesus and having the glory of God rest upon us. You see, grace lifts us, dignifies and beautifies us. God's grace shows up in our lives as His acts of benevolence, charity, mercy, kindness, favor, blessing and clemency bestowed upon us. He adorns us with His grace; however, violent and wicked men and women allow themselves to be used of the Devil to remove God's covering of grace from our lives. Indeed those very acts are committed by people who are selfish, cowardly, unfeeling and vicious; who care nothing about the value of their victims. Unless they repent and cry out for forgiveness, God will one day severely judge every such offender. Jesus says in Matthew 18:7 (NKJV), "Woe unto the world because of offenses, for offenses must come, but woe to that man by whom the offense comes!"

The goal of shame is to bring such destruction and imbalance into an individual's mental, spiritual and emotional makeup that they will never reach their full potential in life and ultimately, they will never fulfill their destiny in the kingdom of God. As He did for His only begotten Son, God wants to deliver us from shame and give us double for our trouble. He wants to give us a double anointing of power, a double anointing of faith, and a double anointing of grace and glory. As the Lord delivers us from shame, He gives us a richer, deeper understanding of the depths of His great love and compassion for us. In the process of deliverance, we experience firsthand the unmatched faithfulness of a God who will go to the ends of the earth to redeem us. You will often find that a person who has been shamed, but who sincerely desires to walk in the will of the Lord, will do public ministry with great fear, but they will do it. These are the ones who, in the words of Dr. Joyce Meyers, will "do it afraid!"

As Jesus Christ hung on the cross, He bore our sin *and* our shame. Hallelujah! Praise God! He became sin for us and has delivered us from the bondages of sin and shame by the power of His blood, which He shed for us. Hebrews 12:2 (NASB) tells us that, "For the joy set before him, he endured the cross, despising the shame." Because He endured such shame and humiliation for us, Philippians 2:9-10 tells us, "Therefore God has exalted him to the highest place and gave him the name that is above every name, that at the name of Jesus every knee should bow, in heaven and on earth and under the earth and every tongue confess that Jesus Christ is Lord to the glory of God the Father." Jesus took on our shame so that we could walk free from the devastating effects of shame and go on to fulfill our purpose in Him.

When the hand of God is upon us to humble us, in His great love for us God never forgets that we are the objects of His affection. He never forgets that we are His precious creation. He never forgets our delicate frame, that we are dust. When He stoops down to place His hand upon us to correct us, discipline us and to unbend the crooked places in our lives, He is firm, but gentle. In Habakkuk 3:2, the prophet cries out to God, leaning into His great compassion, "in wrath remember mercy." David declares, "Your gentleness has made me great" (2 Sam. 22:36, NKJV). God humbles us to teach us life lessons that are for our good and for His glory (Deut. 8:3; James 4:10). He reaches down to pull us up out of slimy pits, out of prisons and caves and dungeons and He sets our feet upon the high places (Hab.3:19). He is radically and passionately committed to abolishing every demonic power that stands in the way of our divine destiny in Him. It was God's mighty power working in David to destroy Goliath, but it was David who picked up the five stones and ran toward the giant to slay him.

When I was just a little girl in kindergarten, I too faced a Goliath. On that woeful day, my dad drove me to school. He had a very sweet and precious habit of either giving me a stick, or a whole pack of Wrigley's chewing gum whenever I would get sick to my stomach. On this particular day, as he dropped me off at school, I don't know if it was because he saw fear in my face or what it was that made him do it, but he handed me a pack of Wrigley's as I got out of the car. There was something about that gesture that made me feel warm and safe as I walked away from him and into the big school building. I didn't have my daddy to take to school with me, but I had the pack of gum that he had given to me and that seemed to suffice for the time being.

As the day wore on in school, I recall sitting in the classroom and having a full bladder, but being too afraid to ask the teacher if I could be excused to go to the restroom. The teacher was leading a song about some frightened little rabbit that was fleeing the presence of a mean old hunter out looking to make a succulent, hot rabbit roast. Eventually, the frightened little rabbit found refuge in the cottage of a kindly old man. All the children's voices were lifted up in song, filling the atmosphere with the words that told of a scared little animal's flight for life. It was a song that I never liked singing. When I finally raised my hand to ask permission to go, it was too late. I had already had an accident. Embarrassed, I exited the classroom and went to the little girl's room, but it was an ugly, scary bathroom to me. The song that we had just finished singing certainly didn't help much to calm my fears either. The gray, cement walls seemed to be too high and they looked awfully cold. The stalls seemed way too big and tall for a tiny little girl like me.

Standing there, in the middle of the scary, horrid looking bathroom, I suddenly remembered the pack of gum that my daddy had given to me. Something about having that pack of gum from my daddy made me feel happy and safe again. I suppose the gum helped me to feel connected to him as I stood in that intimidating place, all alone. I put my hand in my pocket to pull out the pack of gum. I unwrapped a stick and ate it. Just then, to my horror, there stood a very tall and very big girl—my Goliath! She had been watching me eat the stick of gum. She threatened to beat me up and tell the teacher that I had the gum if I did not give her, not one stick, but the entire pack of gum.

I'd like to be able to say that I felled Goliath with a swift kick in the shin and that I ran off victoriously, still clutching the four remaining sticks of gum in my hand. Unfortunately, I have no such heroic story to tell of having conquered my Goliath that day. She scared me, so out of respect for Fear, I reluctantly gave her all but the one stick of gum that I had managed to put in my mouth before she could get to it. It would take many more encounters with various Goliaths down through the years before I was able to overcome my own giants of Fear and Shame. Admittedly, there are times when I still have to wrestle with Fear, but not nearly to the degree that I have in years past.

Because of His great love for us, our Abba Father does not want His dear children enslaved to shame and fear or to any such power that threatens to keep us out of the center of His will. The center of the will of God is where our joy lies, but more importantly, it is the place where God gets the most glory out of our lives. For us to get to that centered place in God, we have to be willing to fight for our destiny. We cannot be too afraid to pick up some stones and throw them at the Enemy, nor claim to be too weak to push some stones out of our way. We must not allow shame to corner us into a debili-tating place of cowardice and underachievement. God empowers us to slay those giants that come to back us into a corner, hinder our progress and to steal our joy (and our gum), but we must be willing to do our part by arming ourselves and hastening to the battle. Most certainly Jesus wept at the tomb of Lazarus, and had purposed to raise him from the dead, but still He said, "Take *ye* away the stone" (John 11:39, KJV).

In humbling us, or in His exhortations to us to humble ourselves, it is never the will of God to destroy us. It is solely our resistance to His touch – aimed at breaking the back of pride, selfishness and rebellion in our lives – that causes us to self-destruct. When we choose to humble ourselves, we will discover that this humility is different from shame in that it embodies (not discounts) every aspect of who we are in Christ, including our uniqueness, our personhood, value, worth and esteem. Having thus considered, this humbling of oneself then chooses to submit all of itself to another person or situ-ation for the greater good, just like that small kernel of wheat that falls to the ground and dies to produce many seeds (John 12:23-28).

In Christ, we see a picture of this type of humility in His struggle in Gethsemane's garden (Matt. 26:36-42). Jesus's choice to humble Himself and be obedient, even to His own death on the cross, was mandated by His knowledge of who He was and by His under-standing of His mission. He chose to be true to His mission for our benefit. In so doing, He opened the gates to eternal life for us to enter. Paul speaks of the humility of Christ in Philippians 2:3-14. In this very scripture, he exhorts us to work out our salvation with fear and trembling through the God-given grace of humility. We work it out with humility, not under the bondages of shame and humiliation.

Some of the most anointed and gifted people I know are those who have endured years of tremendous shame and humiliation. They are highly gifted and anointed because they have brought their garments of shame and humiliation to the feet of Jesus and in exchange, He has given them robes of grace and glory. In their affliction, they did not point the finger of blame *at* God, but rather it was *to* Him that they came for healing, for cleansing and for the reconstruction of their gates. In Isaiah 54:11-12 we read, "O afflicted city, lashed by storms and not comforted, I will build you with stones of turquoise, your foundations with sapphires. I will make your battlements of rubies, your gates of sparkling jewels, and all your walls of precious stones." This is God's promise to us, that out of the depths of His great love and concern for us, He will fortify us and strengthen us who have endured great trials. He will make our walls and gates strong and beautiful. He will reestablish us in "righteousness" (v. 14). These are the children of God whom we call "survivors." They have been to hell and back. They have learned how to wage war in the spirit realm. Having regained their voices and reclaimed their positions of authority and visibility at the gates, they are now formidable foes against the Enemy. They are Satan's worst nightmare. In the hands of God, they are some of His sharpest and most powerful weapons. When we, as God's dear children, suffer disgrace or are dishonored and made to feel embarrassed and unworthy by our cruel Adversary, we have this assurance from Abba Father, "Instead of their shame my people will receive a double portion" (Isa. 61:7). God will make good out of the evil that Satan visits upon our lives and will give us double for our trouble.

Shame leads to disgrace and leaves us feeling that there is nothing in us that is worthy of redemption. Humility leads to honor. The ability to properly distinguish between the two will mean the difference between being forever wedged in what was our soiled past and advancing to regain our rightful positions of authority at the gates. Humility is a vital building material in the reconstruction of our gates.

Chapter 22

Where Are You Headed?
(Dealing with the Wall)

"Now the Angel of the LORD found her by a spring of water in
the wilderness, by a spring on the way to Shur, and He said,
'Hagar, Sarai's maid, where have you come from, and where
are you going?'" Gen. 16:7-8 (NKJV)

"Character cannot be developed in ease and quiet. Only through experience of trial and suffering can the soul be strengthened, vision cleared,
ambition inspired, and success achieved."

-Helen Keller

A few years back, while attending seminary, I wrote a paper
titled *"Where Have You Come From and Where Are You
Going?"* In it I dealt with the plight of the African-American community in the 21st century. I built my thesis around the powerful
scripture taken from Genesis 16:7-8, presenting the line of rea-

soning that it is impossible for any people to know where they are going until they thoroughly examine and gain an understanding of the path or paths that have led them to where they now stand. It is a veritable truth that one cannot know where he is headed until he knows from whence he has come.

To some extent, we can probably all see some aspect of ourselves in the life of the young servant girl of Genesis 16 named Hagar, the mistress of Abram and maidservant to Sarai. Hagar is given to Abram by Sarai, Abram's wife, to conceive the child that Sarai believes will fulfill the prophecy from Genesis 15. However, once Hagar conceives, Sarai begins to mistreat her and to deal with her harshly, believing that Hagar now despises her. We catch up with Hagar in verse 8, who is now on the run and taking a breather from her flight by a spring of water in the desert on the way to *Shur*, which in Hebrew means "a wall."[49] "And the Angel of the LORD found her by a spring of water in the wilderness, by a spring on the way to Shur, and He said, 'Hagar, Sarai's maid, where have you come from, and where are you going?'"

One of the first things we notice in Hagar's encounter with the Holy One at the wall is that He challenges her to know herself, to remember who she is. She is Sarai's maid. She is a servant to royalty. If she could just remember who she is, she would also remember where she came from and what she has been called to do. If she could just remember who she is, all it would take is one look at where she is now, pregnant with promise, yet with her feet planted in the middle of a desert and she would immediately know that she was out of place. However, with her mind under attack, Hagar could only respond, "I am running away…"

She stands in the hot desert, a servant to royalty, but lost; pregnant with promise, but dry; on the verge of a breakthrough, but without a vision to see it. She has run full face into the wall that will not be ignored. It is so high, so deep and so wide that the only way she will be allowed to continue on her journey is to stop and deal with that wall. She is running away, but from what and to what? In truth, it is not really Sarai that she is running away from, but how could she possibly know that when she doesn't even have a sense of who she is or from where she has come?

Like Hagar, we too find ourselves on the run after a barrage of attacks upon our self-esteem has rendered us mentally incapable of continuing along the path that God has marked out for us. Without a renewed mind, we will find ourselves going through the motions of ministry, feeling nothing, but claiming to be doing God's work. We will find ourselves dry, thirsty, visionless and lost, unless and until we allow the Holy Spirit to renew our minds. Many of us will just give up, drop out of the race and become desert nomads if we deny the Holy Spirit His rights at that pivotal place along our journeys called the wall.

We see a similar scenario played out in the scripture found in Numbers 22:23-26. Here we read:

When the donkey saw the angel of the LORD standing in the road with a drawn sword in his hand, she turned off the road into a field. Balaam beat her to get her back on the road. Then the angel of the LORD stood in a narrow path between two vineyards, with walls on both sides. When the donkey saw the angel of the LORD, she pressed close to the wall, crushing Balaam's foot against it. So he beat her again. Then the angel of the LORD moved on ahead and stood in a narrow place where there was no room to turn, either to the right or to the left.

In the passage of scripture above, Balaam, a sorcerer by trade, was being used by God to deliver a message to the wicked Moabites. However, Balaam had a character flaw that perverted his purpose as he journeyed to deliver God's message – he was a greedy man. Though God had strictly warned him to do only what He told him to do, He could see that Balaam's greed was starting to surface and become a motivating factor on his journey to Moab. God used the donkey to halt his journey as he smashed Balaam's foot against the wall, refusing to go another step. There at the wall, Balaam had an encounter with God. The Angel of the LORD informed Balaam that had his donkey not stopped him by crushing his foot against the wall, He surely would have killed Balaam and spared the donkey. Balaam was only allowed to continue on the journey after he considered his ways and repented of the evil that was revealed in his heart.

This same scenario is played out over and over again in our lives when we neglect the condition of our gates. Each time we feel that we have advanced to some long-coveted mile marker along our journey in life, be it in our marriage, our vocation, interpersonal relationships or in ministry, we will invariably hit a wall and try as we may, we can go no further. Frustrated, we will lash out at whatever we perceive to be the thing or the person keeping us from making progress. The very fact that we lash out in fits of violence and rage at innocent people in our lives is only further evidence that something within us is very wrong and needs correcting. We blame the dog, the cat, our parents, our second grade math teacher, the ex, the children, the boss and the pastor when we hit the walls along our journeys. We will put the blame on anything and everything outside of ourselves. Rarely do we take the time to stop and look inward to discover the real reason for the barriers along our pathway to divine purpose

In reality, the holdup is twofold. One part is self-will; the other part is the will of the Lord. We want what we want when we want it, despite the fact that we are fully aware that we do not have the character or the integrity to maintain it and despite the fact that we are fully aware that we have gates that are in desperate need of repair. God simply will not allow us to continue to go merrily along without taking time out to deal with the wall.

That wall has been divinely placed smack dab in the middle of our paths to force us to stop and consider our journey. It is at the wall where, if we will humble ourselves through repentance and allow Him, God will reconstruct our character. He knows that if He allows us to achieve greatness, power and riches without godly character, and authority without integrity, that one of two things will occur: either we will fall, hurting ourselves and others (and great will be that fall), or we will succeed in gaining the world while losing our very souls. Just look at what happened to Judas. Those thirty pieces of silver seemed like a small fortune to him at first, but once he came to his senses, it was too late – the damage had already been done. When he realized that he had betrayed the Son of God, he cast the blood money to the ground and in anguish of soul, he went and hanged himself. He will forever be known to the world as Judas, the betrayer (Matt. 26:46-49; 27:3-10). We must be thankful to our Lord that He knows our journey from beginning to end and is therefore waiting for us at the wall.

I have encountered the Lord at the wall more than once along my journey. After my divorce, more than twenty years ago, I found myself wrestling with the spirit of rage. Years and years of pent up anger dating back to my childhood, years of shame and fear, of anxiety and disappointment in life, of not understanding why God had allowed life to mishandle me so, and of unanswered prayers for deliverance from all of the above had begun to seep out sideways. Although I was never physically or verbally abusive to my two children, they were always with me whenever I went ballistic on perfect strangers in public establishments, so they were always subjected to humiliation simply by their association with me. The best way I can describe the spiritual atmosphere that surrounded me is to simply say that it was highly agitated.

In his book *The Way of the Heart,* Henri Nouwen states that "there are two main enemies of the spiritual life, one is greed; the other is anger. They are the sour fruits of our worldly dependencies. What else is anger than the impulsive response to the experience of being deprived?" [50] If ever I felt, as a customer, I was not being given the kind of service I believed I deserved, whether I was in a restaurant, grocery store, movie theater, mechanic shop, furniture store, school, utility company, bank, or anywhere where public servants had the unfortunate opportunity of serving me, baby, somebody was going to pay! Proverbs 16:32 (NASB) says, "He who is slow to anger is better than the mighty. And he who rules his spirit than he who captures a city."

In all my anger and rage, I thought I was exhibiting strength by using harsh angry words and by being demanding. Don't get me wrong: I was never profane and I never attacked the person for who they were, but my words were harsh concerning the service that I received from them. My attitude was unkind and without consideration for the feelings of the one with whom I voiced my complaint. I genuinely thought that I was "handling my business" by not allowing anyone to treat me poorly simply because I was a woman alone. In truth, I was only showing the world and my children how truly weak and incapable I was of controlling my own spirit. I was telling the world that I was afraid and showing my children how to be a true public fool.

Most times, once my angry outbursts were over and I had managed to get the respect, attention, treatment, or whatever it was that I felt I was being deprived of, I would feel ashamed somewhere way down deep in my spirit. The very next day I would go back to the establishment where I had given vent to my anger to seek out the poor person with whom I had behaved like a mad woman. I would then apologize profusely for my behavior, giving some feeble excuse about having had a rough day, in an attempt to justify my ugliness, but I knew that when I walked away, they still saw me as a fool.

That painful season of my life, marked by such intense rage, was filled with great distress for me because the one thing that I always strove for was to live a life characterized by peace. Peace was something I was desperate for and whenever I reacted so unseemly it was to me like an out-of-body experience that would leave me physically shaken. However, as much as I desired peace, I seemed to have been unable to rule my spirit when I felt disrespected or deprived of my rights. I have often thought that had I been old enough during the Civil Rights Movement, I would have been front and center in the cause, spending half of the movement marching with Dr. King and half with Brother Malcolm. Dr. King would have had to teach me how to exercise more passive resistance, but Brother Malcolm would have, undoubtedly, allowed me to go full throttle!

You see, all of my attempts to manage the world around me proved to be futile, seeing as how I had absolutely no control over the perception that people had of me once I left their presence following one of my abusively brash tirades. Try as I might to justify my behavior, what I really wanted was the empowering to get a grip, but I felt absolutely ill-equipped to do so. I could not change my thought processes. The gate to my mind had been violated long ago in my childhood years. I was a victim then and apparently, as a grown woman now with children of my own, I was still thinking, acting and responding as a victim. Always, I would cringe at the thought of having to go back and look that person in the eyes and apologize, but it was not my idea to apologize. It was the Holy Spirit's idea. Because I desperately wanted to be delivered of this spirit of uncontrolled rage, I humbled myself, repented before God of my ungodly behavior and obediently submitted to His instructions. In my heart, I knew God was disciplining me and that by His Spirit He was leading me to freedom.

These ugly outbursts of rage characterized my behavior for many years until one day, with my two little ones in tow, I was headed back to the store to return a product that did not meet my satisfaction. By now, my children, knowing the routine all too well, said to me, "Mommy, please be calm this time." Being somewhat surprised at the plea, I asked them why they would have said such a thing. "Because when you get mad like that, it's embarrassing to us," they replied. Hearing their reply, my heart sank. All this time I thought I was showing them that I could stand up for myself and that their mommy was not going to let anyone take advantage of "us" as a family just because there was no man accompanying us. I never dreamed that I was causing them so much embarrassment. Next to God, my children meant the world to me, so when I realized that I was hurting them I knew that I had to change my behavior.

In addition to now knowing that my behavior was damaging to my children, I also knew that the Bible says, "Whoever causes one of these little ones who believe in me to sin, it would be better for him if a millstone were hung around his neck, and he were drowned in the depth of the sea" (Matt. 18:6, NASB). Never one to play with God's Word, I became desperate to be right with both God and my children. This marked the beginning of the transformation process in my life. I knew that the only one who could change my behavior was God, by the power of His Spirit, and by the power of His Word.

The Holy Spirit took me on a three-year journey through God's Word, directing me to scriptures that dealt with the feelings of offense that led me to harbor rage, anger, bitterness, and lack of forgiveness in my heart. He then began to teach me about God's mercy, forgiveness and love for me and to impress upon my heart the need for me to extend the same to my offenders. He showed me how to identify the giants within me and how to face them and to do combat with them using His Holy Word as my most effective weapon of war. Because He is the Spirit of Truth, He led me to the truth about my ugly inner self. He skillfully showed me how to take a scripture such as Proverbs 16:32 and walk it out, eat it, live it and breathe it day in and day out until I was completely wrapped up in it, bathed in it, immersed in it and ultimately delivered and changed by it. The process was so intense that I felt I literally became that word, just as Paul says we are to become "living epistles" (2 Cor. 3:3), personifications of the Word of God, living letters. People need to be able to read us and see Jesus, read us and see the Word of God in action, read us and see the way out of darkness. In the process of my own deliverance, I came to understand that it is impossible to have good, sound, durable gates without having the Word of God woven throughout every other material that is used.

It was nothing short of the Word of God that ultimately delivered me from the angry, raging thoughts that controlled my actions for many years. His Word delivered my mind into peace by bringing enlightenment and understanding into the root causes of my anger, which, in actuality, stemmed from a traumatized childhood that left me feeling unprotected and threatened. The entrance of His Word brought light to me just as Psalm 119:130 says it will. I learned that my own anger was aroused in direct response to a real or perceived threat. That understanding empowered me to act and to react to unpleasant or threatening situations with wisdom, rather than uncontrolled, foolish rage – birthed from a troubled past and fueled by ignorance. Undiagnosed, I was constantly misfiring, shooting at phantoms of the real issues because I was simply unaware of what the real underlying issues were. The power of the Word of God peeled back layers of ignorance, just as Hebrews 4:12 says: "… dividing soul and spirit, joints and marrow," discerning the thoughts and intentions of my heart. I definitely came to the conclusion that without the Word of God woven throughout my gates, I was wasting my time trying to rebuild them. We must rebuild on God's Word if we want a firm foundation for our gates.

In the reconstruction of my own gates, the Lord helped me to establish new, healthy boundaries designed to ward off threats. Part of my responsibility and challenge in the reconstructive work was to learn how to walk in deeper levels of love and compassion for God's people, since for so long I had avoided people because people brought threatening behaviors with them. By the power of His Spirit, God helped me to develop new fruit. One primary fruit that He helped me cultivate in the garden of my mind was gentleness. I had to learn how to be gentle with those who I felt were depriving me of something I deserved. Everyone needs gentleness and kindness extended to them. This world can be a very cruel and maddening place. Gentleness is a grace, which if applied, can soften the cruel blows of life.

I had to learn how to not be so hard on myself as well. When the world has been imperfect and out of control for survivors of abuse, who often blame themselves for being the target of their abuser's rage, the neurotic behavior known as perfectionism develops. The thought process of an abused or traumatized child is, "If I can just be perfect enough and not cause anyone any trouble, then they won't get mad at me. By being perfectly good, I can stop the madness." Even as an adult I continued to try to be perfect and to make the world a perfect place. It took me a while, but after years and years of frustration over my own inability to be perfect and to make the world perfect, I finally came to the realization that I had become entangled in a losing battle.

My bend towards perfectionism had its roots in the spirit of fear. The Holy Spirit delivered me from this fear by revealing God's truth to me that my life was securely positioned in the perfect love of my heavenly Father. He reminded me that I no longer had to fear the punishment I believed would ensue as a result of my inability to hold all things together. Jesus had already taken on my punishment and all things were held together by Him (Isa. 53; Col. 1:16, 17), not me. I learned how to lighten up on myself and to trust in the finished work of Calvary to set me free from the Enemy's stronghold. Gentleness became another vital building material for me as I did battle to regain possession of the gate to my mind.

As I radically obeyed God in this work, I saw my old rickety, wooden gate come down, and a new, stronger, functional gate go up. 1 John 4:18 reads, "There is no fear in love. But perfect love drives out all fear, because fear has to do with punishment. The one who fears is not made perfect in love." This was one of several scriptures the Holy Spirit directed me to meditate upon on many occasions as He worked to rebuild my gates.

The Word of God can swallow up the old us and completely transform us into new creations if we will apply it and allow it. In my own journey to wholeness, God's Word clearly gave me insight into where I had come from, where I was in the present moment and where it was that He had purposed to take me. In studying Hebrews 4:12, we come to understand that God's anointed Word is alive! It is breathing, moving and active. God's Word is acting on our behalf to separate all the confusing puzzle pieces of our lives so that we can look at them and understand them as distinct pieces, in and of themselves, yet also understand how they fit together and influence every other part of the whole puzzle. His Word divides soul and spirit, joint and marrow and has the ability to distinguish between what we are thinking and what we really purpose, or intend in our hearts. This is such good news because even when we are messed up, God hears the deepest cry of our hearts to be made whole, to be healed and to be like Him. He sends His Word to rescue us from the pit of sin and despair, even though we do not even fully understand what we are asking to be delivered from. Glory to God! His understanding has no boundaries. It is limitless.

We all need a seemingly ill-timed wall placed strategically along our paths. It is at the wall where the Holy Spirit, the Spirit of Truth meets us, just as He did Balaam and just as He did Hagar, to conduct an inspection of our fruit. Even though we may be spiritually pregnant, operating in ministry, preaching, teaching and being used by God to minister to His body, the Lord exercises His right to inspect our fruit. Though everyone else is convinced that we are the real deal (and we may very well be, just in need of some fine-tuning) the Lord comes to conduct His own inspection. He says, "I see you and I know you." Though no one else can smell our rottenness or taste our bitterness, the Holy Spirit waits for us at the wall of inspection and challenges us to remember who and whose we really are. He challenges us to get better and to do better. He lets us know that no matter where and what we have come from, no matter how low the place from whence we have come, in Him we can be more than that – whatever *that* may be.

We are servants to royalty; ambassadors to the King of Kings and the LORD of Lords (2 Cor. 5:20). We are not our own, but have been purchased with the precious blood of the spotless Lamb of God (1 Cor. 6:19, 20). He chose us in Christ before the foundation of the world (Eph. 1:4). We did not choose ourselves, but rather God chose us to go and bear fruit that will last (John 15:16). Therefore, we do not have the liberty to think that we can disregard our broken, burned down, violated walls and gates and simply run away from our destinies. God, who is the Author and Finisher of our faith, will call us to account. At the wall, He will call us to stand in the midst of His flames as He burns everything off of us that fails to pass His inspection. He will polish us up and finish us off just like silver is refined in the crucible and like gold is tried in the fire.

Hagar had an epiphany after her inspection was complete. She came to realize that she had allowed her very name to dictate her character, for her name means *flight*. When the trials of life had overwhelmed her, rather than standing and facing her giants, Hagar chose the path of least resistance and ran away. In so doing, Hagar missed opportunities that would have served to mature her and to develop her character beyond the mere definition of her name. Though others may not have known that she was fearful and lacking in faith, the Holy One could see past the fact that she was pregnant with a promise and into the depths of her trembling heart. Indeed, it was the Lord who gave her the promise, so He challenged her to stop running and face herself. He challenged her to address her deep-seated character flaw and for her own good, He gave her this command, "Go back to your mistress and submit to her." Hagar could clearly see that God had the 411, not only on her, but on the whole situation. His eyes always see the bigger picture. To her credit, she did not bring excuses or place blame, but in verse 13 we read, "As Hagar responded, she gave this name to the LORD who spoke to her: 'You are the God who sees me,' for she said, 'I have now seen the One who sees me.'" That name is *El-Roi*, "The God who sees me."

Before Hagar had ever become Sarai's servant, she was a runner; she knew it and God knew it. Before she had become pregnant with Abram's seed, before Sarai became jealous of her, before one harsh, abusive word proceeded from Sarai's lips to Hagar, before she hit the trail that morning, running from a bad situation, Hagar had been a runner and she would have continued to run had she not had that blessed encounter at the wall with the One Who Sees into us all. It was her day of visitation; because she recognized it and submitted to it, her character was changed, thus she was able to birth a nation.

God wants no less for each of us than that we fulfill our destinies in Him. It is in fulfilling our destinies that we bring Him the most glory. Jesus said to His Father in John 17:4, "I have brought you glory on earth by completing the work you gave me to do." Jesus was able to cross that finish line victoriously because He knew who He was and He knew where He was headed, therefore Satan was unable to hinder His path. In John chapter 8, Jesus declares Himself to be "the light of the world." Immediately, the Pharisees remind Him that *the rules* state that if a man bears witness of himself, that man's witness is considered worthless and untrue. However, because Jesus knows who He is, He understands that He is the *exception* to the rule; therefore, He gives the Pharisees this response: "Even if I bear witness of Myself, My witness is true, for I know where I came from, and where I am going" (John 8:12-14, NKJV).

In Romans 8:19, we read that even creation groans in eager expectation for the "sons of God" to be revealed. These are the children of God whose gates have been strengthened. They walk in the power and the authority of God. They understand their purpose in God here on the earth and they are determined to bring glory to God by completing the work that God has given them to do.

Who are the sons of God? They are spirit-filled pastors and politicians, business owners, doctors and lawyers, judges and jurors, school teachers and housewives. They are farmers and husbands, mothers and fathers. They are RAs in college dormitories, journalists, editors and moviemakers. They are psychologists and counselors, financiers, athletes, musicians, poets, actors, artists, and photographers and they are all ages, male and female and consist of all nationalities from all walks of life. They stand and sit at the main entrances to the gates of the cities and they control the traffic of both the natural and the spiritual highways and airways.

Every time we move in the direction of radical obedience to our God, we get to take possession of another one of the Enemy's gates. Can you imagine what our world will look like once we, the sons and daughters of God, have captured the gates of our Enemy and regained possession of our own gates? Can you imagine how different the music we listen to would sound if the sons of God had control at the gates to the music industry, or how television programming would change? What we see at the local theater would look very different, as would every magazine rack if the sons of God occupied the seats at those gates. How different would the school curriculum and the information superhighway be? Marriages would be different. Governments and even our churches would operate differently if we, the children of God, would walk in the kind of radical obedience that would allow us to sit in the high places at the gates originally designated for us, the priests, prophets, kings and queens of the Most High God.

It is the heart and the intent of God to grant us complete healing and complete restoration of our gates, but we must also be willing to give God our complete obedience. We are empowered to operate in authority to punish every act of disobedience once our obedience has been completed (2 Cor. 10:6). Jehoash, king of Israel, learned this the hard way when he went down to see the prophet Elisha concerning his ensuing battle with the king of Aram. When Elisha told him to take an arrow and strike the ground, Jehoash only struck the ground three times and stopped. Elisha became angry with him and told him that he should have struck the ground "five or six times; then you would have defeated Aram and completely destroyed it. But now you will defeat it only three times" (2 Kings 13:18-19). This is only one of many scriptures and stories throughout the Bible that drives home the fact that God's instructions require our complete obedience if we desire to walk in the fullness of His plan for our lives. When we fall short of complete obedience, we subject ourselves to some very serious consequences, one of which is our own defeat.

Where you see mention in the Old Testament of a wall or gate being torn down by an enemy, it was a sure indication that a people had been disgraced. A broken down wall or gate left the people behind it exposed to danger and defenseless against future attacks from their enemy (2 Kings 14:13-14). Our failure to guard our gates has been to our disgrace. The violation of our gates has been to our shame and to our disgrace. Years of trying to do life with our walls and gates broken down have left us exposed to repeated attacks and invasion by our Adversary to the point where we no longer even know that we were meant to operate as prophets, priests, kings and queens, to take and maintain dominion of the earth.

Many of us have gotten used to being robbed by the Devil. In some instances, we see him creeping in and out of our gates with our things and we say absolutely nothing! We have gotten used to being stripped, raped, violated, and reduced. We have grown numb to the attacks of our Adversary. We have lowered our expectations to the point where we are afraid to even invest in anything worthy of a king, priest, prophet, or queen for fear that we will lose it anyhow through an unguarded gate. We have allowed the Devil to beat us down and minimize us so, until our confidence in our ability to hold onto and build upon the riches that are befitting an heir and joint-heir of the Son of God is all but gone. I declare that the Devil is a liar! The sons and daughters of God are, even now, being positioned to rise up and regain possession of their gates and take back by force everything that rightfully belongs to them and to their children!

When David and his mighty fighting warriors returned to Ziklag and discovered that the Amalekites had stolen all of their precious possessions, women and children included, they went in hot pursuit of the enemy. The biblical account tells us that when David and his men came upon the enemy, they "fought them from dusk until the evening of the next day" (1 Sam. 30:17). This is exactly how we must respond to the Enemy's thefts in our lives. It is not okay that he has stormed our gates and raided our territory! It is not okay that the Devil and his posse have run off with our possessions! We need to let the Devil know that, not just by our words, but by the actions that we take against him and his kingdom.

David and his warriors fought with everything they had to take back everything they lost, and the Word of God wonderfully records for us that "David recovered *everything* the Amalekites had taken, including his two wives. Nothing was missing: young or old, boy or girl, plunder or anything else they had taken. David "brought everything back" (vv.18-19). We, too, have to be ready to tell the Devil that we are coming after him, in the name of Jesus, to take back everything that he has stolen – if it takes us all night and all the next day, or all year, we will fight him until we have regained possession of everything that we discovered has been missing. We will not give up on our children. We will not give up on our spouses. We will not give up on, or abandon, our incarcerated loved ones to an unjust penal system. We will not give up on evangelizing the lost. We will not give up on our churches, our schools, our communities or our government. We must let the Devil know that we will not give up or give in until we see him running off empty-handed!

My pastor recently preached from this passage of scripture, pointing out that David was largely to blame for the catastrophe of Ziklag because when he left Ziklag, taking all the men with him, he left the women and children completely uncovered. In his sermon, Dr. Vernon articulates that, although David grieved with the rest of the men over their losses and his losses, in his heart he realized that he had made a grave error in leaving the camp uncovered. In so doing, he allowed the enemy to come in unopposed and wreak havoc. It was the word "unopposed" that caught my attention.

Doesn't Ephesians 6:12 say that we "wrestle" against principalities, powers, rulers of darkness and spiritual wickedness in high places? We wrestle, *we fight, we resist, we brawl, contend, struggle,* but to let the Enemy come in unopposed is completely uncharacteristic of a true wrestler. It is clear that God expects us to engage our Adversary in the warfare. In this tragic oversight, the men blamed David too and threatened to stone him. However, David "strengthened himself in the LORD" (v. 6) and got busy with a plan to "confront the enemy" concerning the theft.

In verse 11, we read where David's men found one of the enemy's Egyptian slaves lying in a field, left there by his own master to die. This slave had taken ill and was no longer of any use to his owner. God used this man to lead David straight to the location of the Amalekites. How does this story translate for us? Simply put, it means that even when we have lost possession of our things through a gate that we have unwittingly left unguarded, if God gave us those things, they are rightfully ours and God will be with us if we will only go in passionate pursuit of them. If it is God's will that we recover all, He will even use members of the opposing side to lead us to the holes and caves where the Devil has hidden our property. He will surely empower us to go behind Enemy lines and recover all!

As David and his mighty men set out to return to Ziklag, his men drove the flocks and herds ahead of them that they had recovered from the enemy, as well as the livestock that they had seized from them. David's men were saying, "This is David's plunder!" How rich is that? Not only did David bring back everything that the enemy had stolen from him, but he also took possession of the property of his enemies, which they had most likely stolen from someone else. Remember, everything that the Devil has in his possession is stolen property to which he is not entitled!

In verse 21, we read that there were two hundred warriors who had stayed behind and had not entered the battle because they had been too weak to continue the pursuit of the enemy. As we go in pursuit of our possessions, if God directs us to take possession of the Enemy's things, then we need to take possession without hesitation! God may be using us, who are stronger in battle, to recover stolen property from the Devil on behalf of a brother or sister who has not had the strength to pursue. His promise to Abraham was that obedience was the key that empowered him to take possession of the gates of his enemies. The blessings of Abraham have become our inheritance. Our obedience to the voice of our God will likewise empower us to regain possession of our gates and the gates of our Enemy. As we make our boast in the Lord Who has helped us, we, too will be able to boldly and victoriously declare: "This is my plunder!"

The magnitude of the things that we have lost by way of unguarded gates is staggering. As children of God, our position in Christ alone means that we are heirs to the abundant riches of His kingdom. Many of us have never even walked in any of the power and authority that our Father has intended for us to walk in. It is sad, but true that most of us have not yet come to fully know the significance of our spiritual identity in Christ and Satan fears the day we do.

Final Thoughts

A few years back, my pastor preached a sermon from Genesis 27 that dealt with the importance of a child having the father's blessing. Coming from two angles, he spoke of the blessing of our heavenly Father, as well as the blessing of our earthly fathers. As I sat and listened to that message, the Holy Spirit moved upon my heart to secure my earthly father's blessing. I remember thinking to myself: *Shouldn't the blessing go to one of my brothers? After all, I am the sixth of seven children, next to the last. Of the five preceding me, four of them are men.* However, the prompting from the Holy Spirit would not leave me. Being somewhat fearful, I decided to go to my father and secure his blessing. Furthermore, I had told the Lord that I would do whatever He directed me to do in the process of rebuilding my gates.

The day that I went to my father's house to ask him for his blessing was a turning point in my relationship with him. Yes, he had been the source of a lot of my childhood trauma. During my childhood, my dad was dealing with his own demons that manifested in outbursts of rage. Though he never laid a finger on me in an abusive manner, the spirit that fueled his rage entered my gates and held me captive at the very core of who I was. I became its prisoner, hook, line and sinker. Someone could have called out from across a crowded room, "Hey Fearful, come here!" and I would have responded with, "Be right there!" That is just how fast I was held in its grip.

I spent my childhood absolutely adoring my dad, but at the same time, I was scared to death of him in an unhealthy way. I was afraid of the rage and the damage that that rage could do. It was an unpredictable spirit. Still, to me, my dad was the prophet, priest, and king of our family. I believe that my dad did the best he could as a father and a husband, given his own life experiences and the tools with which he had to work. I also believe that somewhere in his childhood his gates had also been violated in some significant way. There are chapters to the book of his life, written with the finger of God, that I will never get to read, but God knows. Even at the writing of this book, my dad's gates, at the age of eighty-two, are yet in the process of reconstruction. Glory to God! I am always encouraged, whenever my dad and I have our occasional chats, in that I get to see the grace of a loving Savior being applied to his life.

While I recognize the effect that the spirit of rage had upon me as a child, I do not hold my father responsible for any of the misguided choices that I made as a young adult. I also believe that the Holy Spirit used my ability to yet see my dad as *His anointed* to get a directive to me to seek his blessing. It would have been impossible for me to receive such a Word from God without the honor that I still maintained for him in my heart.

The look in my father's eyes when I petitioned him for his blessing seemed to say, "You really want a blessing from *me*?" Yes, I absolutely wanted his blessing! Fear was one of the main giants in my land. To me, the giant was my enemy. As an adult, I knew that my dad was not my enemy, but the little girl that still lived inside of me needed to know that her daddy was not her enemy. He asked me to sit down and he stood over me and repented for any harm that he caused me during my childhood years. Then he pronounced his blessing over me. I have not been the same since that day. My relationship with him has gone to another level of love and respect. My gates have been fortified still stronger as a result of his blessing, and I am living under his blessing today, but more importantly, I am living under the blessings of my heavenly Father.

It is high time we got serious about repairing our gates. However we came to be in the position of being exposed to repeat Enemy invasion, it is the Lord's pleasure to show us love and mercy, just as He did for Hagar and to repair and rebuild our gates. Lamentations 3 reminds us that "the Lord's mercies are new every morning, and His faithfulness is great." Every morning our loving Savior pours His love out over us. He is faithfully interceding for us. He is our God and He is for us. If we belong to Him, the blood of His Son Jesus Christ washes over us and grants us opportunity after opportunity to start anew and to emerge from every temptation, loss, devastation, trial, failure and disappointment stronger in our walk with Him and in our love for Him, stronger in our testimony and stronger in our faith. We emerge a fresh new terror to the kingdom of darkness, wiser, more empowered and more useful vessels for the kingdom of God.

Sometimes, the violation of our gates may leave us walking with a limp for the duration of our lives (Gen. 32:25-31) and to some, our limps may appear to be handicaps. That's okay. Still others may become offended by our limps. That's okay too. However, to us who are limping through life, our ill-perceived handicaps are the proof that we have wrestled with man and with God, and have prevailed. Our limps are the hardcore evidence that the Lord, our God was and is with us. They testify that we are survivors, and more than survivors, God's Word says that we are "more than conquerors through Jesus Christ who loves us so" (Rom. 8:37). Finally, our limps remind the Devil of his one fatal mistake, and that is that he should have finished the job when he had the chance!

It is my prayer and hope that after reading this book, you have gained insight into just how important it is for you to guard your gates. I hope that you now have a better understanding of the significance of every gate to the kingdom of God that exists within each of us. It is vital to the plan of God for our lives and for the lives of our families, our children and our children's children that each of us assumes personal responsibility for guarding our gates henceforth and for doing whatever we must do to get about the task of rebuilding the gates that have been broken down and destroyed. In His radical, obsessive love for us, our Lord will do whatever He must to get us to see how urgent the task is and to assist us in completing it. His unfathomable, passionate love towards us is a definite building material that we must include as we look to rebuild our gates.

Time is winding up. The coming of Jesus is nearer now than it has ever been and there is still much work to be done in the kingdom of God. God wants to use all of His children to accomplish His plan on the earth, but we must ready ourselves so that God can use us effectively wherever He has planted us. Throughout the book, I have noted the building materials that we need to ensure that we are building good, strong gates that will endure repeat Enemy invasion – twenty-one building materials in all:

- Obedience
- Discernment
- Holiness
- Faith
- Trust
- Integrity
- Patience
- Hope
- Truth
- Wisdom
- Faithfulness
- Abiding
- Sanctification
- Stability
- Courage
- Brokenness
- Forgiveness
- Humility
- Word of God
- Gentleness
- Love of God

Revelation 21 promises a day when all of God's children will go home to be with Abba. In the New Jerusalem, we will stand in awe of the majesty, splendor, and beauty of our heavenly Daddy's gates – twelve in all. In Revelation 21 and 22 we are told that each gate is made of one single, beautiful pearl. By every gate stands an angel. On each gate is inscribed the names of the twelve tribes of Israel (21:12-14). We, the children of God, get to walk through those gates and into the Holy City one day soon. Once behind Daddy's gates, we will never have to worry about being attacked, violated, abused, traumatized or robbed again, because every dog, every immoral person, every murderer, idolater and deceiver will be forever prohibited and prevented from passing through God's durable and indestructible gates (22:14-15).

We will never experience shame, lack, fear, death, disappointment, pain or sorrow again. Once we are safe inside Abba's gates, our heavenly Daddy will hold us in His loving arms and wipe away every tear from our eyes (21:2-4). We will all beat our swords into plowshares and our spears into pruning hooks and will study war no more (Micah 4:3). What a glorious day that will be! Until then... we must *stand guard at the gates!*

Then you will know that I, the LORD, am your Savior, your Redeemer, the Mighty One of Jacob. Instead of bronze I will bring you gold, and silver in place of iron. Instead of wood I will bring you bronze, and iron in place of stones, I will make peace your governor and righteousness your ruler. No longer will violence be heard in your land, nor ruin or destruction within your borders, but you will call your walls Salvation and your gates Praise

(Isa. 60:16-18).

ENDNOTES

[1] Strong's Concordance of the Bible, 1990, 52

[2] Helen Gardner, Fred S. Kleiner, and Christin J. Mamiya. *Gardner's Art through the Ages.* 12th ed. Belmont: Thomson/Wadsworth, 2005 (828).

[3] Hannah Hurnard. *Hinds' Feet on High Places.* Carol Stream: Living Books, 1986 (172-73).

[4] Diane Ackerman. *A Natural History of the Senses.* New York: Random House, 1990

[5] Ackerman, 232-233

[6] C.S. Lewis. *The Problem of Pain*, San Francisco: Harper, 2001 (105)

[7] Strong's Concordance of the Bible, 1990, 52

[8] Strong's Concordance of the Bible, 1990, 52

[9] *The World Book Encyclopedia Volume 6.* Buffalo: World Book, 2010 (817).

[10] "Domestic Violence: Fast Facts on Domestic Violence."Uniform Crime Reports, Federal Bureau of Investigation, 1991. http://www.clarkprosecutor.org/

[11] Oliver Townsend. "The Yellow Pimpernel: The Feminist Battles of the 21st Century." *The Yellow Pimpernel.* N.p., n.d. Web. 19 Sept. 2011. http://yellowpimpernel.blogspot.com/2010/02/feminist-battles-of-21st-century.html.

[12] "Domestic Violence: Fast Facts on Domestic Violence."Bureau of Justice Statistics Crime Data Brief. *Intimate Partner Violence.* 1993-2001, February 2003 http://www.clarkprosecutor.org

[13] "Domestic Violence Resource Center | Domestic violence statistics." *Domestic Violence Resource Center.* N.p., n.d. Web. 8 Sept. 2011. http://www.dvrcor.org/domestic/violence/resources

[14] "Domestic Violence: Fast Facts on Domestic Violence." *Welcome to the Clark County Prosecuting Attorney's Office.* N.p., n.d. Web. 8 Sept. 2011. http://www.clarkprosecutor.org

[15] "Domestic Violence: Fast Facts on Domestic Violence." *Welcome to the Clark County Prosecuting Attorney's Office.* N.p., n.d. Web. 8 Sept. 2011. http://www.clarkprosecutor.org

[16] Goode P. Davis and Edwards Park. *The Heart, the Living Pump.* Washington, D.C.: U.S. News Books, 1984 (10).

[17] Davis and Park, 7.

[18] Davis and Park, 111.

[19] Davis and Park, 37.

[20] Davis and Park, 15.

[21] Watchman Nee. *The Release of the Spirit*. Indianapolis: Christian Fellowship, 1965 (80).

[22] Alice Smith. *Beyond the Veil*. Ventura: Renew, 1997 (88).

[23] Phillip Yancy. *Prayer, Does it Make Any Difference?* Grand Rapids: Zondervan, 2006 (185).

[24] Strong's Concordance of the Bible, 1990, 117

[25] A. W. Tozer. *The Pursuit of God*. Camp Hill: Christian Publications, 1948 (50).

[26] *The Hiding Place*. VHS. Directed by James F. Collier. Hollywood, California: Republic Pictures, 1975.

[27] Hunard, 147.

[28] H. Robert Superko and Laura Tucker. *Before the Heart Attacks: A Revolutionary Approach to Detecting, Preventing, and even Reversing Heart Disease*. Emmaus: Rodale, 2003 (6).

[29] Jerry Unseem. "The Art of Lying: Can It Be a Good Thing?" December 20, 1999. *CNNMoney - Business, financial and personal finance news*. N.p., n.d. Web. 7 Sept. 2011. http://money.cnn.com/magazines/fortune/fortune_archive/1999/12/20/270983/index.htm.

[30] Strong's Concordance of the Bible, 1990, 47

[31] Tozer, *Pursuit of God*, (53-55).

[32] Strong's Concordance of the Bible, 1990, 21

[33] Strong's Concordance of the Bible, 1990, 25

[34] Strong's Concordance of the Bible, 1990, 7

[35] *Girl, Interrupted*. DVD. Directed by James Mangold. Culver City: Sony Pictures, 1999.

[36] Strong's Concordance of the Bible, 1990, 24

[37] Strong's Concordance of the Bible, 1990, 36

[38] Strong's Concordance of the Bible, 1990, 63

[39] Dianne Hales and Robert Hales. Caring for the Mind: The Comprehensive Guide to Mental Health. New York: Bantam Books, 1994 (2-3)

[40] Strong's Concordance of the Bible, 1990, 70

[41] Diane Langberg. *Counseling Survivors of Sexual Abuse*. Wheaton: Tyndale House, 1997 (75).

[42] Langberg, 75.

[43] Langberg, 76.

[44] Leanne Payne. The Healing Presence. Colorado Springs: Kingsway, 1991 (192).

[45] Honey, I Shrunk The Devil: Destiny Image Publishers, Inc. 2000, 53

[46] Chris Thurman. The Lies We Tell Ourselves. Nappanee: Thomas Nelson Publishers, 1999 (139, 140).

[47] Jenni Whitehead. "Child abuse and its effect on brain development." http://www.teachingexpertise.com/articles/child-abuse-and-its-effect-on-brain-development-1448 (accessed September 16, 2011).

[48] Nee, 81.

[49] Strong's Concordance of the Bible, 1990, 114

[50] Henri Nouwen. The Way of the Heart: Desert Spirituality and Contemporary Ministry. New York: Seabury Press, 1981 (23).

Who's Guarding the Gates? Study Guide

Nancy L. Robinson

*T*his study guide is designed as a companion to *Who's Guarding the Gates?* by Nancy L. Robinson. As you work through the exercises, questions, and sections written for personal reflection and meditation, you will be challenged in your walk with Jesus Christ, and with others. This study guide can be used for individual, personal spiritual growth as well as for studies in both small and large group settings.

A TIMELY AND AMAZING *M*UST READ

*W*ho's *Guarding the Gates?* is an amazing book that takes a different approach to assuring us of God's love and devotion. The author seems determined that no person who believes should ever feel defeated or feel that their losses in the war between good and evil are permanent. She brings her readers to a higher plane of thinking, in order that they might not limit God by a lack of understanding or faith.

With a remarkable Preface, the author cuts straight to the reader's heart. Any person who picks up this book will be drawn into the author's message of love that she has received from God. Including other forms of wisdom, such as African proverbs, provides another level of credibility for the book. It shows that the author's opinion is not solely based in a Christian worldview, but in basic principles of morality and good sense.- by Vanessa Correa – Xulon Press Editor

CPSIA information can be obtained at www.ICGtesting.com
Printed in the USA
BVOW030024070513

320028BV00002B/4/P